Bill Burnett and Dave Evans

Designing Your New Work Life

Bill Burnett is the executive director of the Stanford Design Program and was a product leader for Apple's groundbreaking PowerBook business. He directs the undergraduate and graduate programs in design at Stanford.

Dave Evans is the codirector of the Stanford Life Design Lab and a cofounder of Electronic Arts, one of the world's largest interactive entertainment companies. He holds a B.S. and M.S. in mechanical engineering from Stanford.

designingyour.life
creativelive.com/DYL

Also by Bill Burnett and Dave Evans

Designing Your Life

Designing Your New
WORK Life

Bill Burnett and Dave Evans

Designing Your New
WORK Life

How to Thrive
and Change
and Find Happiness
—and a New Freedom—
at Work

Originally published as *Designing Your Work Life*

VINTAGE BOOKS
A DIVISION OF PENGUIN RANDOM HOUSE LLC
NEW YORK

The Library of Congress has cataloged the Knopf edition as follows:
Names: Burnett, William (Consulting professor of design), author. |
Evans, David J. (David John), 1953– author.
Title: Designing your new work life: how to thrive and change
and find happiness—and a new freedom—at work /
Bill Burnett and Dave Evans.
Description: First edition. | New York : Alfred A. Knopf, 2020. |
Includes bibliographical references.
Identifiers: LCCN 2019031158 (print) | LCCN 2019031159 (ebook)
Subjects: LCSH: Quality of work life. | Job satisfaction.
Classification: LCC HD6955 .B873 2020 (print) |
LCC HD6955 (ebook) | DDC 650.1—dc23
LC record available at https://lccn.loc.gov/2019031158
LC ebook record available at https://lccn.loc.gov/2019031159

Vintage Books Trade Paperback ISBN: 978-0-593-46745-9
eBook ISBN: 978-0-593-46746-6

Book design by Betty Lew

www.vintagebooks.com

To all the workers everywhere who get up, get dressed, and go get it done every day. Thanks for all you do. We hope that in these pages you find a way to do it with more purpose, meaning, and joy. You deserve it.

To Eliza, Casey, and Ben, my amazing children.

It is a joy to watch you launch as you design your adult lives.

—Bill Burnett

To Dave & Kim, Robbie & Chrissy, Lisa & Donny, Gabe & Nichole, and Rosie.

My first and foremost life design goal has been to be a dad. I am infinitely grateful to you for allowing my deepest longing to be fulfilled. Joining in the dance of your and your children's lives is my greatest joy.

—Dave Evans

Contents

Preface

Your *New* Work Life

We wrote two books.

The first, *Designing Your Life,* was released in 2016. The second, *Designing Your Work Life,* was released on February 25, 2020.

Little did we know at the end of February, as we did media interviews in Manhattan for the launch of our new book, that life was on the verge of changing in ways none of us could have imagined.

A few weeks later, the governor of New York mandated that all nonessential businesses reduce their workforce density by 50 percent, then 25 percent, and then completely. This partial to total workforce reduction happened over the course of three days.

Not just in New York and in California, but across the United States and around the globe.

Schools closed, unemployment skyrocketed, and work as we knew it changed forever.

So yes, weeks before the pandemic we launched a book with the subtitle *How to Thrive and Change and Find Happiness at Work.*

We still believe you can thrive and change and find happiness at work, and know that all of our tools in the first edition of our book remain valuable and useful. But we also know that you need more. We all need more.

So, almost a year after we were in Manhattan and discussed how our second book met people where they were, we are changing the title and updating the book to again meet people where they are.

Welcome to *Designing Your **New** Work Life.*

We've added a whole new section to this book that addresses the work elephant in the room.

And the name of that elephant?

Disruption.

Everything is different, and while we don't know what the future holds, we do know that whatever comes next—in work and in life—won't be like what came before.

And now more than ever, we all need some creative and adaptable tools to cope with the disruption. And within all the chaos and change, there are some really big opportunities to redesign your work life and life life for what we believe will be permanent changes to the world of work.

If you are an employee, one benefit of all this change might be more freedom to work in ways that fit your lifestyle better. If you are a manager, this could mean learning a whole new way to work with your employees, managing for outcomes, with more trust, engagement, and productivity all around. And if you are a business owner or a CEO, what's in the future is an acceleration of where we were going anyway—a more distributed workforce, with talent anywhere, and a far lower cost of operations as the Internet and the home office/kitchen table/camper van replaces those expensive office leases.

For many people—far too many people—there's nothing about how life after the pandemic of 2020–21 differs from life in 2019 that they would call a "benefit." If you've lost your job, your company, or whole sectors of your industry, it feels a lot like crisis and very little like opportunity. Disruptions don't land evenly or play fair, and far too many of us are facing big doses of hard acceptance and painful grief. In particular, our hearts go out to those of you who tragically lost loved ones to COVID-19. We don't pretend that any amount of clever reframing will eliminate the pain of loss, but we do think that handling loss as generatively as possible can help—so you'll find some design tools for that here, too.

As we've said before, designers love problems, and you can't solve a problem you aren't willing to have. So here we are, with a whole new world of problems and a whole new world of change that require us to think differently.

It's time, once again, to think like a designer.

And we are here, in the midst of the chaos, to humbly offer some help.

Some new ideas and tools and reframes.

And while we realize there is no perfect tool kit for everyone's situation, and no easy way back to a more normal life, we believe there is something in our new chapters that will help you navigate these tough times. Pick what works for you and pass the rest along to someone who may need it.

Welcome to Disruption Design and welcome to your new work life.

Designing Your New
WORK Life

Introduction

Making It Work at Work

We wrote a book.

Not this book, another book. Maybe you read it, maybe you didn't. In that book, we taught people how to use design thinking to design their lives. We showed a lot of people how to get off the couch and prototype alternate versions of their lives and their careers. We've taught workshops based on the book, and we've met and heard from thousands of readers whose lives were changed for the better. They've shared their stories with us, and each of their stories is now part of our story. Many of the people who read and loved *Designing Your Life* were people in transition: entering one of life's many inflection points. They needed help with choosing their next step—where to go, what to do, and in some cases, who to be. Their work involved trying to *imagine* a different kind of future or a way to make an unrealized dream real.

That book was about imagining.

This book is about making it real.

We also heard from people who said the Odyssey Plans we suggested were great and all, but it wasn't feasible for them to run off and become a scuba instructor in Bimini because of, well, things like insurance, mortgages, utility bills, and the children who were still in school.

Those people asked us for a different kind of book.

They asked for a book that would meet them where they are

now, and provide tools and ideas that would help them thrive at work.

Look, today's workplace is in continual flux. As companies evolve to be more and more nimble and shift faster and faster to meet changing markets, the workplace is less and less predictable. Increasingly, it's up to workers to define their own happiness and success in this ever-moving landscape. It's also up to smart managers and companies to meet their workers halfway and offer resources (such as this book) that can help create a culture that allows their ever-changing workers to adapt to the ever-changing demands of the workplace as it adapts to the ever-changing demands of the market. Mostly, though, people need tools to invent their own success—over and over—as they change and grow as humans. (Doubly so for the growing ranks of us who are self-employed.) And it's becoming clear that Millennials and Gen Z workers especially *demand* a work experience that is meaningful and that gives them a sense that they are having an impact in the world.

We all want our days infused with meaning and impact.

Most of us spend most of our days at work. So it's no surprise that the workplace is the number one place we go looking to find meaning and impact. Yet most jobs are built around tasks to get done and transactions to manage, and most managers aren't comfortable talking about meaning and impact. When you become the designer of your work life, you can help your boss and your company make your job the job you want. If you own your own business, you can invent it over and over again until it gives you meaning and impact. You can design your work life as an employee or a business owner. Design thinking is for people like you, whether you receive the paycheck or sign the paycheck. This book is full of ideas and tools that will help you not only create more meaning in your life, but also build more joy into each workday.

The workplace isn't just changing—it's restructuring. The Gig Economy, Artificial Intelligence, and the Robots aren't coming, they're already here and they're poised to reshape everything we think we know about work. So smart workers need to prepare themselves to thrive in this new technological reality. We have lots of practical tools in this book to help you respond like a creative designer to this workplace of the future.

If you read *Designing Your Life (DYL),* this book will add to your new design thinking mind-sets to help implement a joyful work life, whatever your Odyssey Plan. If you didn't read our first book (or if you read the first book but didn't do the exercises), this book stands alone to help you use design thinking to design in place, at work—so you can be happier and more fulfilled during those forty, fifty, sixty hours a week you spend working—without having to change jobs or careers, unless you really want to. If you do, we show you how to do that, too.

So it is time to get off the couch and get unstuck at your job. Mostly, it's time to make work work for you!

Something's Not Right

Bonnie is thirty years old and has had five jobs since college. She always begins the same way—with optimism, with excitement, and full of expectations about how this job is going to work for her—but each time she ends up disappointed. The job—each job—lets her down, and she has no idea why. "It just didn't work out," she explains to her parents every time she has to borrow money to make the rent. Bonnie knows her reasons for quitting are vague, but for the life of her she just can't get any clearer than "something is not right, but I don't know what."

Louis is a middle manager at a midsize company where he's worked for fifteen years. Every day he takes the train into work and arrives at the office at exactly 8:15 a.m. He supervises a sales team that sits in perfectly lined-up cubicles, working in perfect disharmony. He's supposed to manage and motivate them, but day after day, Louis walks onto the sales floor and looks around as if he's a visitor to a foreign land.

This is not my company.

None of this matters.

Louis leaves for home on the 5:15 p.m. train. He has two kids in middle school. His mortgage is a third of the way paid off. On the train ride home, as he leans his head against the glass window, watching the world pass him by, the lyrics to a Talking Heads song play over and over in his mind.

And you may ask yourself, "Well, how did I get here?"

Marie is a physician, at the top of her field, who is absolutely bored but isn't about to walk away from a successful medical career. Rajeev is in a job he loves, but there's too much to do and not enough time to do it. Even his overwhelm is overwhelmed. Bruce drives for an app-based car service and does some gigging as a side hustle. While he loves the freedom of making his own schedule, he doesn't love not having a steady paycheck, a clear path to advance his career, or a "real job." Jennifer heads Human Resources at a hi-tech company, and knows the employees are disengaged and underperforming, but nothing in her training has taught her how to help them, so she files away one poor performance review after another.

All of these people we know are unhappy at work. And each has an unhappy story they tell about their job. *It's not working for me. I don't fit at this job. It's too hard to change it, or fix it, but I don't know if I should stay or quit. What should I do next?*

Dysfunctional Belief: *It's not working for me here.*
Reframe: *You can make it work (almost) anywhere.*

Disengaged at Work

If you work forty hours a week, fifty weeks a year (with two weeks off for your skimpy "American" vacation), for forty years—you will have worked 80,000 or more hours. Many of you reading this will average more than fifty hours a week and work well beyond fifty years—which puts you over 125,000 hours. Almost nothing in your life takes more of your time and energy than work.

And yet, in poll after poll, Gallup indicates that approximately 69 percent of American workers are disengaged from their work (a percentage that includes the plain "disengaged" and the angry and resentful "actively disengaged"). Globally, the number of workers unhappy at the place where they spend most of their lives is an astonishing 85 percent. These workers do not go to work with a smile on their face. They often talk about their work as "dreary and boring." And we aren't just talking about people with mundane office jobs or blue-collar workers doing repetitive manual labor, or fast-food workers doing the same at your local burger chain. In our many DYL talks and workshops around the country, we've heard from teachers, CEOs, coaches, doctors, dentists, farmers, bankers, barbers, private equity gurus, librarians, army helicopter pilots, physical therapists, truckers, government bureaucrats, and lawyers (actually, from lots of lawyers), and from men, women, young, middle-aged, old, single, married, divorced—you name it—people, all saying the same thing.

I don't like my job!

As we said, worker disengagement is a global issue, and it is even worse in other countries. More than 93 percent of Japanese workers report themselves in the disengaged category. The Japanese even have a variety of special names for these extra miserable jobs: a shachiku worker (社) translates to "corporate livestock" or "corporate slave worker," and kaisha no inu (会社の犬) translates as "dog of the company." There's even a word, karōshi (過労死), which can be translated as "death by overwork," and there have been numerous high-profile suicides by workers who could no longer tolerate their long hours and harsh working conditions.

So count your blessings, it could be much worse. I mean, who wants to feel like corporate livestock?

The reasons people are not happy at work are many.

It's my job, it's so boring . . .

It's my boss, he's such a micromanager . . .

It's my company, I never get any feedback on how I'm doing . . .

It's my career, I think I picked the wrong one . . .

We hear you. And we are here to tell you that it might not be as bad as you think. If you have a job, that's a start, and you should count yourself as one of the lucky ones. At least you have a little security, a little income, and a place to start your redesign. Lots of people are living gig to gig, and some people are living in the "chronically unemployed" category of labor statistics, and that's a tough place. Fortunately, there are ideas and tools in this book that will be helpful for everyone, no matter the situation.

If you don't have a job yet, there are a lot of great tools in this book to help you find a good one, and also to help ensure that your future job is a place where you can learn, contribute, and grow into who you want to be next.

Our philosophy is that YOU are the designer of your life and your job, and with design thinking, you can make it much better. You can change how your boss reacts to you, change your experience of work altogether, and maybe even have an impact on your company's culture. We believe that we can all learn to design a way to thrive at work and create a workplace that's better for everyone. And the good news is, it's not going to be that hard.

Dysfunctional Belief: *I am a cog in the machine.*
Reframe: *I am a lever that can impact the machine.*
Bonus Reframe: *I'm a human, not a machine, and I deserve a creative and interesting job.*

Think Like a Designer

Before you can start designing and redesigning your work life, you need to learn to think like a designer. We'll explain how to do this, but first you need to understand one really big point: When designing your work life, you need to know that designers don't *think* their way forward. Work designers *build* their way forward. And in order to do that, you need to understand and begin to cultivate the mind-set of a designer. In our first book we had five mind-sets of design thinking—now, for this book, we have six. (It's a bonus mind-set and an important one.) The mind-sets are: curiosity, bias to action, reframing, awareness, radical collaboration, and—the bonus—storytelling.

 Be curious. Get curious, about people, work, and the world, because a designer always starts with a beginner's mind and asks "Why?" Curiosity is your natural human state, and it is the source of the energy you need to get started and get out and meet people who are interesting. *Curiosity* is the most important mind-set of a designer, because it drives inquiry and action and is the start of almost all design activities. Leave your rational skeptic at home (she'll come in handy later when you need to evaluate all of your wonderful options) and get curious. It is a very interesting world out there! And when you're sincerely interested in people and things (i.e., curious), people are happy to engage with you. Remember—interest*ed* is interest*ing*.

 **Try stuff.** This is the *bias to action* step, where your curiosity and questions turn into action in the world. We showed you how you can prototype conversations and experiences in *Designing Your Life;* in this book we will show you a lot more

ways to sneak up on your future and discover what works for you, at work and at home. When you live into this mind-set there is always something to do, a person to talk to, or an experience to try. In this book we will show you how to experiment with all sorts of "Try Stuff" strategies. Designers build their way forward and discover what's right for them, in their jobs and in their lives, with a bias to action.

Reframe problems. *Reframing* is a big idea, and once you get good at it, you will never get stuck again. Designers always start by reframing the problem they're given, because, well, it's hardly ever the right problem. This book is organized around the world of work and the kinds of bad problems that we call "dysfunctional beliefs." These are things you might believe that are simply not true, or are not helpful, or are keeping you stuck. These are beliefs you have about work and life that just aren't working for you anymore. We will show you how to reframe these dysfunctional beliefs and make them into actionable challenges. You'll want to get good at reframing—it is the essential mind-set that helps you get good at solving problems. There's an old expression, "A problem well defined is half solved," and *reframing* will make sure that you define the right problems to work on. And that will lead to some great solutions to your job and life challenges. This is such a big idea, we spend pretty much all of chapter 3 talking about how to do reframing. It's a design superpower.

Know it's a process. In design thinking, you are sometimes out generating lots and lots of ideas. We call this "phase ideation," and it's when you flare out, looking for all the good, bad, and crazy ideas you can find. At other times, you are focusing in on a point of view or a prototype you want to try. In this phase, you are focusing in on a good question or a very specific idea you'd like to test. These two parts of the design thinking process, flare and focus, are fundamentally different, and that's why good designers learn to be mindful of their process. You need to know when it's time to flare and when it's time to focus. You need to know when to ask more questions and when to accept the data you've generated and commit to a path forward. This is especially important if you are on a design team, because everyone needs to be pulling in the same direction if you're going to make progress. And paying attention to the process reassures you that you've touched all the bases, done your empathy research and ideation, and that you are prepared to make a good decision.

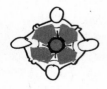

Ask for help. If we want to figure out how to transform our experience of work, we can't sit at home and ruminate; we need to interact with the world of work and workers. We need to ask for help. We call this asking-for-help step "radical collaboration," and when coupled with a bias to action, it results in rapid learning, an abundance of prototype opportunities, and some life-changing experiences. Getting out in the world and talking to lots of different people who are doing interesting things that you are curious about is crucial. This is your design research. And when you radically collaborate, you also discover that you are not alone, that many people are asking the same questions and have the same concerns. When the subject is work, we want to double down on the idea that design is a collaborative process and many of your best ideas are going to come from other people. You just need to ask for help. When you reach out to the world, it's been our experience that the world reaches back. And that changes everything.

Tell your story. Here's the bonus mind-set—storytelling. When you adopt the *tell your story* mind-set, you are always looking for opportunities to reflect on your conversations and experiences, and looking for new ways to engage the world with your story. Everyone loves a good story, and if you're curious, have a bias to action, and build a lot of prototypes, you'll have lots of stories to tell. Becoming a great storyteller is something you can learn, and once learned, storytelling will become one of the primary ways you engage with others and move your job and life design forward. And once you start speaking up, a funny thing happens—the world will start talking back and telling its story, in the form of new friendships, job opportunities, and creative ways to achieve your goals. Remember, in the *curiosity* section above, we said that *interested is interesting*—which is true. And the other half of that idea is that *interesting is interesting,* too. That's what's at the heart of the *storytelling* mind-set. When you combine genuine curiosity with telling your story well, you've got a powerful combination working for you. But before the world can respond, you have to speak first and tell your story. We'll show you how.

Get Sexier

When you adopt this new *storytelling* mind-set, you are tapping into an incredibly powerful stream of human experience—the narrative. Storytelling is a natural element of human evolution. It's how we make meaning of our experience and our lives. It's how we connect with one another. Lisa Bortolotti, professor of philosophy at the University of Birmingham, England, even suggests that telling stories increases sexual attractiveness and improves our chances to reproduce. Dr. Paul J. Zak, director of the Center for Neuroeconomics Studies at Claremont Graduate University, has research that shows "that highly immersive stories can change attitudes, opinions, and behaviors." Telling a new story, especially to yourself, can be a powerful way to change your experience on the job.

That probably explains why the first cavemen and cavewomen, sitting on rocks around that new piece of technology, fire, started telling stories. And humans have never stopped. A good story, and a good storyteller, is always welcome—around the fire, at the office microwave, or on the sidelines of your kid's soccer game. We will show you how to be that person.

Tell your story, get sexier.

And if you're not so happy with your story right now, don't worry. We are going to help you design the work life you want, and in the process rewrite your life's story. We will help you to be more curious, to try stuff, and to cultivate a bias-to-action way of being in the world. Ultimately, we want you to be an engaged and creative force at whatever you do for work. The truth is, if you are fundamentally unhappy with your job, you are fundamentally unhappy with your life.

And that's no way to live.

You need you to be happy at what you do and how you spend your work life. And the world needs more happy and engaged workers.

Throughout this book, we'll tell our own stories and the stories of readers, workshop attendees, and others who have used life design ideas and tools to redesign their jobs, careers, and companies. People just like you who have made it work at work. We'll show you how to design a work life that is productive, engaged, meaningful, and fun.

In the future you are happy at work. You just need to know how to sneak up on that future.

Let's get started . . .

1

Are We There Yet?

> **Dysfunctional Belief:** *Good enough isn't good enough, I want more.*
>
> **Reframe:** *Good enough is GREAT—for now.*

There's a sign over the Design Studio at Stanford that says *You Are Here.* We love that sign, so much so that we made it a chapter title in our first book. The idea behind that sign is simple—before you can figure out where you are going, you need to know where you are, and once you know and accept where you are, you can design your way to where you want to be.

Are We There Yet? is different. As the title suggests, it's about not being content with where you are. It's the same question you hear from kids in the backseat during a long car ride.

Are we there yet?

Are we there?

Are we now?

When will we be there?

Are. We. There. Yet?

There's no joy in that family car ride. It's just a boring means to an end. *Getting there.* Once there, wherever *there* is, that's when they will be happy. Not there yet? Then not happy!

We're not discontented kids in the backseat of the family mini-van, but how many of us live our lives, especially our work lives, as if we are?

How often do we find ourselves waiting to get *there*? That magical place that we wait and wait for—the place where we will finally be content and happy. We think once we have a better job, or more money, or that promotion, we will have finally arrived at the place where things are new and different and magically better. And how many of us make ourselves deeply unhappy thinking this way? The truth is, when we live our lives waiting to get somewhere, the only place we get is stuck.

We have something important to say to you: Wherever you are in your work life, whatever job you are doing, it's good enough. For now.

Not forever.

For now.

Isn't that a relief? *Good enough for now* is one of the big reframes of this book. Cultivating this attitude doesn't mean life or work can't get better, or that things never change, or that you stop learning and growing. On the contrary, changing our internal narrative to "good enough for now" makes it possible for everything in our external situation to transform.

But let's be real: In our society, the message from the media, from our culture, and from all around us is that enough is never enough. That nagging voice in your head, the one that compares you to everybody else, is saying that everyone else has more and I'd be happier if I had *more*, too. You're pretty sure that everyone else already has more than you and you're missing out. You know the voice we're talking about. It plays in an endless loop in your head.

This idea of always needing or wanting "more" can make us

profoundly unhappy, and a little crazy, too. When we're always chasing after the better job, or car, or house, or city, we never stop running. Ever. And this problem is not limited to just "stuff." You can get caught endlessly chasing more peace, more mindfulness, or more magnanimity just as easily as more money. It may be a more noble race—but it's still a trip to frustration and constant not-there-yet-ness. You can use this never-enough, wanting-more, not-good-enough mind-set to ruin just about anything in life.

Psychologists have a term for the endless seeking of more—the *hedonic treadmill* (hedonic = pleasure-seeking). For our purposes, the hedonic treadmill describes a process of being addicted to new experiences and the acquisition of new things. And, like all addictions, each new "high" comes with a big jolt of happy brain chemicals that quickly die off, creating the need for the next "fix." And each time, the high is a little less high, making the pleasure-seeker run faster on the pleasure treadmill, compulsively looking for bigger and better highs. But the problem is that you can never repeat the first "high." Each new thing, each new experience, feels great for a while, and then that feeling fades. In the battle for *more,* you can never win. Trust us when we tell you this journey on the treadmill rarely ends well.

The real question isn't: How much money, time, power, impact, meaning, status, retirement savings, [fill in the blank with your favorite thing to want more of] do you have?

The real question is: How's it going, right now?

A non–life designer, wallowing in the it's-not-good-enough end of the pool, vaguely malcontent with all they have, answers by saying, over and over again, "Not so good. Are we there yet?"

If asked the same question, a life designer would say, "Life is good. Of course, I'm working on my gratitude and managing my

Health/Work/Play/Love dashboard, and I'm always trying to make a more meaningful contribution at work, but I can honestly say that things are good and I'm pretty content with what I have. I have what I need, and that is good enough for now."

The big difference: Life designers have figured out how to get off the "more" treadmill and are living in the point of view that says they have enough, and it is good.

There is plenty of evidence that much of the unhappiness in the world comes from not realizing that we have enough, in many cases more than we need. This unhappiness comes in many forms, but it almost always expresses itself as the feeling that you need . . .

more money
more recognition
more social status
more Instagram followers
more fun . . . , etc.

So what are the warning signs that you might be on a hedonic treadmill and going nowhere? If you find yourself sitting on your new couch, watching your big-screen TV, with your 1,000-watt super 7.1 surround-sound system blasting, and you're feeling lonely—that's a warning sign. If you just spent an hour retouching photos before you posted them to your social media account, trying to make your life look a little more glamorous than it really is—that's a warning sign. And if you find yourself wandering around your local mall, wanting something but finding nothing worth owning, bored to death, and wondering how you got there and what it all means—that's a warning sign. Turn off your computer, silence your smartphone. Run, do not walk, to the nearest beach, forest, or beautiful sunset and stop, take a break, and look around. And to increase your sense of meaning, bring a friend, family member, or other loved one with you. It is a good idea, every so often, to remind ourselves that this is what is real, this is what life is actually all about.

For the last two decades, positive psychology research from the likes of Martin Seligman, Mihaly Csikszentmihalyi, Daniel Goleman, and others has proven that happiness does not come from having "more." Studies of lottery winners show that within a year or so these lucky, richer folks are not any happier than they were before winning. Studies have also shown that people who are happy are enjoying what they get, not wasting their time worrying about getting something they don't need. Research has made it abundantly clear that one of the secrets to a happy life is to learn how to enjoy what you have.

Another secret to a happy life is found in Harvard's Grant Study, which is part of the longest-running longitudinal study of adult human development in Western society. This seventy-plus-year study found that there is no correlation between happiness and how much money you make, your social status, or other external measures of success (this assumes, of course, that you're making a living and can sustain the basics—past that, the science says that money doesn't matter much). What makes life meaningful and what maximizes your happiness and longevity are relationships—who you love and who loves you. And there is a strong correlation between doing something for the benefit of others and living a longer, healthier life. George Vaillant, the last Harvard psychologist in charge of the Grant Study, summarized the entire research with these sentences: "Happiness is love. Full stop."

So, as we go along designing jobs that invite our engagement, let's keep in mind that we are human animals and we work best in relationship with others of our species. Relationships, clubs, churches, communities—that's really what makes the world go around. Create relationships with people, not things—that's one way to get you off the hedonic treadmill.

Good enough for now leaves open the possibility of growth and change but doesn't make changing for change's sake a goal. And it doesn't make getting "more" a priority. It is a powerful reframe and a point of view that puts you in control of what you need in life and what you want to choose to invite into your life.

And it is the number one way to maximize your happiness at work right now. This second. No matter what else is going on in your life and before you even read another word of this book, you can move yourself out of the state of "the unhappy, disengaged worker" and maximize the happiness that is already available by changing your point of view to one where things are *good enough for now.*

Garth's Good Enough for Now

Garth thought he had done everything right. He'd researched the industry, checked out the company, and talked to all the right people in the organization. His interview went great. Sure, the woman who had previously held the position hadn't called him back, but because he had had nothing but positive responses from everyone he did speak to, he accepted the job offer when it came. Garth was now officially a group marketing manager and responsible for several product lines in a large telecommunications company. Garth was happy.

On his second day of work, the elusive woman who hadn't returned his calls during the interview process finally called him back.

"You've been really hard to get ahold of," said Garth.

"Well, don't you know why?" she replied.

In that moment, sitting at his brand-new desk in his brand-new office, Garth's stomach flipped. He took a deep breath. "No, I don't," he said. "Why?"

"They wouldn't let me talk to you because they knew that I would be honest and tell you just how horrible the job is that you now have. It's not at all what it seems. I couldn't get away fast enough."

Garth listened as she explained what was really going on behind the scenes of the company and detailed the nature of the political mess Garth had inherited. She, of course, was thrilled to have been transferred out of state, not that she wanted to move, but she would have gone anywhere just as long as she could get away from the hell that was her old job, and now Garth's new job.

Garth has found himself in about as bad a spot as we can imagine. He made a good choice, based on good information that this new job was going to be great. He made the best decision with the information available. He shouldn't beat himself up because it turns out that some important information was withheld on purpose. Ron Howard, the Stanford professor who is considered the father of decision analysis, says, "Never confuse the quality of a decision with the quality of the outcome— they are really two different things. The only thing you

can control is the quality of your research and the qual-
ity of the resulting decision." This is a critical insight
about decisions and worth remembering. Of course, all
Garth knew was that he was in trouble . . .

Garth hung up the phone and then hung his head. He had no idea what to do. He figured he shouldn't leave a job on his second day, and besides, he was a new dad, and he and his wife had just bought a house, and between that and the baby there was nothing but bills to pay. He knew he couldn't support his family without the income from this job. And how would he ever explain the quick turnover on his résumé to future employers? His position had already been announced in the industry. Any new employer would ask what had happened. It wouldn't look good. There were a million reasons why he had to stay.

He was going to have to tough it out. And after some time he realized that what his predecessor had told him was true—this was a really awful job. Garth's boss was not a great guy. Not even close. It was a pretty bad situation all the way around, and Garth predicted that over time things would go from bad to worse.

And that's exactly what happened.

So Garth had a choice.

He could be miserable every single minute of the day. He could beat himself up for making a bad decision (he did not have the benefit of a class with Professor Howard about the difference between decisions and outcomes). He could turn into one of those people we all know—that person who is always complaining about his job, her boss, the company—but never doing anything about it. Or he could change his point of view and find some way to make the job "good enough for now." So he took the first step designers always take—he *accepted* the situation and, by accepting his situation, he began the process of designing his work life.

First, he decided to plan positive energy breaks at three-hour intervals every day. He would get up from his desk, take a walk around the grounds of the company, then go to the cafeteria and buy an ice-cream cone. He gained weight, but he also found something that made him happy every few hours and helped him feel reengaged with his work when he sat back down at his desk. The day felt less difficult with these scheduled breaks, and Garth felt less like he was doing time in prison.

Buying an ice-cream cone is pretty doable. That was solution number one.

Second, Garth looked around at this large, vast, complicated company and decided he could learn a lot from the smart people there, particularly those outside his Marketing department. He decided to visit the other parts of the organization and learn as much as possible. He especially connected with the Sales department and learned everything there was to learn from them when it came to telecommunications sales. It turned out that having friends in Sales helped him in his marketing job.

Garth's job still sucked—it was not the one he had been promised. But Garth got curious and started talking to people and, because he was learning new things every day, the pay was decent, and he was able to get good work done, he was able to live into the "good enough for now" point of view. And after eighteen months— enough time that it wouldn't look so bad on his résumé—Garth decided to change jobs. Because of some positive recommendations from his friends in Sales, he was able to move to a better job in a much better company. In the end, he left feeling successful, with some great relationships, and with his résumé (and soul) intact.

The *good enough for now* reframe helped Garth, and it is going to help you stop being one of the disengaged at work, stop being a statistic, and begin designing your work life.

Let's be really clear here—we're not trying to tell you to lie to yourself or settle for a miserable job or even for an unsatisfying one. We are suggesting that, to change your point of view and to start moving toward more happiness, it is best to stop waiting for something or someone else to change. You have no control over other people, and little control sometimes of your circumstances (just ask Garth). When we design our work life, we begin by accepting what is, and then find small ways to redesign our circumstances. We get curious, talk to people, try stuff, and start telling a new story. In the process, we find ourselves more engaged, and more energized. All from adopting the point of view that what we have is good enough, for now.

Not for forever.

For now.

Reframe Not Rename

We want to be clear that we are not just telling you to look at the bright side of things, or advising you to blindly choose to decide it's all okay. We aren't ignoring the reality of what might be a really bad work situation. *Good Enough for Now* is a reframe, not a rename.

Renaming is just slapping a new label on the same old mess. Writing *yogurt* on the side of a carton of spoiled milk does not make it taste good—and painting a new *good enough* label on your difficult work situation won't make it better. That's not what Garth did and not what we're recommending.

We've all heard the advice to just make the best of a bad situation. That's not bad advice, but if you only make the best of a bad situation, you are still in a bad situation. It doesn't get at the root of the problem or offer an opportunity to change the situation. You're more cheerfully navigating lousiness, which is an improvement, but not much of one and rather hard to sustain over time.

When you reframe, you are actually completely reorganizing how you structure your perception of a situation (which of course means a new point of view), which fundamentally alters how you focus your attention and deploy your bias to action. When it works, this results in a substantively different story and experience.

Let's analyze Garth's reframe to *good enough for now* with this understanding of the difference between *renaming* and *reframing*. First Garth accepted his situation, and then he reframed it from "getting satisfaction from my job and my boss" to "being around new talented people and learning new things." He also identified something in his situation that would be of real value to his employer (and to Garth) and focused his attention there (in Garth's case, getting Marketing and Sales working together). Garth didn't just put a happy "rename" on a bad job; he designed a whole new outlook and framing (reframing) for his job. He could answer the question "How's it going?" with "It's going pretty well, thanks," and that was an honest answer based on his reframed reality. Sure, the crummy parts of the job persisted, but by accepting his situation and directing his attention to other things, Garth was able to make it work at work.

Now, this doesn't always work. We are realists, and we fully recognize that there are times when your life isn't good enough at all. Tragedies happen, people lose loved ones, or live in joyless or abusive relationships, or have terrible and demeaning jobs. We understand that sometimes things are just rotten and sometimes you have to do something about it. If you are in an abusive job, or being discriminated against, or being asked to do things that are immoral, illegal, or both—run, don't walk, for the exit. Life is too short to put up with that.

But if it is just run-of-the-mill bad—a job that isn't interesting or a company that has a bad culture (or no culture at all)—we advise you to hang in there. We think we know some very effective ways to make a bad job better.

Or at least to make it good enough for now.

Remember, *for now* implies hope, hope that there might be a better outcome in the future, and it gives us a space to prototype into. That's how life designers work—they accept the reality of the situation or job at hand, they look for a reframe, and, by applying a *bias to action* mind-set, they build something—a prototype—then learn something, and do it again. We call this process "building your way forward" and it works in almost any situation. It's a process for taking small steps that eventually set you up for a big success. (Worst-case scenario, you get an ice-cream cone every day.)

And sometimes the best prototype is to just wait a little bit. We are always in such a hurry—taking a little extra time often opens up new possibilities and ways forward.

Good enough is always relative to your situation and your needs. *For now* is also relative, and change, and change for the better, is almost always possible.

And when you think like a designer, you always have a choice.

Just ask Garth.

Dysfunctional Belief: *To have a good work life I need to "go for it" and really shoot for the moon!*
Reframe: *The secret to "good enough for now" is to have a bias to action, but set the bar low, clear it, then do it again, and again.*

Set the Bar Low

You don't like your job, you don't particularly like your boss, you're bored, you think you're underappreciated, and you know you're overworked and probably unknown. Your first impulse is to quit. Start over. Not give a single you-know-what and just let the bridges you burn light your way on out of there.

That's one way.

This book is about a bunch of other ways.

Design thinking can transform your job and change everything. Including you. We're not saying it will always be easy or quick, but we do think it will be satisfying and very doable. Behavior change is difficult. Adopting and living into these new designer mind-sets, like bias to action and reframing, isn't that easy. There's no *shazam* and suddenly you think and act differently. But we do know a few things from the positive psychologists on how to make behavior change a little easier.

It is estimated that 90 percent of New Year's resolutions fail by the time we are three months into the New Year. More than two-thirds of all diets fail. And don't get us started on the number of step trackers and fitness bands that find their way to the junk drawer six months after purchase. At the Stanford Life Design

Lab (d.Life) we've studied these phenomena. Behavior change is tough, and people try too hard, go for too much, and fail, almost every single time. It is another reason why many people are stuck in unhappy jobs and situations—they think they have to make a BIG CHANGE and have tried and failed to change it.

There's another way—and it's called the "Set the Bar Low" method.

Set Small Goals

The Set the Bar Low method is based on some pretty sound psychological studies and behavior change models that suggest that taking small, actionable steps is the best way to establish a new behavior or habit.

Say you are a typical American couch potato, but you've read the studies on the value of exercise for your physical and mental health, and you have decided to start running. You'd like to set a goal of running a marathon, but you've also read that setting a goal as lofty as running a marathon is likely to fail. You want to make a change, and do it right, so the first thing you do is *accept* that this is a problem you are willing to work on. Then, with your bias to action mind-set, you get out a calendar and block out the first two weeks with the goal to "walk 5,000 steps a day." You turn on your smartphone's step counter and note every day how far you've walked. This is a pretty attainable goal—most people walk about 5,000 steps a day anyway—but it gets you in the habit of noticing how far you've walked every day. Noticing is a big deal in behavior change. When you *accept* that you are working on your fitness goals and start *noticing* your progress, you get the ball rolling.

As soon as you have successfully met the goal of walking 5,000 steps every day for a week, you celebrate. For Garth, it was going out for ice cream—you might consider setting a healthier goal. Celebrating is critical, as it gives your brain a little dopamine blast as a reward for successfully making a change. Then you up the goal—say, 7,500 steps a day, then 10,000. After a few weeks at 10,000 steps, you might change the goal to something like "jog a quarter mile." Every two weeks, once you've met your previous goal, you make a small, incremental change. If you fall behind, no problem, just reset your goals and start over—but no ice cream. Your brain needs to pay a penalty for messing up.

You can see where this is going. At a certain point you are ready to walk-jog a 5K race. Then a 10K. And on you go, incrementally, toward that marathon. Signing up for a race also introduces another powerful motivator—accountability. It is best to sign up for these races with a friend and make an agreement to show up and finish the race, together. Studies show that when we create accountability, in this case by committing to a race and agreeing to run and finish the race together, the likelihood of our meeting our commitment increases substantially.

Will you eventually run a marathon? Maybe. But that's not the point. Along the way, your goals may change, and that's okay. It may take six months or so to get up to some serious mileage, and running a marathon might not be what motivates you at that point, but the important thing is that you will have established a method you can rely on for making changes.

Start small, set the bar low, and try something.

Notice What's Working @ Work

In *Designing Your Life,* we had readers try a basic self-awareness exercise called the "Good Time Journal." Here, we'd like you to try a variation on this exercise, which we call the "Good Work Journal." It's a simple tool for noticing and recording what engages you at work, what energizes you, and what puts you into a state of "flow." We recommend doing it as a regular daily practice for a few months in order to get a reliable and accurate understanding of what's working in your work life and what's not.

The basic principle is the same as the Good Time Journal: You observe and record your thoughts, emotions, and behaviors while at work, and then record what you notice about your work and your job. We have a few different categories of "noticing" that are connected to the research about what makes work "good work," and they are:

What did I learn?

What did I initiate?

Who did I help?

This process makes your observations about work explicit and tangible when you write them down. Then you see if anything pops out at you by asking the question *What do I notice?* This will break you out of your stereotypical response to the question *How was your day?* (*Okay, I guess*) and gives you a better sense of what is really going on. Practices like the Good Time Journal and the Good Work Journal help you gain awareness of what's working in your life and what's not. Over time, these practices contribute to a sense of moving in the right direction. And when you get used to setting the bar low and making the small incremental adjustments that come from noticing what's working, it all starts to add up to significant changes in your experience of work.

Below is an example of a Good Work Journal. (All of our worksheets can be downloaded from our website at www.designing yourwork.life.) You make daily entries and then "notice" your answers to the following three questions:

DATE	WHAT DID I LEARN?	WHAT DID I INITIATE?	WHO DID I HELP?
Monday	Learned how to make a pivot table in a spreadsheet.		
Tuesday	Learned that Gladys in Accounting just became a grandmother for the first time.		Helped John in the front office—put paper in the copier.
Wednesday		Organized a "Congratulations card" for Gladys in Accounting.	Helped cleaning staff—put everything on my desk for the carpet cleaners.
Thursday	Learned how to color-code cells in a spreadsheet based on positive or negative values.	Left the break room cleaner than I found it.	

DATE	WHAT DID I LEARN?	WHAT DID I INITIATE?	WHO DID I HELP?
Friday			Showed Celia in Accounting how to conditionally color-code cells in a spreadsheet.
Bonus Day	How to true-up bicycle wheel		Showed a friend in my bike club how to true-up a wheel.
Bonus Day	How to deposit a check by taking a picture with my phone—saving a trip to the bank—YEA!		Showed my partner how to deposit a check with a phone.

1. **What did I learn?** Reflect on your day and your week and ask yourself the question *What did I learn?* Look for small things, something that you've added to all the things you know. It doesn't have to be a big deal. It could be a new process or procedure, a new way to make a PowerPoint slide, or something new about Gladys in Accounting. Also be on the lookout for what we call an "unlearning." That's when, instead of adding to the things you know, you learned that something you thought was true wasn't. You thought the United States is bigger than Russia, and you found out that's not true. (Russia is 1.8 times larger than the United States.)

You thought that nobody liked strawberry ice cream, because you don't, only to discover that it is the fourth-most-popular flavor behind vanilla, chocolate, and butter pecan. (Who knew butter pecan was even on the list?) To feel like your work is working for you, the science says you have to be learning something every day. So notice every day what you learn.

2. **What did I initiate?** In order to feel like a designer in your job, you want to be creating and initiating things, most of the time. When you take it upon yourself to initiate an action, a change, or a new way of doing something, you satisfy what psychologists call an "innate need," and these needs are uniquely human. And when you are getting your innate needs met you feel like you have more control of your world. The best part—you don't need your boss's approval to initiate something. Pick something small, something that you can complete on your own, and you will garner the psychic rewards of being a creator. Some examples: organize everyone signing a birthday card for a fellow employee, clean up the break room after your shift (leave your campsite better than you found it), or build a better spreadsheet with color coding of the most important cells. Set the goal to initiate something new at work at least once a week. You'll be surprised how good this makes you feel. We'd be surprised if some people at work didn't take notice of your newfound initiative.

3. **Who did I help?** The science is clear on the value of helping others. In the Harvard Grant Study that we

mentioned earlier, doing something in the service of others had a very strong correlation to long life and happiness. And just like our intrinsic need for initiation, humans have an intrinsic motivation toward what psychologists call "relatedness." We call it being helpful. So take notice, every day or at least once a week, of something that you have done in the service of the people you work with. Again, small interventions count. Loading the copier with paper before it runs out so that your colleagues don't have to, watering someone's plants when they are on vacation, helping someone solve that weird color-coding problem with their spreadsheet, bringing coffee for your colleague on the night shift, etc. All of these small gestures build good karma around the office and help satisfy an intrinsic motivation—one you might not even know you had.

In the Try Stuff part of this chapter we have included the Good Work Journal exercise, and we encourage you to try it for at least a month. When you start noticing that you are learning new things, initiating useful changes around the office, and helping others enjoy their work, you'll probably notice that your satisfaction with work is increasing. Better yet, you don't need anyone's permission to start doing these things—the change that you are trying to make is entirely in your own hands.

Remember to start with a bias to action, set the bar low, reward yourself when you complete a week's worth of journaling, and, if you lose momentum for a while, no problem. Start back up where you left off, reset the bar, and keep going.

But go easy on the butter pecan ice cream!

A Time for Reflection

We know that it's really hard to separate your work from your life. Not just because so many hours of our lives are spent at work, but because who we are at home and who we are at work are not that different (unless you are a secret spy or living in witness protection). What makes us happy and gives us meaning travels with us from home to work and vice versa. Designing your life is designing your work, and designing your work is also designing your life. And we rarely give ourselves time to reflect on the totality of it all.

You've probably heard of "practicing the Sabbath," which is part of the Jewish tradition of resting from work for one day a week in order to more fully appreciate life. Most faith and wisdom traditions suggest some variation on this weekly practice of stepping back and reflecting on things. It helps us get the most out of our experience. Those traditions contributed to how we ended up with the modern "weekend" of Saturday and Sunday (although now many of us have turned the weekend into another crazy set of obligations).

We recommend that you take five to ten minutes—that's all— once a week on a non-workday, a Saturday or Sunday for most of us, and use that time for what we call our "7th Day Reflection" exercise. To do this well, you first have to understand our specific definition of *reflection* and why we think it's worth a try.

Reflection is the critical step in ensuring that you get more out of both work and life.

To reflect is *to think, ponder, or meditate* on an idea or experience, and when we use the term, we mean to give some quiet, focused attention to select ideas or experiences.

There are two types of life design reflections:

1. **Savoring**
2. **Insight**

By *savoring* we simply mean returning to an experience or thought and reentering and re-remembering it. You do this in a setting where you can give it your full attention, somewhere quiet and comfortable. You participate in the reflection at your own pace, via memory and imagination. Savoring something is inherently valuable in its own right—so a savoring reflection is about focusing on something worthwhile and giving it your honest, undistracted attention. This is the essence of getting more out of (rather than cramming more into) your life. By reengaging your experiences through a savoring reflection, you can more completely engage the fullness of what you're reflecting on, whether it is a social experience, an athletic endeavor, a work accomplishment, an artistic encounter, a new business idea—whatever. Savoring will deepen the experience, secure it in your memory, and expand your understanding of why the experience was valuable. *Voilà!* With a few moments of investment, you got more out of life—for free! Of course, if you document your savoring reflection with a note in your journal, your chance of experiencing more meaning in your life goes way up. It's a practice that pays off time and time again.

The second possible outcome—an insight reflection—is a more elusive beast, and it may or may not happen. Reflection will definitely help you avoid missing insights, but you can't demand an insight after every experience. But we can increase our chances, and invite and enable insights, by reflecting on and savoring our experiences.

Insight reflection usually begins with a question. Insights can be thought of as an ongoing conversation with yourself and your inner world. The insight generally comes by seeing the "bigger picture" behind an experience, or by sensing a deeper structure or emotional framework that gives the experience more importance.

Here's an example of both a savoring reflection and an insight reflection: During the week that Dave was working on this chapter, he had a three-day trip to Saint Louis to speak at a conference. While he was on the road, Dave sent his wife a small flower arrangement. When he got home, his wife gave him a big kiss and a hug and told him how much those flowers meant to her.

While doing his 7th Day savoring reflection on his week, that warm welcome home stood out. It was a brief moment, but when Dave savored it, when he re-remembered it deeply, it was so much sweeter. He was reminded how much he loves his wife, how glad he is to be married to her, how blessed he is to have a wife who is so affectionately grateful. The original hug and kiss were good—but the savored memory in reflection was awesome!

And . . . that brought an insight reflection as well. With all the worldwide trips that have come with being an author—which are pretty big and exciting—he'd lost track of the little things. His wife was almost as excited about those flowers as she was about going to Prague on a book trip with Dave. The insight was simple but profound: The emotional value of things is not proportional to their size. Simply put—never forget the little things!

Don't forget that reflection is *a practice.* That means that to be most effective, it ought to happen regularly. Give our 7th Day Reflection exercise a try for a couple of weeks and then take a moment to reflect on the practice itself; see how it works for you. Reflection is a powerful way to train your capacity for noticing your experience. So go for it, and welcome to "more" for free.

Wait, Are We There Yet?

Designing your work life is a continual process of building your way forward. Start with a bias to action—just do something. Then adopt the "good enough for now" point of view. Try it right now. No matter what isn't working at work, meet our challenge to do something, and accept the reframe that you could make it *good enough for now.* Then identify and resolve your hedonic treadmills and use the Set the Bar Low method for changing bad habits and behaviors. Adopt the practice of a daily Good Work Journal, and notice one or two positive things in your life every single day. Complete a 7th Day Reflection exercise once a week. Savor your experiences, and then dig around in them for insights. You may find that the mind-sets of bias to action and reframing are becoming second nature, and this will cause you to experience your work, whatever it is, in an entirely new way. You will start to notice how much more relaxed and energetic you are. And how much more available you are—to other people and to the opportunities that have started showing up all around you. Pretty soon, good enough for now will start to feel really good. That's because you are no longer asking from the backseat of your life, "Are we there yet?"

You're in the driver's seat.

Using design thinking.

Ready to start right where you are.

Try Stuff

MICRO-GOAL EXERCISE

1. Pick a bad habit you'd like to change, or a new habit or behavior you'd like to make part of your daily routine (exercise more, start a mindfulness practice, have a kitchen that is always clean, etc.).

2. Set some big goals. Write down a clear and measurable description of your eventual goals. (For example: I regularly get three hours of aerobic exercise a week; I meditate thirty minutes every other day, regularly; there are never dishes in the sink and the kitchen is always clean and ready to go for the morning, before I go to bed.)

3. Make the big goals part of your "story." Write a couple of sentences about what you'd get, what the emotional benefit to you would be, if you were to make this new behavior part of your regular routine. (For example: I'd get better health and sleep and feel good about how I look; I'd get a calm and centered approach to life and manage my anger better; I'd get an inviting place to cook and make nutritious meals for my family every day.)

4. Sneak up on the change you want to make with "micro-goals." Plan the first eight weeks (it takes about eight weeks to establish a new normal) of micro-goals, designed to get you partway (maybe 20 percent?) toward your big goal. Make the micro-

goals each week <u>easy</u>, something you think you're
sure you can do. And make sure that whatever goals
you set, you can measure the results.

5. Make sure you reward yourself, at regular intervals,
   for accomplishing your micro-goals.

6. Do not reward yourself if you slip back. And do not
   judge. Change is hard. If you're accomplishing 70
   percent of what you set out to do, you're doing great.
   You will get better and better at this as you go. Reset
   your targets and get back to being on track.

7. At the end of eight weeks, assess your progress
   toward your goal. If you have achieved most of what
   you set out to do (the 70 percent rule), congratulations.
   Now that you're feeling confident with your process,
   keep going. Set the next eight weeks of micro-goals
   and repeat.

There will be a temptation to start increasing the difficulty
of the micro-goals. Be careful—that could cause the process
to fail. Remember, this is the Set the Bar Low method—the
test for micro-goal size is simple: It should look easy and you
should be sure that you can do it. As you gain confidence in
the process, bigger goals might become easier, and that's
okay. But trust your gut and don't overdesign your goals. Stay
patient and keep reinforcing your progress with small suc-
cesses (and celebrations).

We've all heard the phrase, "Be the change you want to
see in the world."

We say, "Go forth and change the world, and yourself—one
small goal at a time."

GOOD WORK JOURNAL

1. Complete a log of your daily activities, using the worksheet provided (or in your own notebook). Note when you are "Learning," "Initiating," and "Helping." Try to do this daily, or at least every few days, and no less than once a week.
2. Continue this daily logging for three to four weeks.
3. At the end of each week, jot down your observations. Then ask yourself, *What do I notice?*
4. Are there any surprises in your observations?
5. Do you find that you have more entries in one of the three categories: learning, initiating, helping? If so, what do you think that means?
6. If you find that entries in one of the three categories are often missing, make a plan to boost your learning, initiating, or helping in the next week.
7. Observe how that intervention made you feel—make a note of that in your journal.

ONE WEEK "GOOD WORK JOURNAL" WORKSHEET

Use this worksheet to reflect on your day and your week and ask yourself three questions: What did I learn?, What did I initiate?, and Who did I help? Research shows that noticing these things will help you get more out of work and increase your engagement on the job. Try to have at least one entry a day.

DATE	WHAT DID I LEARN?	WHAT DID I INITIATE?	WHO DID I HELP?
Monday			
Tuesday			
Wednesday			
Thursday			

Friday			
Bonus Day			
Bonus Day			

7TH DAY REFLECTION EXERCISE

Here's a simple four-step exercise you can do weekly. We recommend making it a regular practice to get the most out of it.

1. Retreat

* Find a quiet spot where you can sit comfortably for five to ten minutes, either at a table or with a surface you can write on (preferably by hand, but typing is okay if you prefer).
* Close your eyes and just breathe for a moment. Take at least three or four full, calming breaths to slow yourself down and be glad that you're alive and have this quiet moment to yourself.

2. Review

- Now, while still keeping your eyes closed, let the last seven days flow before your mind's eye. As you do so, look for two to four moments in your week that you are attracted to and grateful for in retrospect.
- Note: Beware of being "attracted" to problems, conflicts, forgotten to-do items, etc. The mind loves to get caught up in that stuff. When that stuff appears (and it will), just tell yourself, *I'll get to that another time,* and let it go. Don't fight it or attempt to resolve it—both of which will steal all your attention. Just acknowledge it, then let it go and return to your reflection. Yes . . . this takes some practice to get the hang of.
- As you review your week, being attentive to those two to four moments, very briefly jot down just one or two words for each such moment that stands out, so you won't lose it. "Cheerful grocer" or "finished essay" or "appeased boss."

3. Reflect

- When you've got your list, look it over.
- Fully savor each of those moments again—getting the most out of them.
- If one particularly pulls your attention, feel free to journal a bit further about the experience. Nothing long or dramatic—just an entry to capture that experience.

4. Reinforce & Retain

- **Then reinforce your reflection by saying to yourself something like *I'm really glad for these things. With these in mind, it was a good week.* This is putting "good enough for now" to work proactively.**

That's it! And it really does take only five to ten minutes.

Bonus Step—Insights

- **If you notice that any of the moments you identified are offering an insight or a learning you want to capture, write that down, too.**
- **Insights don't always happen, but they're lovely when they do, so be sure and get yours when they're available.**

Bonus Step—Tell Your Story

- **One way of getting the most out of your life is by giving it away—through storytelling.**
- **If others in your household are doing this exercise, too, you can share your reflections.**
- **Most of us get asked, "Hey—how's it going?" at least once a week, if not more often. You could insert a story from your 7th Day Reflection in your answer. "It's going pretty well, actually. Why, just last week the checker at the grocery store ran out to the parking lot to return the credit card I'd dropped—how great is that?"**

What this exercise does is help you decide how to optimize your own experience of your life in your favor. We all do this anyway—focus our attention on some things and not on others. The problem is that most of us focus on the negative or difficult and bias our memory and mind-set negatively.

This exercise has nothing to do with pretending or fantasy. It's all about maximizing reality. The best moments of your week are real—we're just being sure to get the most out of them.

2

Money or Meaning

> **Dysfunctional Belief:** *I must choose money or meaning because I can't have both!*
>
> **Reframe:** *Money versus meaning (like work-life balance) is a false dichotomy. Money and meaning are just two different measurements of what I value.*

Are you Team Money or are you Team Meaning?

It's a question and a choice that a lot of people struggle with.

So, what's it going to be? Money or meaning?

Turns out there's no right answer, because it's the wrong question.

We really don't like false dichotomies, where one thing is pitted against another and it's a zero-sum game. The money-versus-meaning debate is one of those false dichotomies. Although it sure seems like meaningful work and making lots of money are two completely different and often incompatible things, a closer look at the situation tells us it's just not true. Or at least it doesn't have to be that way.

There are doctors working in rural America for very little money and lots of meaning, and there are plastic surgeons doing face-lifts in Los Angeles for lots of money and very little meaning.

There are teachers who have been teaching reading to first- and second-graders for forty years—we know one named Marion who just retired, but not before she taught Bill's daughters to read—whose lives are filled with lots and lots of meaning and just enough money to live comfortably and support their passion for teaching.

There are private-equity gurus who make tons of money, and spend a lot of that money self-medicating with drugs and alcohol, and buying things they don't want or need to distract themselves from their meaningless lives.

There are also burned-out teachers who have lost their love of teaching, and private-equity folks who love the game and find meaning in making capitalism more efficient and more effective.

There is no right answer or wrong answer to the money/meaning question. It's all about living coherently, which means living in tune with what you value. And in order to do that, you need a way to know when you are on the right track and when you are not.

You need to build your compass. (If you've already done this exercise from *Designing Your Life,* you can skip this section.)

The Coherent Life

The coherent life is one lived in such a way that you can clearly connect the dots between who you are, what you believe, and what you are doing. In *Designing Your Life* we explained the two things you need to build your compass—a Workview and a Lifeview.

A Workview is not about your job description, and it's definitely not the "I want a corner office and a company car" wish list. A Workview is a manifesto—it's the set of values you use to define what you think good work is and is not. It is an articulated philosophy of what work means to you. A Workview may address such questions as:

- **Why work?**
- **What's work for?**
- **What does work mean?**
- **How does it relate to the individual, others, society?**
- **What defines good or worthwhile work?**
- **What does money have to do with it?**
- **What does experience, growth, and fulfillment have to do with it?**

A Lifeview sounds big and daunting, but it is simply your own particular ideas about what gives life meaning and what makes life worthwhile. It probably involves others in your family and your community. It may have a spiritual component to it. A Lifeview is what helps us define what matters most. It might address these questions:

- **Why are we here?**
- **What is the meaning/purpose of life?**
- **What is the relationship between the individual and others?**
- **Where do family, country, and the rest of the world fit in?**
- **What is good? What is evil?**
- **Is there a higher power, God, or something transcendent, and if so, how does this impact my life?**

One good reason to have a clearly articulated Workview and a Lifeview, other than trying to live a coherent life, is so you don't end up accidentally living someone else's Workview or Lifeview. Trust us when we tell you it can happen. There are often lots of powerful voices in our head that have no problem articulating our views for us—telling us who to be, how to live, what work to do— and if we aren't careful, we can end up navigating with a compass that doesn't actually belong to us.

Coherence is the goal of this exercise. For example, if your Lifeview says that the way you make your life meaningful is spending time with your immediate and extended family, but you work so much that you forget your kid's birthday and you haven't returned that voicemail from your brother in three weeks, there is going to be some stress in your life that comes from this lack of coherency. Or if your Workview is all about how work should feed your soul, but, as a gig worker, you find that most of your high-paying freelance work is coming from companies whose products you would never buy because they are destroying the environment, you are going to spend a bunch of time rationalizing that you're not really the sellout you seem to be. Again, not so coherent.

Living the coherent life doesn't mean everything lines up perfectly every perfect day of your perfect life. It just means that you are doing your best to live in alignment with your World- and Lifeviews, whatever those may be. If we can see a clear connection between who we are, what we believe, and what we are doing for a living—then we know we are on course. Our compass is working.

Workview Reflection

Write a short reflection about your Workview. We're not looking for a term paper here (and we're not grading you), but we do want you to really write this down. Don't do it in your head. This should take about thirty minutes, and try to shoot for 250 words—less than a page of writing.

Lifeview Reflection

Just as you did with the Workview, please write a reflection on your Lifeview. This should also take no more than thirty minutes, and should be 250 words or so.

The only way to do these reflections incorrectly is not to do them at all. Think like a designer. Be curious. See what you discover. You won't have to read these to an audience (unless you want to—sharing them can be powerful). Just do it. If you are one of the almost 70 percent of people who are disengaged at work, please try to focus on answering the bulleted question prompts at the beginning of this chapter. You might just get to the bottom of your malaise in a matter of minutes.

Seriously, do this exercise right now. After you've written both, see where your Workview and Lifeview complement each other. Notice where you are living a coherent life, and where you are not.

Prepare for an "aha" moment.

We'll wait.

Alcoholics Shouldn't Work in Liquor Stores

For Dave, losing his dad at the age of nine was beyond difficult. He missed growing up with a dad, and it's a loss he still feels to this day. From the time he was young (and notwithstanding his deep-seated desire to be Jacques Cousteau), whenever anyone asked Dave what he wanted to be when he grew up, his answer was always the same.

"I want to be a dad."

This wasn't the cute answer of a somewhat precocious child. Dave really wanted to be a dad, and not any dad—he wanted to be a good dad, the kind of dad who spends lots of time with his kids. He vowed to never be one of those career-focused kind of guys. He was going to be all about family, all the time.

Then he began working in the high-tech industry in Silicon Valley, and he worked hard—fifty, sixty, seventy hours a week. He had a wife and a family, but his job required him to be on the road. He missed dinner most nights, coming in at 10:00 p.m., after the kids were in bed. Dave said he wanted to spend more time at home with his wife and kids, but his actions said something different.

He tried lots of ways to get home earlier, but nothing worked. Dave was baffled when he heard people at work calling him a workaholic. He wasn't addicted to work like the "real" workaholics that he knew. Workaholics cared only about the job and the money, and Dave wasn't that guy.

Except he lived like one.

And his life lacked coherence.

It turned out that Dave actually had attention deficit disorder, which meant he was easily distracted and easily interested. His work was full of interesting things to do, especially in a rapidly growing new technology company in rapidly growing Silicon Valley, so Dave was in a dangerous place.

Dave knew he had a problem, that he wasn't living coherently with his Lifeview and Workview, so he quit his job. He was sure the new job would let him get home in time for dinner.

It didn't work.

So he tried a new boss, a different role, and even a new industry, thinking that would fix his "overwork" problem—he tried it all. But everywhere Dave went, there he was. And he worked as hard and as long because he was as interested in every new shiny conversation that passed in front of him. He couldn't control himself.

And the saddest part of all was that, even when he was home, he wasn't really there for his family. His son wanted to play, but he was asleep in his chair, too tired to play. Dave had become the very opposite of what he had wanted to be when he grew up, a good dad. But he had no idea what to do. The problem required a reframe that was, at the time, bigger than Dave knew how to imagine. But he was sure he wasn't living the coherent life he wanted.

Sometimes life steps in, in the most unexpected way, and shows you a new path. Dave's mom got cancer. Dave knew she had a limited amount of time to live, so he took a leave of absence from his role as vice president of marketing. He wanted to make sure he had the time to focus on his mom. Almost immediately, Dave noticed that something was different. He was spending quality time with his mom, and he knew that was the right thing to do. And he was happy to discover that he also had more time to focus on his family. Things started to feel way more coherent, and he started to be who he knew he wanted to be.

And then something else started happening. A few former employers and friends at other companies began calling Dave to see if he could spare a few hours or a day or two to consult with them on small projects. He said no to some, depending on what his mom and his family needed, and yes to others. Unlike his day job, where he just couldn't say no to a project, the framework of consulting gave Dave a sense of freedom he didn't have as a corporate guy. He had thought briefly about being an independent consultant before, but it seemed a little scary and he wasn't sure he could support the family doing it. But now, having accidentally "prototyped" this new lifestyle (Dave didn't call it prototyping in those days, but that is exactly what he'd been doing), it didn't seem so scary. After his mom died and it was time to go back to work, he never went back. He became a full-time consultant. And while he gave up some money and a fancy title, he was able to buy back time—time to coach his sons' baseball teams, go on vacations with the family, and teach Sunday School. What Dave learned was that he was good at working hard, and he liked to do a lot of work, but working inside a corporation was a bad fit for him. Dave was best suited for the gig economy before there even was a gig economy.

Dave finally accepted that he is actually a workaholic, not because he loves work, but because he can't stop. And just as alcoholics probably shouldn't work in liquor stores, workaholics like Dave shouldn't work in Silicon Valley start-ups where the jobs are never, ever done. As a consultant, Dave was able to bring his Workview and Lifeview into coherence, and he found a way to manage his tendency to overwork. And he's never looked back.

Creating Coherence

Years ago, while waiting for a hamburger at an In-N-Out Burger in Las Vegas, Nevada, Dave and his then nineteen-year-old son struck up a conversation with a long-haul trucker. The trucker boasted, "I've got it made in the shade. I've got the best life of anybody I know." He went on to describe how, after years of being an independent, freelance trucker, who never really knew where his next job was coming from, he had signed up with a corporation where he had a regular route. This life redesign really suited him. His regular route was traveling about 2,500 miles a week, starting up in the Pacific Northwest and looping down around the Southwest and then back to his home out in rural Wyoming, where he had a small farm. He got to spend two and a half days a week at home on his farm. He got to see his kids and his wife every single week.

What a great work-life design! He was one of the happiest people Dave had ever met. He was making a living, he was enjoying his work, and he and his family had figured out a way to design a job that worked for everyone. And what a great role model for Dave's son.

You may not be a long-haul trucker, but if he can design a great work life, so can you. The challenge is to figure out how to follow your compass and create the coherency you need to feel like your life is working for you, like the trucker in Dave's story.

One warning: In the modern workplace people aspire to having their income-producing work also be their meaning-producing work. You're making the impact in the world you most care about and you are getting paid to do it. For many people, and especially when we talk to the Millennials and Gen Z-ers, this is clearly their model for the perfect job or the tailor-made gig.

This is the unicorn.

Seriously.

These people seem to think that you ought to be able to find your passion and get paid to do it. Every day. All day. For lots of money. Most of the time, however, it's just not possible. Most people, even if they find their passion, can't make a living at it.

We are really, really sorry that this is the way the world works—but part of coherency is dealing with reality. So it is time for another Accept. It's time to blow up this somewhat romantic idea about work and remember that this hasn't always been what people expected. For most of the nineteenth and twentieth centuries, people aspired to a simpler idea, where you make money one place and have a life in another. This is and has always been a valid way to live, and we suspect that it's the way most people live today. They just don't admit it—and that's part of what makes them unhappy.

For instance, Dave's "calling," other than being a great dad and now grandad, has been to help young people figure out their lives and to find their own "calling." But for most of his career, as we said, Dave made his living as a consultant, and he helped young people figure out their life on the side. In fact, the first time he ever got paid for doing this important work was at Stanford University, when he went on the payroll at the Life Design Lab, the lab he cofounded with Bill.

In the rest of this chapter we wrestle with the money–meaning dilemma (pinning it down once and for all) and help you to figure out where and what kind of impact you want to make in the world.

So, What Do You *Make*?

We've all been asked the question *What do you make?* (often by people who have no business asking it, but that's a different problem). Whether that question makes you uncomfortable or not—and most people don't like it—it does bring to the surface a very important topic.

What DO you make?

Here's our reframe—making is great. Designers love being makers, and we think everyone should be a maker, too. Now, *what* you make is the question, and it's not just about how much. As Einstein said, "Not everything that can be measured counts, and not everything that counts can be measured." We couldn't agree more, especially when it comes to "counting" money and meaning. We invite you to think differently about your making, which means being clear about what you measure.

Money and meaning are two different ways of "making stuff," so let's put on our smart maker's hat and sort out the money-versus-meaning conundrum. Let's get clear about how we want to measure ourselves as makers, at work and in life.

In the marketplace we generally use *money* as the measure of what we make. When people ask about a job, they always ask, "How much do you make at this job?" The more money you make, the more successful you are in job world, at least in most of the for-profit "market economy."

In the nonprofit world, which we will call the "making a difference economy" from now on, what people make is *impact*. Profits are not the goal; the goal is something like ending malaria, educating kids, or changing the world.

Regardless of whether they work for a nonprofit or a for-profit organization, most people care about both their success in making money and their success in making an impact. Finding and maintaining the right combination supports them in living a meaningful life.

However, that's not the whole story. We also find that, when people do their Workview and Lifeview and create their compass, living more creatively almost always pops up in one way or another. Most people, even those who do not work at a "creative" job, want more creativity in their lives. So it's a good idea to bring your inner artist to this discussion. When we went out and talked to lots of artists (and had empathy for their needs), they told us they value *expression* over everything else—that's how they keep track of what they make.

"I got to write and perform my play."

"I self-published my book of poetry."

"I painted a new painting that I really like."

In the artistic or "creative economy," it is all about the value of putting your ideas, your creative output, out into the world for all to see.

Money, impact, and expression—three different ways for people to measure what they make, at work and in their lives. It's a good way to "measure" how successful you are, and note that it is not another false dichotomy or an either/or situation. Finding your "mix" of all three maker-metrics will increase your sense of success and happiness, so coming up with a good mix for you, for now, of money, impact, and expression is important.

When you get your Maker Mix dialed in, your life is *in tune,* it *sounds* right, it's got a good *vibe.* Getting the right tune, sound, and vibe is what sound engineers do when they mix great music. The tool they use for that is a mixer board. They look like this:

A good sound engineer is expert at getting the right mix of the dozens of tracks that go into a great song. We like simple, and fortunately we think there are really just three tracks you need to manage to get your Maker Mix right. Here they are on our Maker Mix Board.

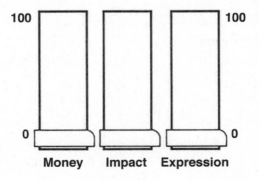

This board shows three kinds of maker outputs that we suggest you measure and manage—for the market economy, we measure the all-mighty dollar; for the making a difference economy, it's all about impact; and in the creativity economy, we measure expression. Like our other graphic tools, the goal is to help you tease out subtleties and understand where you are today, and where you aspire to be tomorrow. You adjust the sliders intuitively and keep adjusting the mix of money, impact, and expression until it feels right. You can always choose a different mix—it's up to you. There are no units—just a range from 0 to 100. You move each slider independently. And yes, we know that there can be overlap (you can get paid for some of your impact, and if you can sell your art, you're getting paid for your expression, too). That's fine, but you don't paint for the money, so intent matters. Just keep adjusting the sliders until your board looks right to you.

Before Bill went to work at Stanford, he was the president of a forty-person consulting company. He enjoyed working with his clients and solving their tough design problems. And sometimes he thought that the products his team was designing would be helpful to the world, and sometimes they were just good product designs. In consulting, you are always working on someone else's

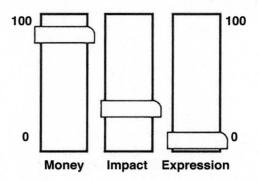

idea, so you can't try to control for impact and expression. He was doing the job mostly to have a fun way of making money. His overall Maker Mix is on page 62—way more moneymaking than impact or expression. And that was fine with Bill—at the time.

Then came the offer to work at Stanford, and the resulting Maker Mix below. Bill took a 50 percent pay cut when he decided to be a full-time academic, so he put his "making money" at a 30. Compared to Warren Buffett's, Bill's moneymaking isn't much, but it's fine for Bill and the work makes him happy. He makes his impact teaching, and his goal is to graduate a thousand smart designers, ready to work on the world's hard problems. He's been working on that goal for twelve years now and he's getting close. Making an Impact—almost there, and at a substantial level of 80. And Bill's future "job" is coming—within the next few years, he plans to transition to the "expression-making" world as a full-time artist—writing and painting to "make a living." Right now, to prepare himself for this future, he's got a studio about four blocks from his house in the Dogpatch neighborhood in San Francisco, and he gets to spend a weekend here and a weekend there work-

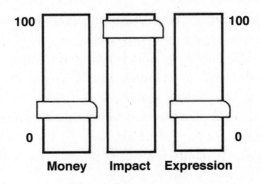

Bill's Current Maker Mix

ing on perfecting his skills as a writer and a painter. Today, his expression-making is still low on his Maker Mix Board, but that's a choice he's made, and it's good enough for now.

Again, the objective is coherence, and a good fit, with your goals and your stage in life. Bill and others like him can say that they are successful, even flourishing, because they are making conscious choices about their Maker Mix.

We believe that happiness in your work life comes from paying attention, and paying attention will help you get your Maker Mix dialed in. The trouble starts when you get your mix, well, mixed up. It's our experience that the people we meet in our workshops and in our classes are unhappy because they have confused the different ways of measuring what they make and are working against themselves. They are at cross-purposes with their own objectives.

For example, the unhappy artist typically confuses the value of her expression-making with moneymaking, and makes a false comparison: "I'm unhappy because I can't sell my paintings. I want my expression to have value—in money."

Or the nonprofit leader of a high-impact after-school program for low-income neighborhoods, keeping kids off the streets and out of gangs, is unhappy because she wants to be paid like a software developer. She is confusing moneymaking with impact-making.

It works the other way around, too. We've met the miserable partner in the big law firm, making seven figures, who's unhappy because he thought practicing law would have an intrinsic impact payoff (fighting for justice and the little guy), when instead he mostly gets paid in money for writing contracts for large multinationals that exploit the environment.

In each of these examples, the pain comes from measuring your success with the wrong yardstick. When you accept and understand the game you're playing, whether it be for money, impact, or expression (and it's always some combination of all three, regardless of what job you're in), you get clear that you value the rewards of the game, according to the rules of the game. Unhappiness comes when you muddy up your mix—trying to play tennis by the rules of golf might be funny, but it's not very productive.

It comes down to making good choices, consistent with your compass and what you value. Many successful and happy artists, poets, and writers, who live to paint, rhyme, and write, choose to do these things on their own terms, not on the market's. If they cared about money, the market's measure of value, they'd have to paint what people wanted to buy (black-velvet paintings of dogs playing poker, anyone?). Or they would have to write stories that they know they could sell (click-bait stories of over-Botoxed celebrities behaving badly, anyone?). They choose not to do this. They choose to be true to their inspirations and passions, and that choice often means that they cannot monetize their art. And, since this is a conscious and coherent life design, they are okay with that, or at least more okay with that than they are with the ugly velvet-dog option.

If it is a choice you make, your life can be good enough, even great, with the things you "choose into."

There's really no built-in reason you can't have it all—money, impact, and self-expression—at least in some measure. People do it all the time—they design clever workarounds that combine their need for impact and expression with a way to make a living doing what they love, mostly. These are the people who start a local theater group or an arts-and-crafts studio in their community. These ventures are typically organized as nonprofits, inherently about impact, and provide a valuable creative service to their communities, all the while allowing the artist-founder the opportunity to do their own work and feed their need for expression. Better yet, these clever, impactful, and expressive people get to surround themselves with people who love the arts, too.

Our friend James is a working musician who, in addition to writing and performing his own stuff (for expression-making), plays in three other bands and does studio work recording jingles for commercials (for moneymaking). James likes to say, "It might mean playing Whitney Houston covers over and over again at wedding after wedding, but I'll take that any day over a regular job." His bumper sticker reads: "The worst day playing music is better than the best day working an office job."

For Bill, after he becomes a full-time artist, his Maker Mix will look like this, with the expression-making becoming his "loudest" track. That means he's in the studio painting and writing most of the time, and that's his (next) idea of success.

Ultimately, and it's worth repeating, it's all about what you make in this world, and money, impact, and expression are three great

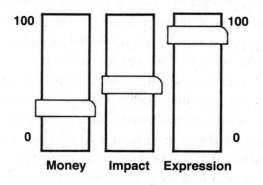

Bill's Next Maker Mix

ways to measure your making. So notice where you are, and then set a goal for where you'd like to be and go for it.

Dysfunctional Belief: *I can't make a living as an artist, dancer, singer, painter . . . fill in the blank.*

Reframe: *I know the money-versus-meaning problem is a false dichotomy, and I'm not letting the market define who I am and what I create. I decide how much money, impact, and self-expression works for me.*

Mapping Your Impact

Of the thousands of people we've met who are designing their work lives, many are struggling with these three questions:

Do I really fit here?

Am I really in the right job/career/company?

Is this really the right contribution and impact I want to make?

These questions are all about the role you are playing and where your impact comes from. Now, this could be the role you play at work, or at a nonprofit, or with something that is not considered work because it is unpaid. If we seek the coherent life, the life where everything fits together, then we are looking for the life where you will experience your impact as well. So we should really be looking closely at what we do—what our role is in the world—and how that role achieves the impact we are looking for. When we talk to people about what makes their job or their role meaningful, they all say that they want to know that the work they do is impacting the world in a positive way. They are just uncertain how to know if that's true.

So we've designed a tool to help you suss out the type and scope of the impact you are having—and we called it the Impact Map. It looks like this:

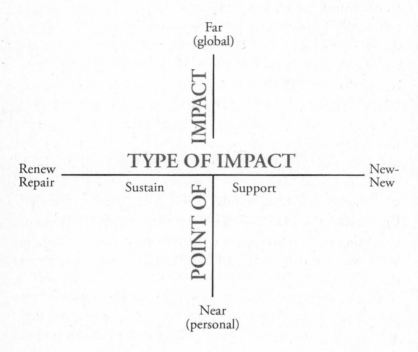

There are two axes on this map—one is about the "type of impact"; one is about where that impact occurs, the "point of impact." On our map, there are basically three different types of impact you can have in the world. One is not better or worse than another, but they are qualitatively different.

- **Renewing and Repairing things**
- **Sustaining and Supporting things**
- **Creating New-New things**

If you are renewing and repairing things, you are rebuilding or fixing existing systems and work in the world. If you are sustaining and supporting things, you are involved in running the systems that run the world and making sure they run well. And if you are creating new-new things, then you are creating whole new processes or systems. These three different ways to have an impact are mapped along the horizontal axis of our Impact Map.

On the vertical axis we map our point of impact—the places where we touch the world—which could be near to us (personal) or far from us (global). It's wherever we connect with the world. The most personal near point of impact is one-on-one, working with another individual to solve a problem or provide a service. Up one click is working with a team of people; one up from there is working with an institution or organization of folks. Working at the systemic and global level is the highest point of impact on the vertical axis.

As we said, there are no "good" quadrants on this map, just places where you've had a job or played a role in an organization. Any organization can be mapped, for-profit or nonprofit, and every role you've had has a place on the map. The map helps tease out some information about your past jobs, and the goal is to help you see a pattern that represents the most satisfying roles for you.

In the Impact Map on page 71, we have an investment banking systems analyst who analyzes companies according to a monetary system of evaluation. She reports that she is very satisfied sustaining and supporting banking, and making it more efficient. The impact of this role is to provide support at the institutional level. The Gates Foundation malaria program manager's job is to manage the project to rid the planet of malaria forever. That's fixing and repairing the world on the global level—a pretty satisfying role if you like working on large-scale systems. Our brain surgeon is also fixing something, something really, really important if he's taking a tumor out of your brain, but he can do this only one brain at a time. He can work only at the individual level. He's not creating something new, he's not inventing new surgical techniques, so he's way down in the lower-left quadrant. But his patients tell him that he had a big impact on their lives! Or take the homeless-center chef who is taking care of people who are in real trouble by feeding them. He's fixing hunger, one homeless person at a time, but he's also working with small groups of people to teach them how to cook, so he puts himself between fixing and supporting. The Google autonomous car development program engineer is trying to eliminate driving for millions of people, and she's creating a fundamentally new form of mobility—one that has never existed before. She's way over on the "new-new" side and semiglobal in scale (not quite global, as there are still lots of places and people not reached by paved roads).

When we are teaching our class at Stanford, we're doing a pretty new thing, and the thing we talk about—life design—is pretty new at most universities, so we'd put it closer to the "new-new" side of the horizontal axis and up in the "groups" point of impact. But we also spend time talking to educators all over the country and running studios to train other colleges to teach Designing Your Life classes at their schools. And in most of the higher education world,

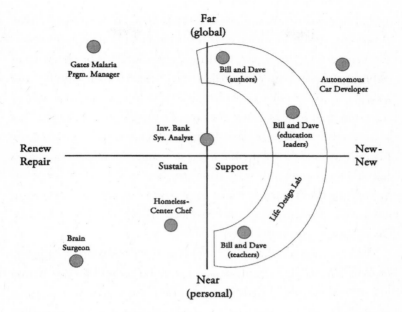

this life design stuff is definitely avant-garde. So it's a very new-new thing, and we are now working at a bigger scale, an institutional scale, because the d.Life Lab is training hundreds of educators and administrators from other colleges and universities, and changing higher education a little. And as authors, our book is published globally, so you can see our different roles on the Impact Map.

In all of these examples, you can see that it's possible to place a role you've had in a couple of different spots and you probably play more than one role in your current job. The goal of mapping your type and point of impact is to see if there are any patterns that might explain how you define and experience impact in one role or another and how that may be changing over time.

For instance, when we interviewed the homeless-center chef, he was clear that he needed some one-on-one connection with the people he served in order to feel his impact. "I tried working at the institutional level. For a while I was the director of the food bank, and it was a very important role. I raised money and awareness about the homeless problem and probably fed more people in that role than I do as a chef. But it didn't work for me, so I took a voluntary demotion, back to being a chef, so that I could see the joy on the faces of the people I was cooking for. When you help a homeless person not just by handing them one bowl of soup but by helping them learn to make soup for two hundred people, you are giving them hope and love that lasts. To feel like I have impact, that's what's important to me."

And we imagine that if we talked to the person organizing the malaria research program for the Gates Foundation, they would say something like, "I admire the folks on the ground in Africa, working in rural villages and handing out mosquito nets to people suffering in these high-malaria-infection zones. They are doing good work, in hard places, but that's not my work. I know I'm having an impact making sure that the millions of dollars that Bill and Melinda have allocated to this cause get spent effectively and efficiently. I'm good with numbers and working with large systems; my signature strengths are best deployed in my job as their program manager. This is what I was put on earth to do."

So you see, two people, two roles with very different types and points of impact, and two very satisfied workers. We want you to be satisfied, too, so later, when we get to the Try Stuff part of this chapter, we invite you to map your impact and see what comes up.

Armed with a clearer idea of what you make in the world, and where you want to have impact, we still have a lot of interesting problems to solve on the way to making it work at work and designing the life you want.

The good news is that designers love problems.

And the first thing that designers do when faced with a persistent, recurring, or hard-to-solve problem is to design a better problem. We call it "reframing." Designers do it all the time, and so can you.

Try Stuff

Note: Before you try out these two new tools, your Maker Mix and your Impact Map, make sure you have a solid compass to guide you. You build your compass by completing a Workview and a Lifeview and examining the coherence between these two things. There is no good or bad Work- or Lifeview. As long as what you've written accurately reflects how you feel (be brutally honest here—this is your reality-based view of work and life, not something you aspire to), it's a good place to start. We recommend revisiting your compass every year or so, or whenever you are contemplating a big change, like changing jobs or careers, or moving to a new city or town, or whenever you start a new chapter in your life. That's when having an accurate compass is the most helpful.

With a solid compass in hand, try these next two exercises to help you sort out the money, impact, and expression conundrum, and to help determine where in the world you are likely to feel you have the most impact.

MAKER MIX EXERCISE

1. The goal of this exercise is to come up with a subjective evaluation of how much moneymaking, impact-making, and expression-making you have in your life right now, your Maker Mix, and how you feel about it. The visualization is simple: You set up your Maker Mix Board to represent your current life mix. Notice once again that there are no right answers— there are lots of good mixes. If lots of expression and little money, or lots of money and little impact, sounds right or seems in tune, then your sliders are right where they should be. And remember, the positions of the sliders on your money/impact/expression mix board are "set" from your gut-level understanding of what is actually the "you are here" state of things.

2. Write a few sentences about how it's going in each of the three areas: moneymaking, impact-making, and expression-making.

3. Adjust the location of each maker slider in your current situation.

4. Ask yourself how you feel about your board.

5. Now build the board you aspire to, the one that you think would represent one manageable step toward a better balance, one that would result in a more coherent life.

6. Brainstorm a couple of simple changes you'd like to make to adjust any one of your "slices."

7. Come up with a few simple prototypes you'd like to try that move a slider a little to change the allocation of

money, impact, and expression in your mix (review the Set the Bar Low method from chapter 1).

MAKER MIX WORKSHEET

This graphic has sliders for three kinds of "maker outputs"— for the market economy, we will adjust **Money** in the mix; for the making a difference economy, we adjust **Impact**; and in the creativity economy, we will dial up **Expression**. Like our other graphic tools, the goal is to help you understand where you are today, and where you aspire to be tomorrow. You move the sliders intuitively and keep adjusting the mix of money, impact, and expression until it feels right. There are no units—just a range from 0 to 100.

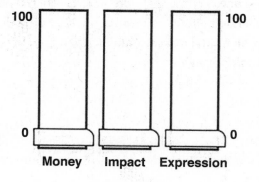

Now design the mix you like in the future. Are you doubling down on money to pay off those students loans—okay push that slider up. Or are you in a season of life where impact and expression are "how you want to get paid." Whatever the mix, make it fit for you.

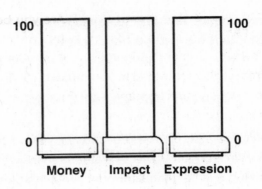

Money   Impact   Expression

Now write down three things that will help you start moving in the direction of your preferred Maker Mix.

_____

_____

_____

_____

_____

_____

_____

_____

_____

Now go out and try a couple of your prototypes and then redo your Maker Mix Board. Did you successfully move one of the sliders? Did something unexpected happen? How did it "sound"? Is life easier to dance to now? Are you starting to realize that you need more expression in your life (after all, you are a creative person, aren't you)? Are you being really clear on how important money is to you (not as much as you thought!)? And are you staying vigilant about identifying any hedonic treadmills embedded in your answers? Tip: The negative aspects of hedonic treadmills are most often associated with the accumulation of money, so be careful with that track.

Check in with yourself and update this simple Maker Mix Board every once in a while, or anytime you think your life coherency might be slipping a little. It is easy to get out of tune in our hyper-busy modern work world. Socrates's "examined life" (you know, the one worth living) requires periodic checkups—the money/impact/expression Maker Mix is another good way to answer the question "How's it going?"

MAP YOUR ROLE EXERCISE

IMPACT MAP WORKSHEET

List 4–6 roles (past, present, and possible future).

A "job" might have several possible roles, each with a distinct place on the map.

_____

_____

_____

_____

_____

_____

Locate the roles on the map.

Far
(global)

IMPACT

TYPE OF IMPACT

Renew
Repair

New-
New

Sustain   Support

POINT OF

Near
(personal)

Reflect:

What do you notice?

What insights does this generate?

What questions does this surface?

_____

_____

_____

_____

_____

_____

_____

1. List four to six of the possible roles you have. And
   don't forget, your job might have multiple roles. You
   might be a production assistant and a planner and on
   the corporate culture committee. So make sure that
   you list all the key roles that you have, and you can
   also list roles you had previously. In fact, it's probably
   a good idea to think about the other roles you have
   had in the past and where they fit. And you may even
   think of some future roles that you've been imagining
   having. The Odyssey Planning exercise from *Designing
   Your Life* includes imagining three completely different
   versions of your next five years of life. If you're doing
   Odyssey Planning, be sure to include some of the roles
   from each of your alternative ideas in your Impact
   Map.

2. Now locate each of the roles you listed within their
   quadrant on the Impact Map. There is no good, better,
   or best quadrant. The tendency is to think that the
   big impact and creating something new is the better
   quadrant. It's not. Ridding the world of malaria is
   no "bigger" in impact than being a brain surgeon,
   particularly if you are the person whose brain got fixed.
   There's no "good place" on the map. On the horizontal
   axis, you are thinking in terms of renew and repair,
   sustain and support, and creating something new. On
   the vertical axis, you are moving from the intimate and
   personal to the global. Maybe you are the caseworker
   taking the personal history of a homeless person—
   that's one-on-one. Or maybe you're raising money
   for the homeless—that's up the y-axis a bit and more

toward a regional impact. **Writing sex-trafficking policy in a windowless basement office at the UN would be operating at the national or even global level, and super-satisfying if that's a good fit for you. One of our students did it all, over time. He went from being a Starbucks barista (supporting individuals' need for daily coffee), to being an emergency 911 dispatcher (remediating a small town's fires and crimes), to finally becoming a county health policy developer (thinking up new ways to enhance wellness across a five-city region). There are no bad spots, just better and worse fits.**

3. **After you've plotted your roles, the next step is to notice stuff (awareness is the first step in any change process) and ask yourself some questions:**
   o **What do I notice? Are there any patterns to this data?**
   o **What insights does this generate?**
   o **What questions surfaced during this exercise? What am I now more curious about?**

Does looking over your Impact Map generate any information about the kinds of roles that were a good fit for you? Did you have a role somewhere on the map that you never liked? Or did you have another role that you didn't think was as important, and you realize now that it was actually quite impactful? If all the jobs you disliked are in one quadrant, that's an important thing to notice. Write down your reflections on your Impact Map.

You are not a static object, and as you grow into roles, your needs and abilities change. The way you perceive impact changes. Be curious about what this exercise reveals. If you find yourself having a bias toward a certain quadrant—for example, I would love to do all my work in the personal/new-new quadrant—then get curious about the skills you need to acquire to play a role in that quadrant.

This tool is one way to get clearer about how to design your roles and your jobs to make sure that you are experiencing meaning and impact. You can also use it to redesign the role you already have by changing either its point of impact or its degree of change.

3

What's the Problem?

Dysfunctional Belief: *My problems at work are insurmountable. I'm totally stuck.*

Reframe: *I'm never totally stuck, because I know how to reframe anything into a Minimum Actionable Problem (MAP).*

We're trying to design a happier life, and a better job, we hope without the hassle of changing jobs, moving towns, or getting liposuction. So that means we're probably dealing with some problems at work. And we have to ask:

What's the problem?

As we said in the last chapter, designers love problems. And we're here to tell you that people can lose days, weeks, months, years, and even decades of their life working on the wrong problem. Figuring out which work problem is actually the problem to work on may be one of the most important decisions you make in designing your work life.

The Art of Reframing

There are lots of skills that contribute to effective *problem-finding*, which we define as identifying the most effective problem to work on—the one that gives you the best chance of coming up with lots of good solutions. Learning the art of *reframing* to find a better problem is by far the most crucial of your life design skills. Great designers are always great at reframing. They can continually (almost annoyingly) be heard to say, "Well . . . what if we looked at it *this way* . . ." Then they describe a new way to look at the problem at hand. When you do this, possible new solutions start percolating to the surface almost immediately.

Reframing. It's a skill and a design superpower.

We get asked all the time: "How'd you DO that?"

"It's magic," we coolly reply.

Well, not really—but it seems like magic when you are good and thoroughly stuck in some problem and in walks someone with a reframe that suddenly busts everything open. That stuck-busting reframe really seems magical—and it makes the reframer look like the ultimate magician.

What is a reframe, anyway? It's a do-over. A problem-framing do-over.

When you define a problem, you are always "framing" it—putting a box (a frame) around it and defining what's in the box and, importantly, what is not. Once the problem is framed, then you get inside that frame and start working on it.

GET IN THE BOX: This is the "box" that people are always trying to "think outside of." The saying "Think outside the box" sounds like there's some way to think in a totally unconstrained and creative way, "unboxed" thinking. Not true. There's always a box. There has to be—your brain can't be all over the universe at once. (Contain yourself!)

Creativity is all about playing around with how you frame your box and how you "play" within that framing.

Step 1: Accept that there is always a box.

Step 2: Remind yourself that you made the box when you framed the question, and you can change the frame when you need new, more helpful solutions.

Minimum Actionable Problem (MAP)

There are lots of problems that *sound* like they have no solutions. For instance, we knew a guy named Bernie and, although he liked his job at a large ground transportation company (we can't tell you which one), he had a problem that had been bothering him for a while. "My boss is just a jerk," said Bernie. "And I'm never going to get any appreciation for the hard work I do around here." We hear this problem, framed pretty much this way, all the time. But it's one of those "problems" that has issues and needs reframing. Exactly what the right reframe is will depend on the specific situation. (By the way, it *always* depends on the specifics: There are no generic reframes. A very famous architect, Mies van der Rohe, director of one of the first design schools on the planet, the Bauhaus, is famous for his phrase "God is in the details.")

Reframing is in the details.

You may have heard of MVP, which stands for Minimum Viable Product. It's a big idea in the world of innovation and entrepreneurship. Start-ups know that getting any new product to market is really, really hard. You don't want to make it any harder than you have to—so the idea is to just build your first product with all the valuable (viable) features and no more. That's a great idea, and it applies to reframing, too, but this time instead of MVP we will call it "MAP," which stands for Minimum Actionable Problem. Once you have reframed your big hairy problem, once you've turned it into its Minimum Actionable Problem, you get to solve a much smaller and more tractable problem.

Life is hard enough on its own. Seriously. If everyone's life was perfect and jobs were hassle-free, nobody would be reading our books. Don't add to the burden by making your problems any bigger than necessary. When it comes to problems, you want to set the bar low and clear it, just as we discussed in chapter 1. Then lather, rinse, repeat.

We find that so-called insurmountable problems like Bernie's are usually either (1) truly inactionable and therefore circumstances to accept and not actionable problems (we call these "gravity problems," because, well, there's nothing you can do about gravity, it just is), or (2) poorly framed problems that we can reframe to make them more actionable.

It's that second group we really want to focus on here. So it's time to learn the art of reframing and cash in on our free do-over. It takes a few tries to get it, and you'll get a lot better with practice. (Like so-called magic, you just need to know how to do the trick.)

Zooming In

Dave's been an independent management consultant for more than twenty-five years. Doing a thorough and penetrating situation analysis at the beginning of any project is crucial. He's something of a pro at situation analysis, and over the years he's developed a very sophisticated approach to this part of his practice. He's boiled the process down to asking just two questions:

Expert Consultant Dave Question #1: What's going on?

(Then he listens to the very long answer the client gives him, he takes a thoughtful pause, and then he asks the second question.)

Expert Consultant Dave Question #2: Okay. Now, what's really going on?

That's it. Really. In any situation where people are stuck and stress abounds, it's not hard to get an answer to Question number 1, and it's exactly the right place to start. Dave would just ask it and start taking notes. After three or five or forty-five minutes of listening to the answer, Dave would move on to the really strategic part of his analysis by asking the insightfully penetrating follow-up question: Now, what's *really* going on?

That has been Dave's number 2 investigative question for decades, and it works about 95 percent of the time in getting to the bottom of the real problem in very short order. In most situations, there's what psychologists like to describe as *the presenting situation* and then there's *the underlying situation.* Question number 1 gets at the presenting situation and Question number 2 gets at the underlying situation.

It's the way to get to your new MAP. Your Minimum Actionable Problem.

The first key to learning how to reframe something is to break open the difference between what's going on and what's *really* going on. The trick to doing that is first zooming in to get rid of stuff in the first description that doesn't need to be there. Then, to get rid of any other baggage you might be carrying, you zoom out to decipher what's really going on, behind the scenes. Let's look at Bernie and the "bad boss" example from earlier:

Step 1: Ask Question #1: "What's going on?"

Bernie's answer: "My boss is just a jerk, so I'm never going to get any appreciation around here."

Step 2: Zoom in to strip out the unnecessary drama.

Start with the question: What personal biases, presumptive reactions, or embedded solutions have found their way into Bernie's description of this problem, biases that are weighing it down unnecessarily? By the way, don't judge Bernie or yourself for making the problem more complicated than it needs to be. It's entirely normal for some drama and emotions to creep into your problem statement. Why? Because we're all human. Bernie has been unhappy for some time. Pain is involved. And while we respect Bernie's legitimate emotions and frustrations, we also humbly suggest that putting extra drama in how you describe the problem distracts you from designing your way out. So, a key step in all reframing is this objective analysis, this zooming in on the real problem.

Now let's see what we find by zooming in and doing some cool, calm, and objective analysis.

Dramatic Component #1: *Jerk*

Jerk is a character judgment Bernie is making about his boss. Is he in fact a jerk, or does he simply not give feedback? And does calling him a jerk really help when Bernie wants to come up with some possible solutions to make his job better? Let's say in this particular instance that Bernie's boss is hardworking, maybe even driven, and he's probably kind to his kids and pets, but his social/ emotional quotient isn't great and he's terrible when it comes to the kind of feedback Bernie wants, because he doesn't give him any. Bernie may not like his boss, if *like* means he'd enjoy having a beer or going bowling with him, but that's a personality thing and not that relevant for this "zoom in" analysis. Bernie's boss is objectively bad at feedback, but broadly categorizing him as a jerk doesn't help Bernie find a solution to his problem.

Let's drop this term; it introduces an unnecessary bias.

Dramatic Component #2: *Just* a jerk

Try saying, "My boss is *just* a jerk . . ." out loud, and really lean into the word *just*. Go ahead, do it now. Hear it? Try it again. Do you hear it—when you get to the word *just*? There's a real edge there, and that means something. It strongly suggests that Bernie's boss is all jerk, all the time. That's tough. And it's probably a little unfair. It is, however, reasonable to conclude that change is unlikely, and it's probably smart not to predict some big "feedback transformation" any day soon. So, without the drama and the exaggeration, let's call it what it is: Bernie's boss is a poor feedback provider, unlikely to change. But that's a far cry from the total universal disaster contained in the statement: *My boss is just a jerk.*

Dramatic Component #3: *Never going to get any*

"Never—any" is the most emotional aspect of Bernie's poorly posed problem statement. Why? Because it includes an inflexible and universal (*never* and *any*) statement that implies two things: one, that the only valid appreciation at work must come from one and only one source, Bernie's boss, and two, without his boss's appreciation, Bernie is "never going to get any." Ever. "Never get any" is an upgrade to Bernie's problem that you don't want, need, or deserve.

This means we have what we call an "anchor problem" here as well, since Bernie has embedded the solution he wants in the problem statement—see the description of anchor and gravity problems later in this chapter. You'll get a great tip on reframing about half the badly framed problems out there.

Step 3: Ask Question #2: What's really going on?

Now we ask the question: What is really going on? This is the critical step where you take the insights from Step 2 and reframe how you describe the problem in a way that defines your new MAP—Minimum Actionable Problem. There are multiple right answers to this reframe, so don't get hung up on getting it right. Just get it *actionable*.

At the d.school we like to start a reframe with the phrase *How might we . . .* for teams or *How might I . . .* for individuals. It's an open and positive way to start the sentence and tends to lead to more generative and creative possibilities. Here are three reframes that give Bernie a MAP that he can work on:

- **MAP 1: My boss rarely gives positive feedback, so *how might I* receive explicit appreciation for my work from someone else in my organization?**
- **MAP 2: My boss has many qualities except being appreciative, so *how might I* get affirmation from other sources whom I respect?**
- **MAP 3: The management approach at my employer does not require giving positive feedback, so *how might I* reframe work satisfaction as coming from my paycheck and look for personal appreciation outside the office?**

With MAP 1, a number of interesting prototype possibilities become obvious. Bernie can set up a coffee meeting with some other managers in his organization and find out how they give feedback. Bernie can solicit feedback from the program managers on the projects he contributes to. And, to ensure his professional integrity, Bernie can practice giving feedback to the people who work with him, doing what's called a "360 review" with anyone who volunteers (they have to opt in), making sure that he is modeling what he thinks are good management practices.

With MAP 2, Bernie has expanded his possible sources of feedback. He remembered a professor at business school who he really liked and occasionally has coffee with. Bernie decided to document his work accomplishments and ask his old professor for some objective feedback. He also respected a buddy of his from grad school, a friend who has gone on to start his own tech company. He decided to ask his friend if he thought the quality of his work was up to start-up standards. Both are credible sources of the feed-back he wanted.

Note that in MAP 3, Bernie continues to believe in Dramatic Component #3—that he will never find appreciation at work because the boss doesn't do it, and Bernie has apparently con-cluded that his particular boss's behavior is a management norm for the whole company. If that's true, and Bernie can find this out by talking to his colleagues in other departments, then maybe this is a reasonable reframe. It means that getting appreciation at this company is a gravity problem (that word again—don't worry, explanation to follow)—it isn't actionable, it's just a really negative part of Bernie's company culture. Once Bernie has that Accept in place, he can focus on reframing a new Minimum Actionable Problem and look to find his appreciation elsewhere. In MAP 3, Bernie accepts the limitations of his company's culture, doesn't get mad, and focuses this one aspect of his energy (desire for apprecia-tion) outside work—at home, in fatherhood, by coaching, at book club, or in church or some other group or club.

The bottom line is that there are lots of ways for Bernie to get feedback and appreciation (or to get whatever resolution he is longing for). All three of these MAP reframes immediately sug-gest prototypes he can try and actions he can take. And Bernie is no longer stuck.

Bonus Round: Zooming Out— What's Really, Really Going On?

There's a handy little bonus that comes along with many (not all, but many) reframes. That bonus analysis helps you get rid of some baggage—stuff you might have been dragging around for a long time. It's hiding in those dramatic components you identified in Step 2 of reframing. The trick is in knowing how to use your curiosity to find it.

In the example above, the dramatic components were "jerk," "*just* a jerk," and "never get any." These are not actually objective elements of the problem; they are elements that added emotional energy to the problem and often made it harder to solve. But these little bits of emotion didn't get in there randomly, and if we can understand what links them so strongly to the problem, we get our bonus.

So first you zoomed in; now you zoom out. When hunting for our baggage-reduction bonus, we need to first adopt a designer's mind-set of curiosity. When Bernie did it, it sounded like; "Hmmmm . . . I wonder if some of this stuff, this negative energy, about my boss, really isn't about my boss. Maybe it is coming from somewhere else?" That stance—one of openness and starting with curiosity—led Bernie to the next question. "Assuming for a moment that were the case, where would all this negative energy be coming from and why is it attached to this problem with my boss?"

Bernie's question opened the possibility for a moment of personal reflection. It can for you, too. Like Bernie, you might want to ponder your question, jot some thoughts in your journal, take a walk, or ask your pet schnauzer what he thinks—whatever fits for you. But take a look inside and see what you notice. Very often the dramatic stuff in a stuck situation includes our own old baggage: old wounds not yet fully healed, sensitivities we just can't seem to dampen, biases no one's talked us out of yet—those sorts of things.

In this case, when Bernie asked himself where this really strong reaction to being underappreciated was coming from, his old scoutmaster came to mind. He was an ex-Marine and loved barking orders to little people in uniform, but he sure wouldn't know how to say "Good work!" or "Hey, nice job!" if his life depended on it. That scoutmaster's lack of appreciation had a pretty big impact on a young, somewhat shy, twelve-year-old Bernie.

Dave actually had that type of scoutmaster. He was a World War II Marine and a veteran of the Battle of the Bulge. He was a terrific guy and the one you wanted next to you if you got lost in the woods with nothing but a penknife and shoelaces, but you couldn't expect any praise or affirmation from this guy. He was fresh out. Fortunately, Dave was pretty good at reframing, even at the ripe old age of twelve. "He's an awful tough SOB and I wish he were nicer, but I know lots of nice people. What I really need is someone to teach me how to backpack and take care of myself outdoors, and this guy sure can do that! Thanks for all that great training, Mr. Smith!"

So Bernie noticed that having some negative history with leaders who lack appreciation skills might be the reason he brought some heightened sensitivity to his company. If so, Bernie's history around not getting feedback might be amplifying his reaction to his boss's admittedly inept style, to both of their detriments.

End bonus round.

The Big Reframe
Zoom-Out Double Bonus

Let's say in Bernie's zooming-out analysis he kept going and the phrase "never going to get any" caught his attention—especially the word *get*, which actually wasn't an important part of his original reframe analysis. But it's got his attention now.

Hmmm . . . get any . . . get any . . . get any . . . Wait! I know. To get something, someone's got to give it to you, right? That's it. I want to receive appreciation that is freely given to me, preferably unsolicited, spontaneous appreciation. What I really want is to get it without asking first. In fact, now that I think about it, my gold standard for appreciation is Mrs. Dunleavy, my third-grade teacher. She was fabulous! I will never forget walking back to class that day after recess when Mrs. Dunleavy saw me from thirty yards away and shouted in front of everybody, "Oh, Bernie! I just read your essay and it was just wonderful. Terrific job, honey!" Man—that was the best day of my life.

So Bernie has an "aha" moment and realizes he's been waiting for a boss, any boss, to be like Mrs. Dunleavy. Aren't we all, in a way, waiting for Mrs. Dunleavy?

Unfortunately, those kinds of bosses are pretty rare. Bernie concludes that he has waited long enough for such a boss and is ready to try another approach. So he gets curious again (curiosity is such fun) and talks to his coworker Basran about this "lack of feedback" problem. Basran tells Bernie that he knows exactly what their mutual boss thinks of *his* work. In fact, he reviews his professional development goals with the boss in a monthly one-on-one meeting. Basran asked for this meeting. Basran didn't wait for the boss to offer. He asked for feedback—and he *got it.*

But that's not spontaneous and freely given, thinks Bernie. That's the way he likes his feedback. That's the way Mrs. Dunleavy did it. Is it really good feedback if he has to ask for it?, he wonders.

And right in that moment Bernie realized he was doing it again; he was embedding one of his preferred solutions (. . . spontaneously given feedback is the "good" kind) in the problem statement, and thereby ruining his chance of an actionable solution.

Bernie's goal is to get unstuck and build his way to a better, more enjoyable work life. He should be designing for actionability—not perfection. Spontaneous feedback might be lovely, but Bernie knows his boss isn't wired that way—and if Basran is getting the kind of feedback he craves, just because he asked for it, Bernie could do that, too.

He could just ask for feedback and he would get it?

Mind. Officially. Blown.

It might not always be quite that easy, but sometimes it just might be. And when it is that easy, you might suddenly hear a bell go off. DING DING DING! DOUBLE BONUS, BONUS!

Every now and then when you do a Zoom Out reflection on your reframe process you score the Big Reframe Double Bonus. You discover that, like Bernie, there is a chance for you to get just what you want, if you just ask for what you need.

This kind of breakthrough reframe doesn't happen too often, but when it does, it is incredibly powerful and freeing.

The Zoom Out Bonus reflection process provides an invitation to outgrow an old problem. After you've reframed a problem, if you find some old baggage lurking in the corner, it might be time to get rid of it. Totally optional, of course—after all, it's just a bonus feature.

Life Is a Multiple-Choice Test

Now that you've got a reframe working and you've redefined the problem—what do you do with your brand-new, small-enough-to-be-actionable MAP? Well, what you don't try to do is solve it. That's right. You heard correctly. Most real problems can't be solved, at least not with a once-and-for-all kind of solution that so many of us are looking for. Life isn't like algebra:

Solve for x using the following equation: $3x + 2 = 11$

Solution: $x = 3$

That nice, clear number 3 is the kind of solution you can really depend on. When you look at it, you *know* it's the *right* answer and your problem is good and solved. The problem is, in our experience, the interesting problems that life asks us to get creative with and reframe are seldom solvable that way. Most of the time the best we can do with our problems is solve them "for now." So it might be more accurate to say that, rather than solving a problem, we're actually just responding to a problem and trying to get it into an acceptable new state. When we've attained that new and more acceptable situation, we've come to a resolution. The problem might not be permanently solved, but it is resolved for now, it is *re-solved.*

Psychologist John Gottman has made the study of human relationships, particularly marriages, his life's work. He has videotaped more than three thousand couples in his "Love Lab" at the University of Washington, and, after coding the heart rate, facial expressions, and body language during thousands of hours of interactions, has come to a startling conclusion. His data says that 70 percent of the problems that couples wrestle with are unsolvable. He calls these "perpetual problems." But that is not necessarily a bad thing. His conclusion is that the couples that stay together for life, what he calls "Master Couples," accept that many of their problems are like this and develop workarounds. They do not let these problems end up destroying their happiness. They seek a "good enough" resolution of these perpetual problems and move on.

We think this is important data that can be extrapolated to most of our hard life problems.

The first step is to recognize that we're going for an acceptable measure of resolution—not the perfect answer. (If this sounds reminiscent of the "good enough for now" idea from chapter 1, that's because it is. Like we said there, good enough for now is a big idea, and it reappears in a number of forms throughout this book.)

Knowing that we're going for an acceptable resolution and we don't have to permanently solve the problem introduces us to the next big idea in designing a resolution for our reframed MAP.

Best Doable Option (BDO)

When we talk with people in "office hours"—whether that person is one of our Stanford students or any one of the thousands of people of all ages we have spoken with over the last few years—we often go through the following routine right after hearing someone describe a messy problem.

"Gosh, Chandra, that sounds like a pretty complex situation you've got there. I can see that you're a little discouraged because you're just not sure if you can ever really understand the problem well enough to come up with a good solution. Is that right?"

"Yes. Yes! That's exactly right. I really don't know how to get started, since I don't fully understand the situation. What do I do?"

"Well, I think you might be in luck. As it turns out, in your situation—as in many, many, complex situations faced by many, many people—you don't have to understand the problem to solve it."

"Wait, what? How does that work?"

"Simple, really. It frequently turns out that many of the really hard problems in life are best treated as multiple-choice tests. You don't really have to figure it all out—all you have to know is enough to choose."

That and the designer's mind-set of bias to action and you are good to go. We call it "finding the Best Doable Option (BDO)."

Think about it. Despite many layers of complexity, lots of times there aren't infinite versions of possible solutions to your problem. And by taking a bias-to-action approach, you get unstuck, make a decision, and move into your future—a future that you chose instead of one that would eventually be chosen for you by inaction. When you get good at recognizing your BDOs, you get good at making actionable choices and are the designer of your future.

Let's take a simple example. Let's say you and your friend don't know what to do for dinner. You don't really know what you want to eat and you don't know where to get it. He looks at you and asks, "Well—what do you *feel* like?" and you really don't know. What do you do?

It's actually an insoluble problem, because you really don't know (and it's probably not worth going to therapy to figure out why you can't answer this simple question). But that doesn't actually matter, because you have only a few doable options that are available to you. Four options, to be exact:

1. **Cook at home**
2. **Go out**
3. **Have something delivered**
4. **Starve**

That's really it. Every other option is just a variation on one of these (and no, eating all the popcorn left between the couch cushions does not count as option 1). So all you really need to know is whether you're going out (2) or staying in (1 or 3), or whether you'd rather just not face it and go to bed (4). You quickly decide that option 4 is out because you're too hungry. Then it's just eat out versus eat in? You're too tired to go out, so it's stay in. Now we're getting somewhere. All that remains is cook or order in? A quick perusal of the cupboards and refrigerator makes it clear that ramen, stale crackers, and cranberry juice may not be what you're really hankering for. So—order in it is! That leaves you with a list of the four restaurants that deliver within a short drive of your place, and you pick one of those. You're done. Bias to action. *And you still don't really know what you want to eat for dinner,* but you are happily (enough) resolved and thoroughly enjoy the kung pao chicken and snow peas when it arrives.

That's how it works.

It turns out that lots of problems, even after being well reframed, are difficult if not impossible to fully understand. But in most cases you have only a finite number of viable alternatives, so you don't need to "understand" your problem, in all its existential glory, you just need to know enough to pick from among the doable options.

BDO, not BTO

The trick here is to remind yourself that you're going for the Best Doable Option (BDO), which is not the same as the Best Theoretical Option (BTO).

It is very tempting to want to find the BTO. That's the option that you think you *should* be able to figure out; it's the one you *deserve;* and it's the one that probably doesn't actually exist! It's only in your head. If you really did know exactly what you wanted for dinner, then your BTO becomes a BDO, but the fact is you don't know! (And frankly, if you did, what are the chances that there's a Hungarian goulash place nearby that's open at this hour?)

When you're distracted by the idea of the BTO, all the BDOs—the things you can actually do, like ordering kung pao chicken or a Philly cheesesteak sandwich—seem like a compromise. They're all "settling," and you don't want to settle. But you aren't actually settling, because an option that doesn't exist in reality isn't an option—it's just an idea. Designers are all about making things—real things. We want you to real-ize your dreams, not just dream them. So formulate the list of actually available options, then pick the best one. The Best Doable Option. And don't let worrying about the nonexistent Best Theoretical Option steal your enjoyment of your chosen BDO.

Got it? Great.

Bill took an economics class when he was a freshman, and he was introduced to a concept that economists call "satisficing." It's a funny word, a combination of *satisfy* and *suffice*. Wikipedia defines it this way:

"**Satisficing** is a decision-making strategy or cognitive heuristic [a formula for making a decision] that entails searching through the available alternatives until an acceptability threshold is met."

When you choose the Best Doable Option, you are actually performing a sophisticated economic analysis of your "acceptability threshold" and acting like the chairman of the Federal Reserve to promote the best possible "decision economy."

Congratulations, the Nobel Prize Committee should be on the phone shortly.

Now, please pass the kung pao!

The Terrible Twins

There are two types of problems that get people stuck on all the time: anchor problems and gravity problems. These terrible twins have trapped people many times.

Anchor Problems: These guys are just like a physical anchor; they hold us in place and prevent our forward motion. They keep us stuck, and, if we are going to practice good work design, it is important to notice when we are stuck with an anchor problem.

Nathaniel wants to go sailing every weekend, but he can't afford a boat. So Nathaniel thinks his problem is: "How do I buy a boat when I have no money?"

Chelsea's start-up is maturing and has stopped growing 100 percent a year, and the company isn't naming any new directors in the near future. Chelsea wants to be promoted to director, and so she frames her problem this way: "How do I get a director title when they aren't promoting anyone anymore?"

You get the idea. An anchor problem occurs because we actually define the problem as one of our preferred solutions; we embed a solution in the problem. In other words, an anchor problem isn't really a problem at all—it's an unnegotiable and, unfortunately for you, unavailable solution masquerading as the problem. We marry ourselves to a solution that just isn't going to happen.

The way to cut the anchor loose and get free again is to reframe the problem and brainstorm alternatives. If we do the reframing steps outlined above, we'll quickly discover that "buy a boat" is a single solution to a problem that can be solved in many ways. That invites us to reframe the problem as: "How can Nathaniel go sailing regularly on his limited budget?" That problem is actionable. It's bounded (by Nathaniel's budget), but it has more than just one possible solution, so he isn't anchored to something that won't move.

There are lots of ways that Nathaniel can go sailing every weekend, and some are even better than buying a boat. He can go down to the docks and, for no costs to him at all, volunteer to crew someone else's boat (there's almost always a no-show on sailing weekends). Or Nathaniel can join a sailing club and have many different boats to sail. And so on.

This example points out how reframing energizes the life design process. When you open up a problem with a reframe, it opens up lots of possibilities (Best Doable Options) that you can prototype. Learning interesting things about the sailing world and meeting lots of sailors and boat people along the way is a pretty fun project in itself. So it's not just about the solutions you come up with; the whole design experience (which includes getting curious, talking to people, trying stuff, and telling your story) is part of the fun of a well-lived and joyful life.

Chelsea's problem can be reframed similarly. Examining the question quickly reveals that Chelsea is assuming that getting one of the almost extinct director promotions is the only way to be happy at her company. Again, Chelsea has embedded one solution into her problem and is anchored. Does she really just want to get promoted, or is she bored and looking for a new challenge at work? If it's the latter, we can draft a reframe like: "How can Chelsea find a different role in the company that will help her learn new skills and maybe grow her career in the process?" That really opens up lots of options. Chelsea can move to the same job in a new division, or retrain and take a completely new job. And if in the process of learning new things Chelsea learns that she really wants a bigger role in management, she'll have increased confidence and might decide to take on the challenge of interviewing at other companies. Again, the reframe opens up possibilities that energize Chelsea's curiosity and get her prototyping. Reframing will get you moving toward a Best Doable Option that can result in a better design for your life at work—and that's what we're after.

What we've learned over the years of working with people is that anchor problems are often about fear. Rather than trying something new and maybe failing, it is sometimes more comfortable to hold on to our familiar, impossible-to-solve problem—our anchor. The inaccessibility of that preferred solution is a great place to hide. We may not get what we want, but at least we didn't have to confront our fear of failure.

Don't let this be your story. Be courageous when you have

to be. Remember, courage isn't the absence of fear; courage is action in the face of fear. So it's okay to be a little scared as you're doing all this, but just try to keep moving and not get stuck.

Gravity Problems: We also tend to get mired in what we call "gravity problems." In our travels we come across gravity problems all the time.

John really wants to be a poet, but poets just don't make enough money to live on in our culture. How can John make a good living as a poet?

Francis has been out of work for five years raising her children. Everyone tells her that there is bias against people who been out of work, and it's going to be much harder for her to get a job. How does Francis avoid that unfair bias?

These are both gravity problems because, in life design, if it's not actionable, it's not a problem. It's a situation, a circumstance, a fact of life, and, while it might be a drag and it probably is unfair, it's like gravity. It's not a problem because there's no effective action you can take, and if you can't take action, it can't be "solved."

The key is not to get stuck on a problem that you effectively have no chance of solving. Don't get us wrong, we are all for aggressive and world-changing goals. Please do fight City Hall. Oppose injustice. Work for women's rights. Combat global warming. Fight to end homelessness. Support fair pay for poets. If that's your cause, go for it, and we wish you the best.

But if you didn't sign up for that fight, then it's a gravity problem for you. If you accept that reality, you'll be free to reframe your gravity problems into something actionable. Then you design a way to get what you want, and participate in the world in a way that is satisfying and matters to you.

To help John, our frustrated poet, we must help him accept and then reframe his gravity problem. John wants to "make a good living as a poet."

Let's first accept that poets do not generally get paid much for writing poems. We imagine that most poets proudly belong to the starving-artist club. And we think that poetry is wonderful and important and we really need more of it in our society, but John has to accept that it is not valued much in the market economy. Expression yes, money—not so much.

Okay, a moment of sadness for John and our poor poets.

This is an "accept first" gravity problem because there's no there *there* (just like there's no there *there* in trying to repeal the law of gravity). Once we accept the problem, we are free to ask John what he really wants, and it's obvious—to write poetry. That, in turn, can be reframed as having the opportunity to write poetry and perform poetry and to do as much as he can with poetry, thereby maximizing his expression, without worrying about how poetry is going to make money. So a good reframe for John might be: "I'm curious, how might I discover how poets enjoy and sustain their art while making a living doing other things?" That opens up a lot of prototyping potential. John could check out poetry slams; he could join a poetry circle (he didn't even know that was a thing until he got curious and talked to people). John could write a poetry blog and start submitting his poems to poetry journals or, better yet, start his own poetry journal. John could practice some radical collaboration and start talking to literary agents who represent poets and authors. They could introduce John to professionally failed poets who found their way to a happy life as amateur poets.

John could also reframe this poetry/money problem another way by saying, "How can I learn to live on what I'd make working only ten hours a week so I can be an almost-full-time poet?" One of our students, Auggie, decided to work on a problem just like that. His observation was that being wealthy means having more resources than you'll ever need. One way to do that is to spend a lot of time and energy on making money and collecting resources. The other way to do it is to radically reduce what you need. So he decided to do a radical reframe—he decided he was going to learn to live incredibly inexpensively—at about 10 percent of a typical person's budget—in order to radically free up his time. His first prototype was to get rid of everything he wasn't willing to carry, all the time. He got down to fifteen pounds of stuff in a smallish daypack about the same size as everyone else's book bag. He works three months a year, to make about 10 percent of what his friends make, and takes the other nine to travel and do all the things that "rich" people say they are going to do but don't have time for.

He considers himself wealthy.

John could take this approach and become the "rich poet" he's always dreamed of being. It's just a matter of lowering his need for money below his 10 percent income target. It is really about under-standing what you want, and how far you are willing to go for it.

The point is that *you are in charge* of how you define your problem and how radical a design solution you are willing to build. You may not be willing to try Auggie's solution—most people do not consider it a "doable option." But if you are careful about finding the right problem and you get good at reframing your problems in a way that gives you the creative freedom to prototype lots of solutions, you will have the best (available) chance at finding yourself in a job and life you enjoy.

That's all we're after here—we want to give you the best shot possible at living the best work life and life life for you.

Reframing problems is your go-to superpower for both.

If you get confused about the difference between anchor and gravity problems, remember that with an anchor you are stuck on a solution, and with gravity you are stuck on a non-problem. And by this definition, gravity and anchor problems aren't really "problems" (i.e., actionable challenges) at all. They're either circumstances or unattainable solutions masquerading as problems, and in so doing they are keeping you stuck.

Meanwhile, there are, of course, lots of legitimate, real problems that need solving in life—that feel completely overwhelming. In fact, the problem of overwhelm can be so overwhelming, we've decided it deserves a chapter of its own.

Try Stuff

THE MINIMUM ACTIONABLE PROBLEM (MAP) TOOLKIT

Let's practice taking a look at our problems, a real problem in our work and/or our life, and see if we can remove the drama and cut the problem down to size. Let's take a stab at coming up with our MAP.

1. Pick a problem that you would like to work on. It could be a problem that you are having at work, like the "feedback problem" we talked about, or even one of Gottman's "perpetual problems" from your relationship. But make sure it's a real problem, and one that you've been stuck on for a while.

2. Write the problem down, as clearly as you can. Writing it out will help you understand the "frame" that is implicit in the way you state the problem.

3. First, examine the problem for any biases, embedded solutions, drama, or emotional components. This is challenging, because we often do not see our own biases. To do this well requires radical honesty, a healthy dose of Accept, and maybe the help of a friend.

4. If you are struggling to state the problem objectively, ask a friend to help. Read them your problem statement and ask them to help you detect biases, embedded solutions, drama, or emotional components. Let them help you find a couple of MAPs.

5. Once you have a few ideas about how to reframe your problem into a MAP, put your more objective, nonbiased reframe in the form of a *How might we . . .* or a *How might I . . .* statement.

6. Once you have a few MAPed problems, brainstorm (maybe with your friend again) at least three different prototypes that you could try to resolve your problem. Remember: We are setting the bar low here, accepting that a lot of problems can't be fully solved, and looking for a few good ideas for a re-solution for the MAP.

Best Doable Option (BDO) Exercise

1. Pick a problem that you want to work on or something that you are actually working on and would like to find a good solution to.

2. Brainstorm at least five solutions to the problem as you currently understand it.

3. Examine the options you've brainstormed and sort them into BTO and BDO categories

4. Now eliminate your BTOs and focus on your BDOs. Resolve to have a bias to action, pick one, and execute it.

5. Ask yourself, *How do I feel?* Remind yourself that, with that decision behind you, you now have more time to devote to other things. With that decision behind you (and be sure to separate the quality of the decision from the quality of the outcome), you are now free to tackle whatever is next.

Go ahead and MAP your problems and tackle your BDOs. Once you get used to handling your problems this way, you should discover that you have more time for the good stuff and are spending less time mulling over problems that do not deserve the attention.

4
My Overwhelm Is Overwhelmed

Dysfunctional Belief: *I can't possibly do all this work, and I'm overwhelmed.*
Reframe: *I chose my way into this and I can design my way out.*

We're going to pause this book for a brief Public Service Announcement about overwhelm.

It's not going to be a long message, because if you're overwhelmed, the last thing we want to do is, well, overwhelm you further. If you're reading this because you do not like your job—and know there must be a nicer, richer, handsomer job out there for you somewhere—we would be remiss if we didn't explain that not everyone who dislikes their job actually dislikes their job. Sometimes we like what we are doing; we are just doing too much of it. We love our work but don't like our situation, because we are dealing with task lists and inboxes that are replicating and growing and invading our lives like aliens in a science-fiction movie. We know we are getting swallowed up, and we can't escape. It doesn't matter what type of work situation you're in—corporate executive, small-company employee, self-employed contractor. It can happen to anyone. Overwhelm is an equal-opportunity ailment.

Sometimes our work problem is that we have too damn much of a good thing, and this good thing transforms into a life-sucking monster that just wants to eat our brain, turn us into strangers to our loved ones, and maybe even make us ill in the process. So sometimes we are overwhelmed by too much good stuff at work. Not always, but sometimes.

We can also be overwhelmed by too much bad stuff at work. And sometimes it is a combination of the two.

The important thing is not to let overwhelm turn into burnout. We can help you design your way out of overwhelm. Burnout is a completely different beast. When you get all the way to burnout, it's almost impossible to design your way forward without first addressing its very real mental and physical effects. So, quickly, let's take a look at that.

If you're not sure if you've crossed from garden-variety over-whelm to burnout, know that the Mayo Clinic defines job burnout this way: "Job burnout is a special type of work-related stress—a state of physical or emotional exhaustion that also involves a sense of reduced accomplishment and loss of personal identity." They have a ten-part questionnaire that you can use to decide if you are experiencing the symptoms of burnout.

Ask yourself the following questions:

- **Have you become cynical or overly critical at work?**
- **Do you have to drag yourself to work and have trouble getting started once you arrive?**
- **Have you become irritable or impatient with coworkers, customers, or clients?**

- Do you lack the energy to be consistently productive?
- Do you lack satisfaction from your achievements?
- Do you feel disillusioned about your job?
- Are you using food, drugs, or alcohol to feel better or to simply not to feel anything?
- Have your sleep habits or appetite changed?
- Are you troubled by unexplained headaches, backaches, or other physical complaints?

Answering yes to two or more of these questions might indicate that you are burned out, or well on your way.

So how do we get from overwhelm to burnout? Mayo attributes it to a number of potential causes and triggers, such as:

- **Lack of control.** You are not able to influence decisions that affect your job, such as your schedule, assignments, or workload.
- **Unclear job expectations.** You're unclear about the degree of authority you have or what your supervisor expects from you.
- **Dysfunctional workplace dynamics.** You work with an office bully, you feel undermined by colleagues, your boss micromanages your work, or there are lots of "office politics" that you don't understand (see the next chapter to get help with office politics).
- **Mismatch in values.** If your values differ from the way your employer does business or handles grievances, the mismatch can eventually take a toll.
- **Poor job fit.** Your job doesn't fit your interests and skills, or you are underemployed and bored all the time.

- **Overwhelmed with tasks.** Your job is chaotic and there is too much to do.
- **Lack of social support.** You feel isolated at work and in your personal life.
- **Work–life imbalance.** Your work takes up so much of your time that you don't have the energy to spend time with your family and friends.

Look, ignored or unaddressed job burnout can have significant consequences.

But we're not doctors.

We don't play them on television.

Or in books.

If you think your overwhelm is really burnout and needs professional-level intervention, then please go get that. A handy book from design guys is not a substitute for professional assistance for a diagnosable condition. Get some help if you need it.

Now.

Meanwhile, let's look at the run-of-the-mill sorts of overwhelm.

Everyday Overwhelm

General overwhelm comes in a few different flavors. Flavor one is what we like to call the "Hydra Overwhelm." The Hydra is a nine-headed Greek monster that grew two new heads every time one was chopped off. Sound a little like your current job? Jobs that have too many parts, or too many people to report to, are often unmanageable and can lead to overwhelm. This often happens when an organization is leaned out to the point that everyone is doing two or three jobs at once. Or maybe the company is growing so fast that managers are managing more tasks and people than they can manage.

You might have Hydra Overwhelm if:

- **You have too many different responsibilities.**
- **You are reporting to too many managers (more than one) at the same time or are running too many client projects or side hustles concurrently.**
- **You are consolidating important data from too many different sources.**
- **You have to deliver status information and/or reports to too many people.**
- **You regularly use legacy systems that are cumbersome and poorly designed.**
- **You lack control or are micromanaged.**
- **You are working in isolation.**

Flavor two is called the "Happy Overwhelm." This is where you just have too much of a good thing and too many cool things to do, and you mistakenly volunteered to do them all. Your job is challenging but fun, the people you work with are great, and the projects you get offered are all high-impact and worth doing. You are just doing too many of them.

Both Hydra Overwhelm and Happy Overwhelm are pretty straightforward and in fact share the same solution—with slightly different implementations. You need to do less and get control of your time. This is where the old design adage *less is more* comes in handy. How you manage this "task reduction" depends on the Hydra or Happy Overwhelm you are experiencing.

The Nine-Headed Monster

In Hydra Overwhelm, you want to get rid of, or get permission to drop, the too many things on your plate. Start by looking over the list of possible Hydra sources listed above to get your juices flowing, then make your own list of all the tasks you are doing. Make it objective, but list everything. Then, and this can be hard, pick one or two items on the list you can modify, work around, or even skip completely. Remember the Set the Bar Low method and pick simple changes that you can initiate yourself. Things like:

- **If the root cause of the overwhelm is consolidating data from too many sources, ask Accounting to give you one spreadsheet, not six, consolidating the monthly budget numbers. Explain (with empathy for Accounting) that this will lead to more accurate forecasts, to everyone's advantage.**
- **If the root cause of the overwhelm is working in isolation, take the lead on organizing a Monday Munchies Run (a snack run with your colleagues), and a Wednesday Walk-a-Thon (an organized walk around the building for a midday stretch), and even a Friday Freestyle (a lunch conversation with coworkers about news of the day—but no politics, office or otherwise).**

You'll probably surprise yourself once you start brainstorming ways to reduce your task list or connect more with your coworkers. You are more in charge of your Hydra than you think. However, unless you are your own boss, there are some solutions to Hydra Overwhelm that you'll likely need permission from the higher-ups to implement. The best way to get the solutions you need approved is to start with empathy for your boss's needs, and frame your requested change in those terms.

"Boss," you say, "here's the situation. I'm getting swamped with stuff that really has nothing to do with what we're trying to get done around here, and it's reducing my productivity. This isn't good for me, the team, or you. I could be a lot more effective, and get the stuff that you think is critical done faster, but I need your help. I need to . . .

- ". . . come in later on Thursdays . . ."
- ". . . upgrade from the 1998 version to the 2015 version of [your key software app] . . ."
- ". . . change the weekly report to a monthly report . . ."
- ". . . split my internal clients into two groups: A's and B's (I've got a list for you right here) so that I can guarantee twenty-four-hour turnaround for the A's (like always) but ninety-six hours for the B's . . ."
- Or . . . or . . . You get the idea.

The only way to change your Hydra Overwhelm situation is to change something. Figure out what small incremental move you could make—the one with the greatest impact and the most probable endorsement from your boss—and give it your best shot. You probably expect your boss to reject your idea, but you might be surprised. If you start with empathy for the boss's situation, you are much more likely to get approval, especially if you use a trial, an experiment, or a prototype as the framing for your request. Lots of our students, clients, and readers have made significant changes in their workload with this method.

Mayra, one of our workshop attendees, proposed prototyping a change: not doing the weekly asset reports for one week. The report was a pain in the neck to produce and she was pretty sure no one cared about it. She checked with her boss to see if it was okay, and he said she could try it (prototype it) for one month. After one week, there were no emails, no complaints, nothing—so she didn't do the report the next week. After four weeks of no reports and no complaints, she went to her boss and said, "Boss, I'd like to discuss the weekly-asset-report prototype we talked about."

Boss: How did it go?

Mayra: The results are in. I haven't done those reports for four weeks in a row and no one has complained.

Boss: I didn't even notice you'd stopped!

Mayra: Yes. The prototype revealed that you never read that report and no one else does, either. I'd like to stop doing it and spend that time on organizing our sales data better. You said that was your number one priority, getting better sales information out to the field.

Boss: Okay, but we've always done the asset report—maybe you could do them quarterly. If, after a year, no one comments on the quarterly reports, you can drop them entirely. That a deal?

Mayra: Deal.

Boss: Great, now get that important sales-data project going.

What Mayra's story teaches us is that things might be more negotiable than you think they are. And Mayra played it smart. The key to negotiating out of Mayra's busy work, the asset report that no one was reading, was understanding that there was more strategic work to be done, and suggesting a low-risk prototype to get data about a possible redesign of her tasks.

Mayra also moved from disengaged (doing busywork reports that no one reads is a great way to create a really disengaged worker) to feeling like her work was of strategic importance. A double win.

So the path forward is . . . well, straightforward. We encourage you to start prototyping small changes to your task list. You will discover that you have more agency than you think, and whether you have to ask for permission to try something or not, you are the initiator. And initiation is one of the things you're keeping track of with your Good Work Journal, right?

So Much Happy

Happy Overwhelm is a little different. Since you chose all of the things that are overwhelming you, Happy Overwhelm often comes with more flexibility and a higher degree of electiveness to your options. The number one solution to Happy Overwhelm is delegation. Of course, you have to be willing to let go of one or more of the many cool, fun, impactful, amazing things you get to do every day. But you'll get to do some of those amazing things longer and avoid the potential for burnout if you learn to share the joy. Since the fun, challenging, interesting things that are overwhelming you are attractive, you can very likely give them to your colleagues easily. (This is very unlike the Hydra Overwhelm problem, where the issue is getting rid of stuff that no one wants to do.)

If you really want to get a lot of time and energy back, you should give away your most prized and high-visibility activities.

Those are the easiest ones to find takers, and giving them away frees up a lot of time. For instance, Dave used to do all the section facilitator trainings for the Stanford Designing Your Life course. He'd done these dozens of times and had built a decent set of handouts for the training—and loved doing it—but he needed to let something go. He asked one of our Life Design Lab fellows (who had seen him do it just once) to lead the next session. He did great—to Dave's astonishment. Dave never did it again. A few quarters later, Dave sat in on the facilitator training being done by yet another staffer—and it was way better than it was when Dave did it.

Dave's delegation worked—he got more time and the facilitation training got better.

Of course, we are not just workers. Sometimes, when you have Happy Overwhelm, you need to delegate some stuff at home.

When Bill worked at Apple and joined the brand-new Power-Book group, they were putting the final touches on Apple's first laptop. Code-named Tim, it was released as the PowerBook 170 and it took the industry by storm. Bill jumped in and, as the mechanical project lead, took on the next laptop project. Code-named Suntory, it was being designed in a joint venture with Sony, and this meant Bill was on a plane to Tokyo almost every month. And because the product line was so successful, new portable projects were popping up faster than Apple could hire. Bill took on another laptop project, code-named Asahi, and another, code-named Bonsai (Bill really liked Japanese code names). Around this time, Bill and his wife, Cynthia, had their second child. With two young children in the house, a wife with a full-time job as a business consultant (traveling every week), and Bill needing to travel to Japan every few weeks, he found himself deep into Happy

Overwhelm. There was no time to do anything right, and some things were just not getting done. Remember, Bill volunteered, even lobbied, happily, for all these projects. Bill was deep into in-over-his-head overwhelm.

About six months into this disaster, Bill and his wife called a time-out. They decided that their current life was not sustainable. They got together and looked carefully at their work to see if they wanted to back out of anything they were doing. Cynthia was just out of business school, and building credibility in her consulting firm was important, so they decided together that she had made a good choice and they would find a way to support her in this new career. Bill realized that this was a special time at Apple: they were inventing a whole new business, and it had grown to more than a billion dollars in revenue. He was unlikely to have a chance to be involved in anything this exciting, so they decided to support Bill working and traveling this much.

Having made those decisions about work, they then made a list of all the things they had to do, things they would not compromise on, like being around to raise their children. They made a list of things they could delegate to someone, things that were not that important, like cooking, doing the laundry, mowing the lawn, and cleaning the house. They calculated that if they didn't do these things, they would have enough time for each other and for their kids. They would have enough time for the important stuff.

There was just one problem: They didn't have the money to delegate these tasks to someone else.

So Bill went to his boss at Apple and told this story: "Right now is a critical time for our group. We are riding a tiger, in the fastest-growing part of Apple's business, portable computers. We are setting the standard for the industry and, right now, we have more projects than people and we can't hire fast enough to keep up. I'm all in, one hundred and ten percent, and I recognize that this is a very special opportunity to be part of something amazing. That's why I volunteered to do three projects at once. At the same time, everyone else in my role is doing just one project. I've figured out that to sustain this level of commitment and to make time for my family, I need to outsource a bunch of things in my life, and that's going to cost a lot of money. I need a raise."

It was good storytelling. It was true. And he got the raise. Not right away—he needed to prove that he could take on the three-project challenge and make it work. But he and his wife made it work by delegating out from under their Happy Overwhelm.

SHOUT-OUT TO SMALL-BUSINESS OWNERS—AVOID THE OWNER'S TRAP

If you're a small-business owner, you're at particular risk for overwhelm (especially Hyper-Overwhelm, described next). Many business owners feel trapped—trapped in a box that they think they can't get out of because, well, they made the box. If this is you and your business has you in overwhelm too much of the time—the only boss you can talk to is you. You own not only the company, but also the processes and procedures and roles and responsibilities. You own the *how* of the company as well as the *what*—and that sense of personal ownership and responsibility can keep you in a special brand of stuck.

Everything in this book and in our first book applies to you.

You can design your way out of being stuck and out of over-whelm the same way an employee or a consultant or a gig worker does. You can design your work life right where you are. The mind-sets are the same. And you don't have to ask permission.

But your particular brand of stuck, the one that has out-siders scratching their heads and wondering why, if it's your company and you're in charge, you don't just make the changes you want to make, is often harder to recognize.

Those outsiders are right, but since they couldn't possibly understand your business or appreciate all you are doing, you just ignore them and work harder. The ironic thing about being a business owner is that most people who choose that path do so in order to chart their own course and work on their own terms. They want autonomy, so they strike out on their own. Then once the business gets going, they often feel less autonomy than many corporate employees do.

So business owners have a high risk of getting stuck in overwhelm, but there is a way out.

STEP 1: REMEMBER YOU ARE *STILL* IN CHARGE.

What subtly happens over time is the business gets in charge of you—not you in charge of the business. Sure, you've got tons of responsibilities and obligations and people and cus-tomers depending on you, but it *is* yours to run and man-age as you see fit. You aren't any less powerful or any less in charge than when you started your business—you're just busier.

STEP 2: THERE'S ONLY ONE RULE—OBEY IT!

In any business or institution, whether it's for-profit or non-profit, there is only one inviolable rule—don't run out of money. As long as you are selling enough products or services, or garnering sufficient contributions from donors to cover your expenses—you get to stay in business. The ink at the bottom of your spreadsheets has to be black—not red. If it's stuck in red, you're in the process of going out of business (and if that's the issue, then you need different help that is probably in a different book). This rule is incredibly freeing! As an owner, you can literally do anything you want as long as you can afford to keep the doors open (and pay your taxes, not break laws, etc.). You can reduce or expand your offerings. You can sell off part of the business to make it simpler to run. You can apply pretty much all the ideas in this book to your situation. Even if you need to make dramatic changes to the business to get out of overwhelm, you can *because you are in charge.*

That's it.

Ellie, a former neighbor of Dave's, ran a successful local restaurant for years. It's a relentless business because people want to eat pretty much every day. She got tired of the relentlessness but couldn't figure out how to change her overwhelmed situation. Then she realized that it was up to her—it was *her restaurant.* **She remembered why she opened it in the first place—to make great Mexican food that people enjoyed—and realized that had nothing to do with a big room full of tables. It's about the food. She ended up closing the restaurant and buying a food truck. She got rid of the rent. She cut her staff and her hours. She traded 10 percent of her money in order to lose 100 percent of her overwhelm.**

She redesigned her business to work for her. You can, too.

Hyper-Overwhelm—a Special Case

The last flavor of overwhelm is a special case, and you usually find it in new organizations or start-ups. We call it "Hyper-Overwhelm." This is where management and staff are building the plane and trying to fly it at the same time. There are no organizational norms to follow and very little support infrastructure (in fact, that may be one of your jobs—build the support infrastructure—but who has the time?). The enterprise is having great success and scaling rapidly and that means seventy-, eighty-, and even ninety-hour workweeks, because the job is never done. It's exhilarating, challenging, and ultimately exhausting. Being a leader or early team member in a small business or high-growth start-up is not for the faint of heart, nor does it make for short workdays. If this is the path you are on, try to think of your day-to-day work as a marathon, not a sprint.

What that really means is you need to implement a particular version of storytelling's "good enough for now" story, through a reframe and possibly some negotiated compromises with key people close to you (we're seldom in this situation alone). What really sustains this solution "for now" is the new narrative—which illustrates the power of the *storytelling* mind-set. Perhaps the best way to explain all this is with a story . . .

Once upon a time, Dave asked Bill if he wanted to collaborate on an idea Dave had about teaching college students how to figure out what to do with their lives using design thinking. That conversation turned into one of the most popular electives at Stanford University, Designing Your Life.

Once that course got going, it really got going!

In fact, it just about exploded. And that put Dave into the condition of Hyper-Overwhelm. You see, the Life Design Lab really is a start-up, and in the early days, like most start-ups, it was just the founders doing the best they could, working lots of long hours. And then when it started to work, there was no one to delegate to.

It was all work all the time, and it all came together one late night in Palo Alto.

Dave was walking out to the parking lot at Stanford, looked at his watch, and saw that it was 8:00 p.m. "Shoot," said Dave. Actually, he strung quite a few words together and said something stronger than "shoot."

He got into the car and called his wife.

"Hi, honey."

"Well, hello, dear," she said.

"I'm so sorry," said Dave. "I did it again. I've clearly missed our seven-thirty dinner date."

You see, Wednesday was dinner-date night at Dave's house and he was supposed to be home, an hour's commute away. So by 8:00 p.m., it was clear that Dave's wife, Claudia, had figured out that he would not be home half an hour ago.

This was not the first time this had happened.

"Well?" she asked.

"It just blew up on me again. A whole bunch of students showed up for office hours that weren't scheduled, and then I got a message that the vice provost of undergraduate education wanted me to swing by the office and talk about where things could go in the future, and that's a meeting I really couldn't avoid. So when you put it all together with those extra student conversations, the time just disappeared again. I'm so sorry, honey. I blew it. I'll be there as soon as I can."

"Oh," said Claudia, "you must be so happy!"

This wasn't the response Dave had been expecting. Maybe he had misheard her.

"W-What?" he stammered.

"Well, you must be so happy, because this is exactly what you want. I mean, everything you've told me says 'This is perfect.' More students are coming to office hours, and talking to students is your favorite thing. And then you're hearing from the Provost Office, which means you're now starting to have an impact at the institutional level. What you and Bill are doing is starting to make a difference. That's exactly what you'd hoped for. So it's really working. You must be so happy!"

Dave thought about it for a minute.

"Well . . . yes. Yes, that's right. I am so happy. I just called to let you know how wonderful things are, and how the wonderful things have inadvertently caused me to miss dinner again. Thank you, darling."

"Why, you're welcome. I'll see you when you get home."

Now, the first and most important moral of the story is this: Marry well.

The smartest thing Dave ever did was to design his life to be happy by marrying well, to a brilliant and fabulous partner.

That being said—there are other things to learn from this story.

You see, what's going on in a Hyper-Overwhelm situation is that lots of good things are happening but there are way too many of them. And you're not in a situation like a Happy Overwhelm, where you can actually delegate out, because there's nobody to delegate to.

When this story took place, the Life Design Lab was barely funded, so Dave was teaching three classes a quarter, every quarter, and there was no one to delegate to (except Bill, who was also in start-up Hyper-Overwhelm). It was also during this time that Dave was trying to establish the credibility of the Life Design Lab. So Bill and Dave were still very much hands-on in this Life Design start-up.

It was a really good time. It was exciting. But it was overwhelming.

For Dave it was too much, but he knew that it was too much . . . for now. He figured he could find a way to tough it out and get through start-up mode and then he could downgrade Hyper-Overwhelm into Happy Overwhelm and start managing it better.

For Dave, his new story went something like this:

Old story: "Oh my gosh, I've got too much to do," or, "Oh my gosh, here comes another meeting I can barely fit in," and then, "I blew it," or, "I can't do this."

New story: "Wow, I'm fortunate to finally get to realize my goal of making a difference in higher education and in students' lives. It may feel tough sometimes, but this won't last forever, and it's what I wanted all my life, and although I'm really busy now, I'm going to enjoy it while it lasts."

The moral of the story is that the way you manage Hyper-

Overwhelm, assuming you choose to be in this "start-up," is to change the story. It has to be short—two or three sentences—and it has to be something you can remember. This way, when the invitation to feel terrible shows up, you can quickly reframe it and catch yourself before you blow your mood and you blow your attention.

There's an old proverb that says, "You cannot prevent the birds from flying over your head. But you need not let them make a nest in your hair." Which means bad thoughts will come (including dysfunctional, destructive, mood-destroying thoughts), but you don't have to wrestle with them, or let them make a permanent home in your mind. Practice replacing these thoughts with your much better story.

One important caveat: You are not alone! You see, when you're in Hyper-Overwhelm, there are almost always other people affected. For your new story to work, you want them in on the deal. They need to be willing to say, "It's working for me now, too."

If you can get your key partners, intimates, and collaborators to join you in temporarily embracing your Hyper-Overwhelm, things will go much more smoothly for everyone. There will always be a few adjustments you make to prioritize your partner's issues, but for the most part, because you choose into (together) your Hyper-Involvement with your start-up, you can work your way through it. And when you get to the other side of your Hyper-Overwhelm (remember, it's just *for now*), it is all the more sweet because you did it together. And that's exactly what Dave did (and, oh, is he *sooo* happy).

Overwhelm happens to all of us at one time or another. Our message by now should be clear—overwhelm can be managed, and it is a temporary condition of your job and your life. You are the designer and you are in control.

And now back to your regularly scheduled work life.

Try Stuff

GETTING OVER OVERWHELM

1. **Overwhelmed (Y/N)?** Ask yourself if you feel continually overwhelmed—do you have this problem or was it just one tough week? If yes, continue. If no, go play Frisbee or walk the dog—you deserve it.

2. **Burned Out (Y/N)?** Check if you're actually burned out or overwhelmed by reviewing the burnout indicator questions. If you think you are headed for burnout, put the book down and immediately find yourself a therapist specializing in burnout and get good support. If not burned out, continue.

3. **Pick Your Flavor of Overwhelm: Hydra, Happy, or Hyper.** Review the characteristics of Hydra, Happy, and Hyper-Overwhelm. Decide which description best fits your circumstances and start designing your way out.

4. **Hydra and Happy—Implementation**

   a. **Less Is More List:** Make your Less Is More List of things to drop, delegate, or renegotiate. Notice that

implementing this is quite different in Happy versus
Hydra Overwhelm, but the goal is the same—
something has to go. Make a list.

b. <u>The Boss or Colleague Giving Plan</u>: If you're in
Hydra, you'll have to renegotiate some relief, most
likely starting with your boss. Figure out what your
top Less Is More items are and the best pitch you
can come up with to get your boss on board, then
arrange that negotiation meeting. If you're in Happy,
you'll likely be able to delegate to colleagues (who,
if you remembered to pick tasty things to give
away, will be easy to find), so plan what to hand
off and to whom. Then plan those meetings and
the delegation process (it may take a few steps to
competently release something, but hang in there, it
will eventually work).

c. <u>Execute</u>: There's no substitute for good execution.
Get started with your boss and your colleagues and
follow up on all the details. You'll feel better almost
immediately.

5. <u>Hyper Implementation Plan</u>

a. <u>Reframe</u>: Figure out how to reposition your
situation in a way that lets you get the most out of
it despite the fact that it's costly (for now . . .). You
may need to enlist the help of a friend, colleague,
spouse, or partner to get this figured out.

b. <u>Better storytelling</u>: Make up the new story that
reframes your situation as an advantage. See
Dave's example and write this new story for

yourself. It should be less than 250 words. Read it aloud to yourself every morning for two weeks (i.e., until you make it true).

c. <u>Negotiate:</u> Figure out what compromises others will need to make (for now . . .) in order for your Hyper reframe to work effectively. Your Hyper-Overwhelm is probably having the biggest effect on those people closest to you. If you enlist help from these folks in your reframe and new story, your chance of success increases. Be prepared to work through some issues and complaints from your intimates— don't be defensive and work toward a story that works for everyone.

d. <u>Check In:</u> After six to eight weeks, have a check-in meeting with yourself and your closest partners in this Hyper situation, asking, "How's it going?" This will ensure that your approach to getting through your season of Hyper-Overwhelm is working for everyone. If things are good with everyone, keep going. If not, figure out what needs updating (the reframe, the story, or the negotiation) and put the needed fixes in place. And be sure to make the changes necessary to get out of Hyper—it's not a place you want to live permanently.

5

Mind-set, Grit, and the ARC of Your Career

> **Dysfunctional Belief:** *I don't like my job, and I don't know what to do.*
> **Reframe:** *You have the power to reframe and redesign any situation and any job.*

Some days feel longer than others.

When you are disengaged at work, each day can feel longer than the day before it, and there is nothing, not even another cat video, that will make the endless tick-tock of the clock move a little faster so that you can commute home and complain to your family (or your cat) just how much your boss/work/clients/job/company sucks. Your current plan: Collect your pay, do your time, and eventually you will retire and then start really living. You'll do what the company asks you to do, report to your manager, nod and smile at your coworkers, all the while knowing that when you retire none of this will matter. When you were young you never dreamed of selling insurance. Or writing technical manuals for software companies. Or installing pool covers for other people's pools. But somehow this is where you ended up.

Sound familiar? If it does, you are part of the almost 70 percent of the workforce who are disengaged and not satisfied with the majority of the way they are spending their hours/day/week/life. So what are you going to do about it?

Who are you going to hold accountable?

Spoiler alert.

There's only one place you can get job satisfaction. It doesn't come from a different job or a different company, and it's not found somewhere in your orientation packet from Human Resources. Your company cannot give it to you, although they could do a better job of enabling it. So, as a designer of your job and career, where does job satisfaction come from? Read on . . .

Who's the Boss of Me?

When we feel stuck in our lives, we tend to externalize the blame: The bad things that are keeping me stuck are caused by someone or something else, not me.

It's not my fault that my job sucks—have you met my boss?

It's the company's fault that the culture sucks, and that's why everyone here is unhappy.

My partner doesn't understand me and will never support my dream to become a Cirque du Soleil clown.

But, if we are being completely honest with ourselves, it's not always true that other people are keeping us from being happy. Of course, those bad bosses and bad companies are certainly not helping any, but at some point you have to ask yourself, *Who's the boss of me?*

In life design there's only one answer.

You are the creative agent in your life, and you have the power to make the changes that you need and want. It will take some effort and it may take some time (because we're going to set the bar low and sneak up on these changes), but ultimately the answer to that question is clear.

You are the boss of you.

If you don't like that answer, talk to your boss.

If you want more engagement, satisfaction, and meaningful work, it's time to redesign your experience of work. And the first place to start is with you—your attitudes and mind-sets that create the story of your job and career.

Grow Your Mind-set

Research from our Stanford colleague psychology professor Carol Dweck suggests that people can generally be divided into having two ways of thinking about life, two dominant mind-sets—fixed and growth. A fixed-mind-set person believes that their intelligence and abilities are fixed, natural "talents" that cannot be changed. When they succeed at something, it is because of their natural abilities. When they fail, same reason—they "just aren't good at that."

I'm just not creative.

I can't do sales.

I'm terrible at math.

On the other hand, a growth-mind-set person believes that, although everyone starts with different natural abilities, their intelligence and talents can be developed. They can learn and master new things. The attribute their success to hard work and practice, not to something innate. Dweck writes, "Believing that your qualities are carved in stone—the fixed mind-set—creates an urgency to prove yourself over and over . . . [while a] growth mind-set is based on the belief that your basic qualities are things you can cultivate through your efforts, your strategies, and help from others . . . [and] that a person's true potential is unknown [and unknowable] . . ."

These two ways of approaching the world and its challenges create profoundly different outcomes. Fixed-mind-set folks tend to be more fragile when it comes to setbacks, and tend to give up sooner because "it's not my fault, I'm not good at that." People with a growth mind-set tend to be more persistant and more willing to work hard to achieve a goal, even if they aren't very good at it when they start.

There is even some evidence from fMRI scans of the brain (one way to see which brain circuits are active during a task) that these mind-set differences are neurological. For instance, when subjects are put inside an fMRI machine and asked hard questions, and then given feedback on their answers, the brain patterns of the two mind-sets are startlingly different.

"People with a fixed mind-set were only interested when the feedback reflected on their ability. Their brain waves showed them paying close attention when they were told whether their answers were right or wrong. But when they (the fixed mind-setters) were presented with information that could help them learn, there was no sign of interest. Even when they'd gotten an answer wrong, they were not interested in learning what the right answer was. Only people with a growth mind-set paid close attention to information that could stretch their knowledge. Only for them was learning a priority."

The fact that a fixed or growth mind-set seems hardwired in our brain does not mean that we are doomed to those constraints. There is a lot of evidence that your brain can wire up new circuits in response to training. So when you start the process of designing a job that you love, you should think about training yourself to develop a growth mind-set. Studies show that adopting and developing a growth mind-set will increase your desire to learn (curiosity), your embrace of challenge, your ability to learn from criticism and the examples of others, and also your ability to see hard work and practice as the path to mastering anything you set out to do.

Dysfunctional Belief: *I'm not good at math and I'm never going to get better. There are a bunch of things I can't do, and there are people who are far more talented than I am. I'm stuck with my abilities and I can't get better.*

Reframe: *That's your fixed mind-set talking, and it's not telling you the truth. The truth is, with a growth mind-set and a lot of hard work and practice, you can probably accomplish almost anything you set your mind to. Talent isn't the reason other people are doing so well; they are working hard to get better.*

The fixed versus growth mind-set story is a little too binary. Research shows that we are all a mixture of fixed and growth mind-sets, and we operate somewhere on a continuum from one to the other. If you feel you fall more on the fixed end of the mind-set spectrum, there are things you can do to move toward a growth mind-set. If growth mind-set is already your default, you can make it better with practice.

The first step is learning to identify when you slip into a fixed mind-set. Ask yourself what triggers this way of seeing the world. Is it when you hit a problem you can't solve (*I'm dumb*), when you procrastinate (*I'm lazy*) or when you fail to speak up for yourself (*I'm shy*) or fail to take a stand about an injustice (*I'm a coward*)?

By the way, the above are examples of negative self-talk, or using the *storytelling* mind-set in a negative way. When you say things to yourself like "I'm dumb," or, "I'm stupid and lazy," you are telling yourself a story. Tell that story enough times and you will start believing it.

To reverse the process, get good at noticing when your fixed mind-set is in charge—do not judge it, just notice. Next, use the power of reframing to change your problem and utilize the power of your *storytelling* mind-set to "change the narrative, change the outcome."

Every time you find yourself in a fixed mind-set, notice the story you're telling, reframe, and tell a better story. For instance, instead of "I'm dumb," how about this story:

"I'm really struggling with this problem and I need some new ideas. I could seek out a new problem-solving strategy (get curious), I could ask for help (radical collaboration), and I could give myself more time and work harder on the basics I'm going to need before I tackle this problem."

That's a better story!

Or instead of "I'm stupid and lazy," how about this story:

"I notice myself not wanting to get started on this problem; I'm procrastinating. I could start by making sure I have all of the information, research, and materials I need to get started (awareness). I could reframe the task (reframing) and find new ways to get going to get the same results. I could make a list of the benefits of completing this task, and that will motivate me to get started."

Get it? It's about changing your internal story.

The final step in moving more toward a growth mind-set is to ask yourself, *What can I learn today? Can I reframe the challenges of my to-do list around the objectives of learning and growth? And can I use what I learn in the service of others—can I be a teacher today?* (By the way, great teachers are always great storytellers.) Learning, growing, and sharing your experiences are great ways to reinforce a growth mind-set.

Your first order of business is to adopt and develop your growth mind-set! Make a plan to maintain your transformation to this new mind-set. It will definitely take practice and reinforcement to make a growth mind-set the natural way you approach problem solving.

Once you have embraced this way of thinking, and you're working hard to make your job the one you want, you are inevitably going to hit some setbacks. And that's when the psychology of resilience comes in. Because when the going gets tough, the tough get gritty.

Getting Gritty

Grit.

It's the best predictor of who will finish the grueling seven weeks of basic training, also known as the "Beast," that all West Point recruits must endure, or who will pass an even more rigorous

Green Beret Special Forces Selection Course, which includes running miles carrying heavy packs, crawling through mud and water under barbed wire, and a variety of other nasty challenges. It's the best predictor of who will be the highest-producing salesperson and who will outperform even the most naturally gifted athletes. Grit is the thing!

Angela Duckworth, a psychology professor at the University of Pennsylvania and the author of *Grit: The Power of Passion and Perseverance,* has developed a way of measuring grit, and you can take the Grit Scale test here: angeladuckworth.com/grit-scale.

Although people obviously have varying natural abilities, it turns out, according to Duckworth's research, that talent, IQ, and natural ability have almost zero correlation to success under difficult conditions. It is the ability to persevere that separates the successful from those who quit. So in designing your work life, grit is an important thing to cultivate. And there are ways to develop a more resilient and gritty mind-set.

There are four factors that Duckworth calls "the psychological assets that mature paragons of grit have in common."

1. **Everything starts with enjoying what you do. To persevere, you need to be intrinsically interested in your subject (more on intrinsic motivation coming up). We'd add the designer's mind-set of curiosity, a potential precursor to interest, to this asset.**
2. **Next comes the capacity to practice. You must devote yourself to the kind of deliberate and well-informed practice that leads to mastery. And you must practice, every day, every week, every year—there is no end to practice—it is an end in and of itself.**

3. **Third is purpose. You have to believe that your work matters to something and someone greater than yourself.**
4. **And, finally, you have to be a hopeful person. Hope is what keeps you going even when things get tough and your plans aren't working. Hope is related to optimism and a deeper sense that your mission is ultimately possible.**

Cultivating your curiosity and interests, practicing hard to become a master at your craft or subject, defining your purpose in something greater than yourself, and remaining hopeful will lead to an increase in your grit and your ability to accomplish what you set out to do. Sounds a lot like the mind-sets of a great job and life designer.

Research shows that working on this every day is a much better use of your time than viewing cat videos or watching the clock or complaining about your job.

Okay, maybe there's not official research correlating cat-video-watching to grit cultivation, but if there were, trust us when we tell you that grit would win every single time.

If you've cultivated your growth mind-set and are getting good and gritty, it's time to look at what motivates us to work in the first place. Because, as the manager and boss of you, you need to know how to best motivate your key employee.

The ARC of Your Career

> **Dysfunctional Belief:** *I'm not happy in my job, and I have no idea how to make it better.*
>
> **Reframe:** *I recognize my intrinsic motivations and I know how to increase my autonomy, relatedness, and competence.*

At the end of the workday, we are the one responsible for making our job feel challenging and fun. Whether we are driving a bus or driving a corporate merger, this is true for any and every job. And to make our job fun and rewarding, we need to again turn to the psychologists. The research on human motivation, called "self-determination theory," says that we are intrinsically motivated animals, and, in addition to responding to external motivations, a full understanding of human motivation requires an understanding of our innate psychological needs for *A*utonomy, *R*elatedness, and *C*ompetence (ARC).

Now, some of you may be putting on the brakes right now.

Psychological needs? That's great in theory, but I need cash. That will motivate me and get me engaged with my work faster than anything. Let's discuss the ARC of my bank account!

Good question, and of course we need to have our financial needs met. But research shows that humans are weirdly motivated by things other than cash, especially when they have enough to live on—things like curiosity and the inherent challenge of solving puzzles. In his book *Drive: The Surprising Truth About What Motivates Us,* Dan Pink describes some strange results from the psychology of motivation as revealed by self-determination theory.

... human motivation seemed to operate by laws that ran counter to what most scientists and citizens believed ... we [thought we] knew what got people going. Rewards—especially cold, hard cash—intensified interest and enhanced performance. [However, what the self-determination theory psychologists found] was almost the opposite. When money is used as an external reward for some activity, the subjects lose intrinsic interest for the activity ... Human beings ... have an inherent tendency to seek out novelty and challenges, to extend and exercise their capacities, to explore, and to learn.

Dan was describing the work of Edward Deci, a pioneering psychologist who, along with Richard Ryan and others, has spent the last forty years developing the notion that, along with our primitive external motivations (the drive for food, shelter, safety, etc.), humans have powerful intrinsic motivations that are in some ways their own reward. In other words, humans will do things because they are just interesting. We are curious animals. And Deci and Ryan and others have demonstrated that you can mess up the intrinsic reward system (solving a puzzle because it's interesting) by introducing extrinsic rewards (like paying people to complete the same puzzle). When you pay people for tasks that utilize the intrinsic reward system, their performance actually goes down.

That's the weird paradox.

So let's look at our innate psychological needs for autonomy, relatedness, and competence.

Autonomy, at its most basic, is the need to control our own life. It's a human drive and an innate psychological need. We all want to be in a position at work where we are able to control aspects of what we do, who we do it with, and when we do it. Deci and Ryan write, "At a phenomenological level, human autonomy is reflected in the experience of integrity, volition, and vitality that accompanies self-regulated action . . ."

At work, you develop your autonomy by showing up in the work that you do and deciding to do it as good or better than is required. When you get in the habit of overdelivering on the job, good things start to happen.

Ann is a shift supervisor at a fast-food restaurant. Her daily tasks are pretty fixed, and she has been trained to run her shift according to the best practices in the industry. She's taken classes at the famed Hamburger University and has learned a very orderly and specific way to maximize the throughput and profitability of her restaurant. You'd think, in a job like hers, there is no room for autonomy. But that's not the case. Ann follows the rules and runs a tight ship, and her shifts are marked by their orderliness and good behavior. But Ann also overdelivers for her shift workers. She brings in some fresh flowers every other day, and places them next to the time clock to brighten up the work environment. She is very generous with her time, helping new staff to learn the rules and processes that make the food. One time, Ann noticed that the transition between shifts was a lot messier than it needed to be, so, without asking permission, she set out to fix it. She arranged for an informal coffee between the three shift supervisors, and they talked about the fact that there was no incentive to "leave the campsite better than you found it"—and shift workers, in a hurry to get home, often ignored the mess they were passing on to the next shift. This resulted in a messy kitchen (a potential health hazard) and some botched orders. Ann proposed "prototyping" a new schedule that designated one employee as the "shift master, overlapper." Their incentive would be tied to making the transition seamless. They all agree to try this for a month and the results were great—no more lost orders and a cleaner, happier workplace.

Ann is full of other ways to make her workplace more efficient and, more important, more fun. "When I hear singing coming from the prep line, and the maintenance staff is making a game out of who can clean the grease trap the fastest, then I know my crew is working together well. And my shifts have the highest rate of staff retention, nobody quits me—and that's getting noticed by the top management."

If Ann can generate autonomy in her fast-food job, so can you.

Relatedness is about connecting to your people and your community. We develop and sustain our relatedness by engaging with our fellow workers, collaborating well on projects, and being empathetic to the needs of those we work with and work for. The drive for connection is a strong human motivator and a basic component of our evolutionary history. Humans, by themselves, are not very strong or fast animals. In the wild, almost all predators are faster and more deadly. We had to learn to live together, and hunt together, in order to survive. As we evolved, the best survival strategy was to form strong family and tribal groups. This intrinsic need for relatedness shows up at work, too.

Think of a time when you were energized and jazzed by being part of a bigger project or purpose. Being part of a team and working hard for that team shows up in many aspects of our lives—from sports, to community groups, to social movements—and radical collaboration is a form of relatedness that designers do naturally.

In contrast, being isolated in a matrix of sterile cubicles, working all by yourself, on tasks that have no obvious connection to the mission of the team, tribe, or company is not a healthy work environment and is not likely to be where you do your best work.

Increasing your relatedness will increase your happiness—at work and in life.

When Bill was just out of Stanford, having finished his master's degree in product design, one of his professors, who had started a very successful tech company called Convergent Technology, offered Bill a job on a special project that was in "super-secret stealth mode." That was the start of one of the best work experiences he ever had. Convergent Technology had a reputation for being a tough place to work; the CEO was fond of calling it "the Marine Corps of Silicon Valley," and he ran a very tight ship. Bill was one of three mechanical engineers, on a small team of about twenty people, trying to design and manufacture what was at the time the world's smallest portable personal computer. To do this, the team would work long days and well into the night. There was an expression at Convergent: "There's a week in a weekend"— the logic being that there are forty-eight hours in a weekend and you need to sleep only eight! Bill worked many "weekend weeks," including some where he never slept at all. He remembers leaving work "early" one Sunday to go to his mom's birthday party and having to stop at a department store on the way to buy a clean shirt to wear because he hadn't had time to do laundry in three weeks. The deadlines were intense, and the potential for failure was real. The team was pushing every technology to its limit and there was more than $20 million on the line—a very big investment in 1983.

Despite this rather grim description of long hours and lots of stress, this is still one of the best jobs Bill ever had. The radical collaboration and teamwork were phenomenal, everyone was doing something they had never done before, and everyone had one another's back. There were weeks of pure flow, where the task at hand was right on the edge of challenging the laws of physics, and late nights in the lab when they finally got the motherboard to run for the first time and it said, "Hello World."

Champagne was served.

The team that Bill worked with, some thirty-five years ago, still remembers the experience fondly. They used to have annual reunions, for years and years, after the project was over. If Bill runs into one of his old teammates he knows he's in for a long conversation, savoring the memory of how it felt to be on that team.

And, by the way, the groundbreaking portable computer that they made, the WorkSlate, was a complete business failure. The company shut down the WorkSlate division about a year after the launch. No one on that project got rich, and no one can point to the success of the product as the reason for the way they feel today. It was about the people and the journey—it always is.

**WorkSlate Computer by
Convergent Technologies, circa 1983**

Competence is just what it sounds like. We all want to be good at what we do. Some of us even want to be the best at what we do. We develop our competency by (and there is an element of grit in this one) practicing our craft until we have achieved what others would call mastery, and then going on to "out-master" ourselves through even more concerted practice. Your grit and ability to persevere is key here. Competence feels intrinsically good. That's why it is important to be able to identify with the value of the work we do. To do work well, we need to develop our skills, and if we're developing skills we truly care about, we will be driven to improve our competence. In contrast, if we are not engaged in our job, then we really don't care about improving, much less mastering, the skills required to do the job well.

There are two common areas where we need to invest in growing our competency: our areas of natural strength that are useful in our work and our areas of natural weakness, which are required in our job. In the former, the idea is to take your natural strengths (like leading small groups of people) and pushing yourself to the next level (becoming a world-class teaming expert). It's easy to rely on our natural strengths "as is" and just enjoy them. But to fully reap the benefits of your strengths, you want to grow them.

The reverse is equally true. Most of us encounter tasks in our work that we just aren't good at but are absolutely required. For instance, if you're going to be a university instructor, you have to be good at public speaking.

And Bill wasn't.

Bill is naturally an introvert. He prefers working one-on-one or with small groups—or alone. He likes having leadership impact (he's a great strategist), but he does not relish being in the front of the room—especially a large room. And that's exactly what teachers of popular classes have to do over and over. Bill loved being a teacher, developing students, conceiving design thinking curricula, and leading the design program staff. But he didn't love that front-of-the-room part and recognized that he had to learn to do it if he was going to do his job. He watched the top-rated teachers and talked to them about their approach to learn what they did. He studied the science of communication through public speaking so he knew what actually worked to deliver messages that matter and stick. And he practiced. He taught and taught and taught again, and got constructive feedback on his teaching from colleagues and students. It wasn't that much fun, initially. He felt clumsy, and he was getting more criticism than affirmation—which no one really enjoys. But he was committed (some grit is involved) and he truly believed that good speaking wasn't genetic and could be learned (he had a growth mind-set). And it worked. Bill regularly gets good teaching evaluations and Bill enjoys teaching—both seeing students learn and doing the job well. He's really enjoying his competence as a teacher and public speaker.

When there's a gap between your skills and your job's requirements, make it an opportunity to grow. It takes a lot of work, but on the other side are terrific benefits for you and those you work with and serve.

Bill is still an introvert, so after teaching all day he's happy . . . and exhausted. The best thing for Bill to do after a day in the front of the classroom is to go home and take a nap. By contrast, Dave is an extrovert. So after a day of teaching, Dave wants to ride his bike for two hours to blow off the extra energy, and then keep his wife up late, telling her stories about class. Bill and Dave both love teaching and have worked hard to build a high level of competence in it, but they still experience it in different and personal ways. When pushing your competency to attain true mastery at something, it's personal—you have to make it your own and do it in a way that fits you.

The drive for autonomy, relatedness, and competence is part of your humanness; these qualities are part of your intrinsic motivation system. Everyone has these motivations, and when you can satisfy these motivations at work, you are likely to do your best work, feel more connected to your colleagues, and experience your work as meaningful. This is what it means to develop the ARC of your career.

SHOUT-OUT TO MANAGERS

As a manager, you can design opportunities for your employees to experience autonomy, relatedness, and competence. It's in your best interest as an employer to encourage the conditions that allow your employees to create ARC on the job. You should be constantly asking yourself: *Am I allowing employees to meet their fundamental need for independence and autonomy? Do I trust them? Are my teams self-directed? Are my people learning on the job?*

If you are not encouraging ARC on the job, it might be time to check your disengagement rates. And your job retention rates. It costs anywhere from 20 percent to 200 percent of an employee's salary to replace that employee, with the highest number being spent to replace key employees, managers, and executives. These costs aren't reflected in your bottom line, but can be measured in lowered productivity, decreased morale, and increased stress, all leading to the potential burnout of your staff. The people who don't quit are often left to work harder, covering for the employee who quit, while you hire a replacement. All of this adds to the time spent interviewing, the costs of recruitment, and training new staff. If you think your employees are leaving over money—think again! People don't quit jobs—they quit bosses. Investing in raising the ARC of your employees is a direct investment in your success as a manager.

Passion Is Not the Starting Point

We don't believe in the idea that if you know your passion, you know what to do with your life. Passion—a kind of self-organizing singular drive toward an objective—is rare. And the research shows that passion is generally something that emerges in response to working hard in an area of interest. Therefore, you may not know your passion for years. We've noticed that when a true passion does surface early in life, it happens more often than not in people who are drawn to a life in the arts. Dancers, singers, designers, and creatives of all stripes have a higher percentage of "start with your passion" motivation than most. And that makes sense. These are people whose Maker Mix is overwhelmingly focused on expression—which is a more inside-out (or intrinsic) than outside-in (or extrinsic) type of work motivation. The artist's work satisfaction comes mostly from within. For most of the rest of us, our work is extrinsic—interdependent on other people, situations, systems, etc. A fireman has trucks, special equipment, a large team of very specially trained crewmembers, and a complex relationship with the city government, the police, and the local populace. Most careers are like that—with lots of complex interdependencies beyond yourself—so it takes years of living in the world and experiencing lots of situations to discern where you really fit (which is why the research tells us that it takes most people until their midthirties to really feel at home in their careers).

Don't be concerned that you are not yet passionate about your work. Passion may take time to form. To build on the process of passion-building, stay curious and pay attention to what attracts you. You can notice at each step of your career, *if you are paying attention,* whether the thing you're doing is leading, more or less, in the direction of a passion. There are a few key indicators that something will *not* lead to your passion:

* **You are getting bored with the tasks you do as part of your job.**
* **You are not willing to "stay late" on any of your projects.**
* **You are not working to perfect the skills it takes to be really good.**
* **You are not keeping up with what is going on in your field.**
* **You are not curious about what others in your profession are doing.**

Our advice is to concentrate on designing a job you love, right now—which includes one that maximizes your growth mind-set, builds up your grit, and pays attention to your internal and intrinsic motivators—and the odds are good that you will find your passion in it.

We all want a meaningful job and work that matters. And the good news is you are the boss, so get curious and start prototyping toward a better job. Change your self-talk from doubtful to positive and tell that story out loud. Develop yourself in concert with your intrinsic motivations to be an autonomous and creative worker, and to collaborate with others. Work hard to gain mastery in your field and focus on what you need to make your job meaningful. When you approach work and life with a growth mind-set, and when you are your grittiest self, you create work that matters, to you and potentially to the world.

There are, of course, other things going on at work—mysterious things that we're not in charge of and don't always understand. Undercurrents and power plays. We are talking about office politics. In the next chapter we'll explore how to deal with these particular types of challenges, and why it's in your best political interest to do so.

Try Stuff

Here's a simple checklist that you can use to calibrate where you're at when it comes to creating a meaningful job and work that matters. Fill in the questionnaire with different jobs—current and past. Don't forget, you might have a "job"

that you do not get paid for. Fill out a checklist for that job as well—you might learn something about where meaning and passion come from in your life.

Job description: _____

Rate whether you mostly agree (yes) or mostly disagree (no) with the following statements about the job listed above.		
QUESTIONNAIRE	YES	NO
1—I enjoy almost every day at this job.		
2—This job is one of the stepping-stones in my career, and I want to do a good job in order to have better opportunities in the future.		
3—I am more interested in this job than I was when I started.		
4—I think I might be moving toward or potentially have found my calling with this job.		
5—I enjoy learning new things on this job, almost every day.		
6—Setbacks at work don't discourage me. I don't give up easily.		
7—I like setting personal and professional goals, and I use this job to accomplish my goals.		

QUESTIONNAIRE	YES	NO
8—I have the autonomy to do this job the way that I think is best.		
9—I enjoy collaborating with my peers at this job. It is one of the best parts of this job.		
10—I'm working hard to get better and better at this job. Someday I hope to master all the elements of this job, move on to the next level, and keep getting better and better.		

Scoring
Give yourself one point for every "yes" answer.

1–2 points You are working for a living; your current job is probably just a job.

3–4 points You are enjoying your job, and you may be working on a career.

5–6 points You are getting grittier, and working on something you value.

7–8 points You might have found your calling.

9–10 points Excellent! I wish I had your job, and probably your life.

6

Power and Politics

Dysfunctional Belief: *I do not understand how things work at my job; it's all about the office politics.*
Reframe: *I can learn how to succeed by learning how to manage influence, authority, and power.*

We're going to get political.

Not that kind of political—work political.

Listen, we understand. You don't like politics. You don't understand politics. And thanks, but no thanks, it's all drama and it's just not your thing.

We get it.

We also get the simple truth that in order to succeed at designing your work life, it's critical to understand the power structures that exist at work. There's no way to get what you want unless you understand how power and influence work within your company. You must get political.

While some changes can be made easily because you control the circumstances, others involve people with more authority than you, and that's where politics becomes important.

Look, certain people are the brokers of *yes*.

We first have to start by understanding how change, any change at the office, happens. Ask yourself, any time you've seen something change where you work, what happened just before that change? The answer is a decision. If we changed the carpet, if we got a new copier, if we sold the company to some multinational banking operation, if we decided to buy trucks and stop renting them—any and all changes happen because of a decision.

A decision caused the change. Directly.

So, ask yourself, *What is required at work to make a decision?*

It's not time, or luck, or good looks. It's authority. To make a change happen, you need to be the person who has that authority.

If you're the senior buyer at Acme Trucking, then you're the one deciding whether the company is going to stop renting and start buying trucks because, in the long run, you think that's going to be cheaper. So you have the authority to make the decision to buy a bunch of trucks. You're the one in charge. The same goes for the head of operations who decided to change the carpet in the lobby. Or the owner of the company who decided to sell the company to the Swiss company that's made a great offer. For any decision to get made and stick, you have to have the authority to pull it off.

The question then becomes: Is that all there is to it? Authoritarians make decisions and that makes the world go around? No, the world isn't that simple. An awful lot of other voices are in the air around decisions, so there must be something else going on, and that's the wielding of influence.

Influence that matters acts on the people with the authority who are making decisions, often by providing an informed opinion on the pros and cons of the decision in question. So if you've been influential on a decision that resulted in a change, your influence was well received by the authoritarians. That is a form of power in any organization.

Making a lot of noise and trying to insert yourself into the decision process might look like it's being influential, but it's not. If the wannabe influencer doesn't have an impact on the decision, he or she isn't one. Influence equals having an impact on the authoritarians who are making decisions that cause changes to occur.

At the core of it, the true definition of politics is the wielding of influence.

When we can understand not just what influence is (action on authority), but also where it comes from and how it operates, then we can be more effective when we want to exert influence and navigate office politics. And that makes our work life simpler and more effective.

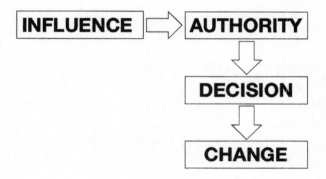

The Power Potpourri

Authority is the power to make decisions.

Influence is a form of power that acts upon authority.

Now for a little 2x2 model: In the Influence and Authority chart on page 158, you can have a lot of authority or not much, or you can have a lot of influence or not much.

Looking at the chart, this means we have roughly four kinds of people in every organization. We have influential authoritarians (IA), we have non-influential authoritarians (NIA), we have influential non-authoritarians (INA), and the non-influential non-authoritarians (NINA).

Let's briefly look at each of these four different kinds of people and power in an organization.

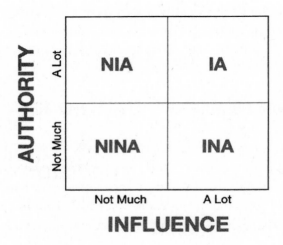

NINA

At the bottom left we have the non-influential non-authoritarian. These are people who have neither influence nor authority. These are not particularly powerful people and, by the way, there's nothing wrong with NINAs. Every organization should have lots of them; they get a lot of stuff done. And if you got rid of all the

NINAs in an organization, the population of workers would simply redistribute themselves on this chart. There are always people in all four quadrants of this chart; it's just a description of the population of people in any situation.

We're not judging anybody. We're just describing the ways things work. Most people are NINAs—they are valuable and important but not necessarily influential in the making of big decisions. The teacher in the classroom. The clerk in the store. Most of the doctors in your local hospital. The freshman congressperson in Washington, D.C. They're all NINAs.

NIA

At the top left we have the non-influential authoritarians. NIAs are people who are relatively high up in the organization, but they're not particularly influential. They're not necessarily people in charge of terribly important stuff. Sometimes the facilities director who's taking care of the office cubicles and the copiers is in an authoritative position, but they're not really influential. They might have a big budget because the building rent is really high, but they are not involved with the strategic direction of the organization.

It can also be a place where people who have sort of outlived their welcome get kicked upstairs. These become the auxiliary autocrats. People who are high up but don't seem to be doing much of anything. Maybe they made a big contribution in the past and so they got a big promotion and were kept around, but the strategic direction of the company has left them behind. They exist, they're not critical players, but most organizations have a few of them.

INA

The right side of this chart is the power zone. This is where people have influence. INAs are the influential non-authoritarians. These are people in the organization who get listened to. Actually, Dave is an INA these days at the Stanford lab. As part of a leadership succession plan, Dave and Bill hired a terrific managing director for the Stanford Life Design Lab. She works for Bill (who is the executive director of the entire Stanford Design Program, so he's the big boss and definitely an IA) and she took on almost all of Dave's managerial responsibilities. Everyone in the lab reports to her, and she reports to Bill. Dave's still around and does some teaching and coaching, but he's not authoritative. But since he started this thing twelve years ago and coauthored the book with Bill and still has pretty good ideas, he has lots of influence but no authority.

You see these kinds of people in every organization: It's the really forward-thinking classroom teacher who has the ear of the principal when she's considering changing something. It's the waiter who's always consulted about any and all menu or décor changes because the owner knows she's really got her finger on the pulse of the customers. It's the phone service agent at the IRS help desk group who the regional manager always turns to for advice when it comes to improving the website design. It's Dave. They're all INAs.

IA

Last but not least, we have people who are both authoritative and influential. These are people who get listened to because they have important things to say, and they have positions of authority so they can make decisions. These are the real power players.

The Big Boss (CEO, owner, president, general manager, battalion commander) is almost always an IA. But there are others, too. It all has to do with one's area of responsibility—which usually presents itself as control over the sizing and use of budgets and funds. The city manager, a permanent staffer who oversees a large budget *and* how it gets spent, is arguably more an IA than is the mayor who gets reelected every two years (so can be easily waited out and worked around). The head coach of an NFL team is usually in the third level of management, as he reports up to a general manager, who reports up to the owner. But the head coach is clearly an IA, since he has the biggest responsibility for the most important thing the team does—win games to get into the playoffs (where the big money resides). It's a risky job, it's win or get fired, but an NFL head coach is perhaps the most powerful person in the organization when he's winning.

The Value Proposition

Understanding the Influence and Authority chart is a good first step, but how do you use this model to increase your influence and have greater power? Basically, you do that by being strategically and culturally aligned with the business and other influencers, and by creating a history of contribution that is recognized by others in power. Influence is therefore the sum of the value you contribute and the recognition you get from contributing that value.

Influence = Value + Recognition

It's all about value. This is a really important idea to understand, and it's going to get you over your negative feelings about politics. When we're talking about politics, we're talking about the wielding of influence, the kind of influence that acts on authority, authority with the power to make decisions. And that influence comes from a very legitimate place; it comes from the real value you create, strategically and culturally aligned, for your organization.

People who are given the authority to make decisions are supposed to be moving the organization forward, collaboratively, toward success. If you are one of those people at work, you have goals. You have a strategy. You're trying to get something done— like trying to build and sell these new autonomous cars or trying to make sure that people have a good experience in your corner grocery store. Whatever decisions you use your authority to make, they are supposed to be part of creating success for the business, our partners, and our customers.

So, if Angela is the decision-maker who has authority, who does she listen to? Well, a decision-maker will listen to you if she thinks you have good ideas that will help the company do more valuable things and be more successful. She doesn't listen to you because she likes your dress, or because you used to date her cousin. (Sometimes *those* are the reasons, and that's bad politics, but it's pretty rare.) Most influencers became influential, and get listened to by the Angelas, because their advice and counsel can add value.

So how do you become an influencer? It's really simple. You add value to the organization, meaning you help it be more successful, by being useful and doing great work. It is important that the value you add is strategically aligned with the organization's direction and is recognized by people who can do something about it, the ones with the authority to make decisions.

If you add value and nobody knows, that's a noble contribution, but it won't make you influential. If you try to get recognized by being noisy or popular but you don't do anything valuable, it might work briefly, but that will wear off quickly. Real influence comes from a repeat record of adding value and being recognized for it. This is a good thing. Decision-makers need influencers, because without them they're left on their own to figure out everything. So a healthy ecosystem of authority and influence, our definition of healthy office politics, actually makes for a stronger organization.

Are you liking politics more now?

Bad Politics

Occasionally things do go bad. Politics turn ugly. And nobody wants that. Ugly politics are noisy, they're costly, they hurt people, and they sometimes involve things breaking or getting burned to the ground. Sometimes they end up with everyone losing their jobs and the company shutting down.

There are generally two ways that bad politics can happen. The first is when someone in the organization pulls a power play. And the second is when there's a values crisis in the company.

First, let's distinguish between a power play and a power struggle. A power struggle is when people with legitimate opinions get into a conflict about what the right thing to do is. If we go back to our example about renting verses buying trucks for a company, and let's say there's one group that's really in favor of renting trucks, because then we can update the fleet more easily. And another group is really in favor of buying trucks, because we can finance them at a lower cost. Both sides have honest opinions, and it is a legitimate struggle to make a good decision. There's a conflict, and two parts of the organization with equal power disagree, and that is not actually a bad thing. That's a legitimate power struggle, and that's okay. Resolving the decision and moving on is going to make the company stronger. In a power struggle, everybody involved wants to do the right thing for the organization, but they just don't agree on what the right thing is.

In a power play, somebody's not trying to do the right thing for the company, they're trying to do the right thing for themselves. Let's say that, in the truck example, Arie is really pushing for buying trucks instead of renting because Arie has a cousin who is a truck broker, and what she's really trying to do is make a bunch of money for her cousin by getting the company to buy trucks from him. It has nothing to do with helping the company. That's a power play, not aligned with or good for the company's strategy, and that's not okay.

The second reason politics go bad is when there's a values crisis in the company.

Let's say Gus has this corner grocery store and he has been running it successfully for years. But lately the customers are starting to disappear. He's had regular customers for a long time, but now they're aging, and new people are moving into the neighborhood, and they tend to buy online and are more interested in going to that big chain that sells organics and supplements. Gus isn't sure how to get these new folks to try his store, and he is in some real trouble. In fact, he's starting to lose money and starting to panic.

When you are experiencing challenges to your business model and don't know what to do, when you are not really sure what a good decision looks like, that's when organizations, large and small, run into a values crisis. In this case, the equation

Influence = Value + Recognition no longer works, because we're not sure what "value" really means. Gus isn't sure whether it is more valuable to paint bigger window signs or build a bigger presence on social media (which didn't exist thirty years ago when he started his successful store). Is it more valuable to stock more organic food for these new "foodie" customers or start a home delivery service? And when you don't really know (1) why you are failing and (2) what to do about it, you don't have a strategy. And that's when you get chaos and a crisis of values.

When you don't know how to make a good decision, you make decisions randomly. People start picking the person whose ideas sound the coolest or who has the loudest voice. Suddenly it's decision du jour, and things are changing constantly and without a clear direction. When nobody knows a good decision from a bad one, it can get pretty ugly pretty fast.

And this isn't just about little corner grocery stores caught up in changing demographics. It can happen in any organization that is undergoing lots of stress or value confusion. During the time that Bill was at Apple, Steve Jobs was gone (he came back years later) and the company went through three CEOs. Each one brought a new vision for the company, and pretty soon no one was sure just exactly what they were supposed to be doing. The metrics for a "good decision" kept changing, and bad politics soon followed. People argued to fund their pet projects, not because they were on-strategy (there was none) but because they wanted to accumulate personal power.

We have seen things go bad, in a start-up of just three people, when the cofounders couldn't agree on a strategy. Instead of working to get better research and "build their way forward" together, two of the founders (who were friends at a previous company) gang up on the third and a power play ensues. The third founder is ousted, and it ends up being costly. The ousted founder usually comes back, right around the public offering, and sues to recover what he or she thinks is their fair share of the company. It's a mess, it's unnecessary, and it happens more often than you might think.

So when there is either a power play going on because somebody's in it for themselves or there's a values crisis and nobody knows how to make a good choice, the situation can result in bad politics that get out of control. Our advice: You want to be careful in those situations to make sure you don't get caught up in the mess. You have to stay close enough to the situation to know what's going on, but not so close that you get burned. Most bad political scenarios don't last long. Someone eventually comes in to clean up the mess and, if you can identify who those people are and make yourself useful to them, you can end up on the healthy side of things again. Just be a savvy political observer and keep adding value that's visible to the right influencers and authorities—something good will come of it.

Organize This

Most people have seen a traditional organizational chart. These are authority-based charts that show the hierarchy of who is above whom and who is below in any organization. Boss. Minor boss. Middle managers. Workers. This is the way that people have drawn organization charts for centuries. The only problem is it doesn't tell the true story because the way authority and influence work in a company is not two-dimensional—it's three-dimensional.

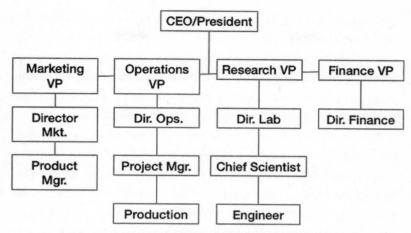

Typical two-dimensional organization chart

Here's a three-dimensional organization chart that is a much more accurate description of the way things really are:

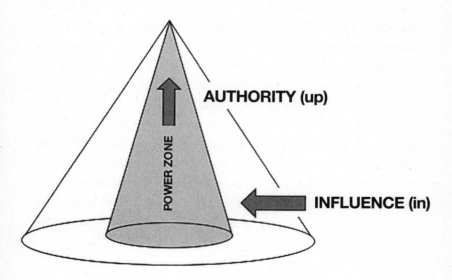

In a traditional organization chart, all you see are the lines of authority, but this three-dimensional chart includes both authority and influence. As we have just explained, both are critically important. This diagram shows you in three dimensions that, when you go up, just like in a regular org chart, you go up in authority, so the higher up in that cone, the more authority you have.

But also as you move in closer to the center on the x-axis, not just up, you're moving into higher levels of influence. You are moving into the power zone. In the power zone the influential non-authoritarians and the influential authoritarians, the INAs and the IAs, are the ones to watch. The less powerful influencers are on the outside. (Note: You can go up in the cone without going into the power zone, and that's how you become a NIA, a non-influential authoritarian.)

This 3-D model is a much more accurate representation of how power and influence, and the people who wield it, really work in the organization. And if we could turn this 3-D model into a hologram and have it jump off the page, we would also make it spin (maybe we could do that in our next book), because this model of influence and authority is dynamic. The power/influence scene at work is never static; things are always in motion. If you stop moving, if you're not working hard at adding value, then what's likely to happen is the centrifugal force of this spinning model is going to pull you out and away from the power zone. In this model, you have to be making a contribution to hold your position.

If you're making more and more and more value contributions, you go further and further into the power zone. You become more influential. If you make less of a value contribution, you start sliding out.

So a smart designer reframes his or her understanding of his or her organization to match this three-dimensional, moving system and works to increase his or her power and influence. And that is how things get done in business.

FOR THE SELF-EMPLOYED: As you read this chapter, you may be saying to yourself, *Whew! It's so great to be self-employed and not have to deal with all of this!* Actually, this chapter is more important for the self-employed than for any other group. Sure, you don't *live* inside a traditional organization and no one keeps sending you updated org charts, but you almost assuredly *work* within organizations. Clients are usually companies (and even when clients are individuals, politics still matter—they're just less complex). The reason is simple. As a contractor, you have no authority power in the organization. You have to work through the power of others who are employed there. That means you rely entirely on *influence* to get things done, so you have to be especially effective and artful in the practice of healthy politics. Dave was an unauthoritative, non-employee consultant who didn't get a corporate paycheck for more than twenty years. He succeeded or failed entirely based on his ability to work effectively within the political and influence power structures of his clients' companies. It's not that hard, and we promise you'll get the hang of it.

Using Your X-ray Vision

So now that you understand power, influence, and politics, you have a form of X-ray vision that allows you to see through company walls. Once you understand that influence is making an impact on good decisions, and that causes change, you can start to see through the politics of decision-making and it all starts to make sense.

With your new X-ray vision, you can identify, understand, and recognize who is and who is not an influencer, and you can see how influence affects decisions, even if you are not in the room when the decision gets made. You understand the valuation process and how it acts on decisions. Once you start seeing these business situations more clearly, it doesn't take long to realize how these new political insights put you in a position of power over your own work life. You get organizationally smart by recognizing the way decisions are actually made, org chart notwithstanding. And if you can get in alignment with the people who have the power, whether it's authority power and/or influence power, and work on adding recognizable value, you will be engaging the political realities in a very healthy way—and not just "playing politics."

What you don't want to do is stand around all day, yelling on the corner like a street evangelist, screaming, "We should not buy trucks!"

That's volume.

Not value.

Getting louder doesn't make you influential; it just makes you annoying.

Pete and the Power Nurse

Pete is a physician—one of those good old family doctors and general practitioners. He lives in a large metropolitan area, so there are big research hospitals nearby, but there are also still some small local neighborhood clinics. He works part-time in one of those small clinics and part-time in his own private practice. And Pete is not just a doctor; he also happens to be a total computer nerd. He has been since he joined the ham radio club (look it up) in junior high school.

It turns out the small clinic where he works part-time was thinking about putting in a new electronic medical records system, an EMR. Pete really wanted to get involved in implementing this system because, you know, he's a computer nerd who's really good at that stuff and he thought he could help them do a good job. But Pete was just a part-time family doctor at the clinic, so he wasn't someone who anybody would think to ask about how they should implement the EMR system.

In office hours one day, Pete was talking to Dave about this and complaining about not having any influence on the EMR implementation, so Dave asked him to tell him about what was going on at the clinic in general, not just about the EMR project. Dave knew that for Pete to be successful in this situation, he had to be aligned with what was going on at the clinic—he had to know what was valuable and not valuable to the organization—because that would be the basis for figuring out how to make an impact on the EMR decision.

"Well, we're growing," said Pete, "but we can't afford a bigger building, so we're staying open longer hours. It turns out that people really like to come to the local clinic at night, so we're running multiple night shifts. That's a little more complex, particularly for the nurses, and let me tell you, you really want to watch out for Esther these days."

"Oh, who is Esther, Pete?"

"Well, Esther is the chief of nursing at the clinic. She has been there a long time and she keeps getting promoted, and by the way things really work, you'd think she's running the place."

Dave said, "Tell me more."

"Well, since we're running three shifts a day, not just one, different nurses on different shifts are working with different patients. The handoff from one shift to the next has to be done properly, or patients could be at risk, and the whole thing has become very process-oriented. Esther really likes that, she's really good at process, and she makes sure that everybody follows the rules. And she's on the EMR implementation team, advising them about the nurses' concerns."

Then Pete went on to tell Dave about the EMR implementation.

"You know, the director of the clinic and the head of Information Technology are the ones in charge; they have the authority to make the decision. They really want to go to electronic medical records, because that's going to be easier for them to get paid by the insurance companies. But they aren't thinking about the impact it will have on patient care."

Dave asked Pete the following question: "Once the EMR system is implemented, wouldn't everybody have to enter the data while they're working with the patients, and wouldn't that have a big effect on everyone, particularly the nurses?"

"Sure," said Pete. "In fact, I know Esther's a little frustrated because she wants more input on how the EMR system is going to affect her nurses and the overall quality of patient care. But she's told me that she gets a little flustered when the discussions get technical and doesn't always feel listened to."

And that's when Pete's X-ray vision, his new understanding of politics, influence, and how decisions get made in organizations, came into play. Pete realized that Esther was probably a major influencer in the organization (she had been promoted several times) and had expressed a desire to increase her influence over the EMR implementation. Dave suggested that Pete call up Esther, invite her for a coffee, and share with her that he, like her, really cared about the quality of patient care. He should also share that he could "speak computer" and that he understood how to demand that a good user interface and easy-to-use software be part of the EMR implementation. Dave also suggested he tell her how he thought EMR could improve the quality of the nursing experience, something that she was very concerned about.

A couple of weeks later, Pete came back and said, "It was magic. I got together with Esther, we sat down, we were talking about the EMR project, and now I'm on the EMR team. I'm influencing one of the major players on the team, Esther, and we are both aligned around improving patient care. And this is one of the best project teams I've ever worked on."

To some, Pete was just a part-time general practitioner with no influence. Nobody knew or cared about his expertise with software. But because Pete identified that Esther was influential and found out what she cared about in terms of adding value, and made himself valuable to her as the guy who could figure out what kind of user-friendly software interface for an EMR system would improve patient outcomes by implementing her procedures in software, he suddenly found himself inside the influence zone for that project, and was, in fact, influential.

Pete got political.

And he and the organization benefited.

The bottom line: When designing your work life, we want you to be able to take this newfound X-ray vision, and the knowledge that organizations are three-dimensional, whirling pyramids of influence and authority, and make it work for you. Politics, in healthy organizations, is about making the organization run better. Once you can see (through walls, even) what's going on, and understand how the power and politics work, then you can decide what kind of influencer you want to be. Align yourself with the organization's strategies and goals, and make sure that you are values-aligned with your own compass, and we predict good things will happen.

Because that's just good politics.

And once you start getting the hang of relating to and wielding influence more effectively, then you might want to try your hand at pulling off one of the most powerful moves you can make in your career—redesigning your job right where you are.

Try Stuff

THE POWER-SORT EXERCISE

This is a very simple and often surprisingly insightful exercise. Draw a 2x2 table and label each quadrant IA, NIA, INA, and NINA, as shown.

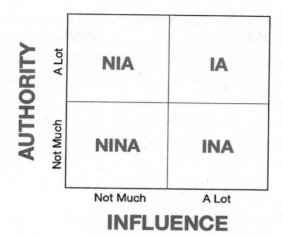

Think about an ongoing issue you're encountering at work (like the EMR project at Pete's clinic), and to the left of your box write the names of all the people involved—even peripherally—in that issue. Then sort those names into the quadrant that best describes that person's influence and authority.

The end result is that everyone is identified according to their relationship to the "power zone." Then ask yourself the following questions:

1. What do you notice?
2. Did anyone end up in a box that surprised you?
3. What information do you need to complete assigning people to boxes?

If you're like most people in these situations, sorting out the influencers from the NINAs and getting clear information on the rest of the political positioning of all the players provides a powerful insight as to how your organization really works and who makes decisions. Once you know that, it helps clarify what you might do next (and especially what you might not want to do).

7

Don't Resign, Redesign!

> **Dysfunctional Belief:** *I have a bad job, and I need to quit!*
> **Reframe:** *There are no bad jobs, just jobs that fit badly, and I can redesign right where I am to make my own "good" job.*

Sometimes you hate your job, or you are bored by your job, or you aren't challenged by your job, or you never saw this job as a permanent thing but here it is twenty years later and you are stuck doing what you have always done.

All of that can be true.

Except for the part about being stuck. Designers don't get stuck, because they know how to get unstuck. And quitting is rarely their first option.

So we're going to be explicit—don't quit. Yet.

That might be exactly what you don't want to hear right now, and we absolutely don't mean never quit. Nor do we think you have to stay where you are regardless (there's a whole chapter on quitting well coming up next, because everybody quits a job eventually). What we do observe, however, is that people put themselves through the pain and risk of quitting and starting over when in fact the raw materials to redesign a significantly improved work experience are within reach right where they are. Redesigning isn't easy, but it's a lot easier than starting over, so let's at least under-stand the redesign option and try a few ideas before we make any rash decisions.

You've got a couple of things going for you right there where you are—in the job you now have and in the company that knows you. If you've worked for any significant amount of time in your company, you've most likely developed a solid internal network and support system. You also know in detail all the things that are right and wrong where you are. As in any other intimate relation-ship, time reveals the foibles and warts of colleagues, bosses, and companies just as it does parents, partners, and friends. We all get frustrated, impatient, and tired of feeling like we're just putting up with the way things are. But before you jump to a new place where you'll have to start all over again (and soon discover a whole new set of warts), let's see if you can redesign your situation without the cost and risk of changing employers.

We're going to show you how to change your work so that it inspires and challenges you again, and fits you like your favorite jeans. We've helped a lot of people just like you diagnose and fix a bad fit, and in the process, we've come up with four redesign strate-gies that you can try when you want to redesign your work life. Depending on your circumstance, one of these strategies should help you get unstuck.

1. **Reframe and reenlist to the job you have by finding a different story for and relationship to your work, crafted by realigning your activities around your organization's priorities—making you more valuable in the process.**
2. **Remodel your job through a combination of cosmetic and structural modifications that better align with your**

interests while utilizing more of your signature strengths, resulting in improved performance that makes your boss happier and improved engagement that makes you happier.

3. **Relocate.** Slide laterally into a new role that's within reach, even if it's not obvious at first. Either it's an existing opening or a new position created just for you.

4. **Reinvent.** Launch a new career. It's the You 2.0 Program, but at the same company, in a completely different kind of role for which you've prepared and retrained to give you a major career refresh and your employer continued access to a loyal and valuable team member.

Dysfunctional Belief: *My job sucks, and I need to go to another company to get a better one.*

Reframe: *Before you quit, make sure that you have maximized all of your available options in place where you work. The better job (or gig) you seek may be the one right next to you.*

Look, we know it's tempting to look for a new job or a new career in a new company or jump into (or out of) self-employment. That's what most people think of first when they feel like their work just isn't working. But in life and work design, we believe in iteration. We've helped hundreds of thousands of people use design thinking to improve their lives, and by utilizing one of these four redesign strategies, we think there's an excellent chance you can renew and refresh your work life. And . . . you can't lose by trying these ideas, because even if you end up concluding that you do want to leave and find a new job elsewhere, your redesign efforts will put you in a much better position both to start looking for the new job in a new company and eventually to do a great job of quitting your current job well.

Caveat—the Toxic Workplace

WARNING: SOME JOBS ARE NOT WORTH IT!

If your workplace is toxic, if you are not being treated with respect, and/or if you're being harassed or abused, by all means quit as soon as you can. No one should have to put up with an unsafe workplace just for a job. And if your boss is an "asshole," you should read our colleague Bob Sutton's book *The No Asshole Rule* and his companion book, *The Asshole Survival Guide.* Sutton's books are both a comprehensive review of the academic research on toxic bosses (yes, you can actually get a Ph.D. for studying this stuff) and a practical guide on what to do about them. They are both a fun read and have sound advice on how to deal with assholes, in the workplace and in life.

If you suspect that your situation is indeed toxic, then do your homework to be sure that's the case. Then, if it is, proceed directly to chapter 8 for quitting tips and get on with your life somewhere else.

Your Secret Weapon

Assuming the place where you work is bigger than about one hundred employees, it probably has lots of different jobs available. And we are going to make another assumption—almost every job is important to the company's success or it wouldn't exist. Since you are literally an "insider" (you work there, right?), these jobs are naturally more visible and more available to you, certainly more visible than they are to poor John Q. Public, who doesn't have an insider's connections.

So, once you've made the decision to "change jobs," why not try and land one of these internally available jobs first? You have a built-in network, you can set up prototype conversations more easily, and your built-in social and political capital can work to your advantage.

Compared to an outside hire, you have many unfair advantages. You are a known talent at the company and, even if you have outgrown your current job, you are inherently a less risky hire than an outsider. And, since you're a good life designer and you have nurtured your internal network, you probably have some advocates for your talents and potential. All of these advantages mean that you are more likely to find your good "next job" with an internal search strategy, are more likely to get selected (if you tell your story well), and are more likely to succeed in your new job because you did your research and understand the company culture. You know what a good fit looks like.

One caveat: All of this advice assumes that you've had some success in your current position and that you have advocates and supporters where you work. So now is the time to take a hard look at your performance on the job and assess your assets and liabilities.

Design thinking isn't magical thinking. If you really haven't put your best effort into your current job, you probably need to do some soul-searching and might need to pause your job redesign until you get that situation addressed. If you're looking for a new job internally, you need to start as a valued employee in your current role. A generally understood management principle is: Don't transfer problems, fix them first. If you are a problem employee—fixing yourself in your current role is Step #0 that precedes Step #1 in any of our redesign strategies. It's okay, time is on your side, just do what you need to do. We'll be right here when you get back.

Strategy #1—Reframe and Reenlist

This strategy has an easy part and a harder part. Let's start with the easy part, which is—you end up just keeping your current job but liking it a whole lot more. By that we don't mean just start chanting "I like it, I like it, I like it" three times every fifteen minutes. That's not likely to work very well. Some changes have to be made, but in this strategy those changes are made by you. Now for the harder part—which is coming up with a reframed relationship with your job that enables you to successfully reenlist and go forward more happily. If you're a person for whom this design approach applies, then probably what's happened is things have changed at the company (or whichever kind of employer you've got) since you first started doing this job. Once upon a time the job worked a lot better for you than it does now, but the accumulation of changes both inside and outside the organization has created a new context and those changes have made the job a lot worse for you.

The outdoor extreme experience training company Outward Bound has a motto: "If you can't get out of it, get into it!" That's what we're going to do here. We're going to start with the assumption that those same changes that have made the job seem so lousy also include the raw material for reframing the job and redesigning your relationship to it.

A Tough Job for a Good Reason

John works for a midsize aerospace manufacturing company in Tennessee. He joined the company right out of technical school and progressed steadily from his original job as a line assembler, to a line technician who debugs manufacturing fixtures, to a quality manager who is responsible for making sure that the widgets the company manufactures meet all of the requirements for the demanding applications required to fly on a commercial airliner.

John is proud of the job he does and the company he works for. He tells his friends, "We make the parts that make the airplanes fly, and fly safely." After sixteen years with the company, John felt that he had achieved a certain coherency between his work and his values and felt pretty good about the choices he had made in his life.

Then, one day about a year ago, John was summoned to an "all-hands" meeting where his boss's boss's boss explained that the company had been sold to a private equity firm in a "leveraged buyout." John wasn't certain he understood what had actually happened, but was reassured by the big, big boss that "nothing would change" and that the company would continue to have the positive work culture it was known for.

Despite the reassurances, things changed almost immediately. And not for the better.

New production quotas were established, raising the number of widgets that were to be manufactured by 18.5 percent. The new management made it clear that they felt the old management wasn't delivering competitive results and it was time to clean things up. Most of the old managers that John knew well took an early-retirement offer, but that offer didn't extend to employees at John's level.

It really wasn't all that surprising that the new owners wanted the company to increase production. New owners almost always want to make some changes and assume they can do better than the other guys. John figured they'd learn soon enough that pushing too hard would impact quality, which isn't acceptable in the aerospace business, and things would settle down after a little while. He tried to just go with the flow. John did what he could to adapt to the new management demands: He started working longer hours to catch up with the increased production, and soon he was working on Saturdays and sometimes Sundays. John was concerned that the increased production was putting quality at risk—there just wasn't enough time to scale up the quality department to meet the new demands. He raised this issue with his new manager but was told that he would have to adapt to the new schedule or else he could "find something else to do." It looked like the increased production demands were actually here to stay and John was stuck.

He could not leave this job.

You see, John had a son with a chronic medical condition—one that required expensive immunotherapy drugs and constant medical supervision. The cost of this care was almost twice John's take-home pay, but luckily the company had a great health insurance plan and John's out-of-pocket expenses were manageable. Changing companies and insurance plans was out of the question—this was the only aerospace company near John's home, and his son's preexisting condition made getting insurance tricky, if not impossible, if he changed employers. John's son was getting better, but it would be at least another year before the doctors could say he was out of the woods.

There's stuck. And then there's really stuck.

John was really stuck.

Have you ever been in a situation like this: stuck in a bad job for a good reason? Maybe you took a risk and moved to a new city for a job and it didn't turn out to be what you expected. You loved the new location, but not the new job. Or maybe you got a new boss with whom you didn't exactly see eye to eye. Or your company's market started collapsing, and everyone got stressed out, and the job you loved turned into the job that's no fun anymore.

Or maybe, like John, your company just got new owners and, well, it's like it's a completely different company. You come to work every day at the same place, sit at the same desk, and mostly do the same job—but everything you used to count on has changed.

We all like consistency, and change can be frightening—especially when it has to do with our financial security and the security of our family. It wasn't John's fault that his company was sold, it wasn't his fault that the conditions for success had changed, and it certainly wasn't his fault that his son was sick. All of these circumstances were difficult, and even unfair, but that's the way things worked out.

The way he looked at it, John had only three choices.

He could get angry at his new bosses who were making what he considered unreasonable demands, and he could declare this situation unfair and be self-righteously outraged. He could take his grievances to his new management and argue that things should return to normal—the way things were when he was happy.

Most likely, this wouldn't work, and potentially, it could get John fired. He might be "right" about the recent changes, but he could easily end up "dead right" and terminated. John felt this option was too risky, and besides, he didn't like being angry all the time (and his wife and son didn't like it, either).

John's second option was he could decide that he would show up at work and just go through the motions. After all, he needed the paycheck and the insurance for his son. He could do enough to not get fired and to keep his job, but stop caring about the work and just try not to notice. Surveys by Gallup suggest that this is the tactic that 69 percent of U.S. workers take—they simply disengage from caring about their jobs. It happens all the time.

But John's gut told him that this wasn't a good approach. He had a feeling that if he took this approach it might fundamentally change who he was, and not for the better. He would lose some of the coherency and integrity with which he lived and worked. That was a price he wasn't willing to pay. Showing up like a working zombie wasn't a John way, even for a little while.

So John took the third approach. He decided that since his work situation had changed, it was time for him to reframe his approach to his job and create a new context for his work. He decided that he would stay in his job for the next two years, and then reevaluate. He made that commitment for the safety and security of his family—to make sure that his son would receive the medical attention he desperately needed. Once he made that choice, and decided that his two years were his "good enough for now" strategy, he suddenly felt relieved (he was no longer exhausting himself by rehearsing whether to quit or not every hour on the hour) and he felt a little more energized (now that he knew he was staying a while he decided to try and make the most of it). He realized that both he and his employer deserved an engaged employee—one who did a competent job while at work. Over one weekend, he decided to reenlist as the company's dedicated quality manager for at least the next two years. Starting on Monday, he would show up every day and do that competent job—respecting the needs of his employer and respecting his own need to live a life of integrity. That meant that, every day, John needed to remember his "why" and shift his mind-set from maximizing his career satisfaction to maximizing his family's safety and health. It took a little getting used to—changing our "why" is not always easy—but little by little, John adapted his work strategy to this new context, and the results were surprising.

A few months into his reenlistment (which of course he didn't tell his boss about), he developed new relationships with some of his new coworkers, and, whenever the job got too stressful or demanding, he was able to back it off just a little, without giving up or getting angry. He learned to negotiate reasonable boundaries between his demanding job and time with his son and his family. He finally found some ways to speed up the quality-assurance process to maintain an acceptable 15 percent production increase. John had to admit that without the pressure from the new owners, he never would have made the extra effort needed to come up with those improvements. The new quality measures he designed were making reliable products that fully met their customers' specifications—and John took pride in making them faster than they ever had. John even made it through a round of layoffs (often when things start changing, they keep changing for a while), and throughout it all was able to keep up a positive attitude about what he was contributing to the company. Most important, he stopped trying to manage what was out of his control. Two years later, John reenlisted for another two years, after which his son's treatments should be done and . . . well, who knows.

Sometimes reframing our role and realigning our activities around a new context, a new "why," can make all the difference.

It certainly did for John.

The strategy of reframe and reenlist is all about how to make the best of a difficult situation. It doesn't always work. If John were forced to produce products that didn't meet safe quality levels, he'd have to decide if he could in good conscience stay there despite the huge risk of losing his medical coverage. And it doesn't always last. After two years, John might decide it's not worth it to re-up again. But if you can't afford to move, reframe and reenlist is a good way to make it good enough for now.

It's quite straightforward: (1) Accept the new reality. (2) Identify new sources of "why" that you can use as your rationale for your job. (3) Reframe your relationship to the job and company. (4) Reenlist and live into it. (5) Look for new benefits and sources of satisfaction along the way to make it good enough . . . for now.

Strategy #2—Remodel

You can give your current job an overhaul and get a whole new lease on life by making either a cosmetic change or a structural change. By cosmetic change, we don't just mean a new hairdo. We mean making changes that are significant—new paint, new carpets, new furniture, and a whole new sound system—which in combination make for a very new experience, but which don't require knocking any walls down. Usually, you can do these sorts of remodels without getting much if any permission from higher-ups. Structural changes are bigger and more involved—like knocking out a wall to combine the kitchen and family room into a great room that opens out onto a relandscaped yard. It's a big project, but you can probably do it without a second mortgage, and no moving trucks are involved.

Just Eight Cups of Coffee— Cosmetic Changes

Ann was able to make a cosmetic change that thoroughly reinvigorated her experience of her job, and she did it all on her own, with no prior permission. Ann was a senior sales representative for a financial services firm that mostly sold loans to small businesses. Business was good. Ann was effective, well appreciated, and fairly compensated. The company was growing. And Ann was not unhappy, really, but she was a little restless and occasionally a bit bored. She'd been at the company about three years and got the "senior" title ten months ago. She liked what she did, but she wanted something more. She didn't really want to get promoted to her boss's job, because then she'd spend all her time managing and none of it actually selling, and she liked selling and talking to prospects and customers. She didn't really want to move into operations, either, so . . . now what?

Ann asked herself what she was already doing that she'd like to do more of if she could. Almost instantly, she answered her own question: Interviewing! Since the company was growing, they were hiring new staff regularly, and she loved interviewing new candidates—both for sales jobs in her area and for other roles in the company. She loved getting to know people and helping them figure out how they fit in. More than a few people she had interviewed came back after they'd been hired to get her advice and knock ideas around. They just liked talking to Ann. She loved those conversations, too—and that was the inspiration for her remodel.

You see, Ann was a natural people developer—a great listener and incredibly empathetic and intuitive, which is why she's a natural in outside sales. But those same strengths make her a good inside coach, too. She was already being successful "on the side" in helping a few people perform better and solve internal work problems. Why not help lots of people regularly instead of a few people just now and then? She started small, by prototyping in quiet but effective ways. She went to four people (each from a different department) who had already come to her for help and had appreciated her insights, and she asked if they'd like to try getting together regularly to discuss performance improvements or problem-solving. They all jumped at the chance. Ann scheduled a coffee before work with each of them, then another one three weeks later. So, in less than a month's time she had eight coaching sessions (without using that term, of course) and all it cost her was eight cups of coffee, each lasting about thirty minutes before work. No big deal. Ann didn't offer additional meetings because she wanted to see what the others would do. Three of them asked for another coffee meeting at the end of their second session, and that's all Ann needed to know. She accepted those requests and asked each of those three people if they thought anyone else in their department would enjoy having such conversations. They all did and said they'd ask around. Within a few weeks she had eight people asking for her time from five different departments.

Before she booked appointments with all those people, Ann had her regular monthly one-on-one meeting with her boss, the sales director. In that meeting she mentioned the coffee meetings she'd been having with the new employees and the fact that she had quite a few requests to do more of them. She told her boss that she loved doing it and was doing it all "on the side" with no loss of attention to her sales duties, but thought that her boss would like to know, if only because it made the sales group look good. "Well . . . sounds fine to me. I wish more people were taking that kind of initiative, Ann. Good job!" the sales director responded. (Most managers are happy about people adding extra value that doesn't detract from their existing responsibilities. Doing more for the company is usually not a hard thing to sell.)

Ann managed it so that she had to come in thirty minutes early to work only three days a week, which was not difficult at all, and that allowed her to maintain nine active internal coaching clients at a time. While it was a small impact on her schedule, it had a huge impact on her experience of her job. Every week she was making a difference in a colleague's life. She got to know all the departments in the company much better, and that made her a smarter salesperson. She got recognized in the lunchroom by an ever-growing group of people, and so she just felt more at home and more appreciated as an employee. Eventually, the HR director got wind of Ann's morning coffee club and asked her out to lunch to hear just how all this had happened. She wondered if there might be others with Ann's skills who could do the same sort of thing, and would Ann be willing to join a company task force to develop an internal coaching program? Ann's boss gave her a day a week to work on the task force for three months, and the program launched successfully. Ann happily stayed in her sales job (she loved sales—she just wanted something more) and her boss offered to let her keep a half-day a week free for coaching permanently. Ann never asked permission. She never stopped doing her job. She crafted a minor remodel at work resulting in a major improvement in her satisfaction on the job.

Wonder if this might work for you? Like Ann, start with what's already happening at work that you most enjoy, then prototype doing more of it in ways that make it easy on your employer to like what you're doing. If it works, just keep building your way forward to a more joyful job.

Sometimes cosmetic changes aren't enough. No amount of re-arranging the furniture will change the shape of the room, and then it becomes time to knock down some walls. When the walls you want to knock down are part of your job description, you've got some work to do—and you need to be smart about your redesign.

Let's Knock Out This Wall— Structural Changes

Sarah was always a nerd.

In high school she preferred being on the fighting robots team to the field hockey team, and writing code to make her robots even more destructive was more fun than whatever most of her friends were doing on social media. When she went off to MIT to study programming and robotics, she was sure that she had found her own particular version of heaven. This was her tribe—people who loved the intricate complexities of control systems and feedback loops and making machines do exactly what you want them to do.

Sarah graduated near the top of her class at MIT and got a job in a highly sought-after Silicon Valley company. At first she was happy, writing code and building things that were hard to build. She loved the software team she was on, all coders and all as introverted as she was. No one seemed to care that she was a nerd, as long as she delivered great code on time that ran fast and didn't break under heavy testing.

After a few years, Sarah was promoted to a team lead position. At first she thought this was a great idea—getting promoted was always a good thing (right?), and the raise that came with the promotion was substantial. She enjoyed leading discussions on how to architect a new piece of code, or helping her teammates come up with a new debugging utility to make their code-writing go faster. But the job also meant she had to go to biweekly meetings on budgets and schedules and other administrative stuff that she didn't enjoy at all. These meetings were very uncomfortable for her. When it was her turn, she had to talk in front of management to report on the progress her team was making and defend and update her team's budget and schedule. It was all difficult for her, but the schedule and budget part was just the worst and was invariably the most contentious part of those uncomfortable meetings. And those meetings just kept coming. Every. Other. Week.

That part of the new job was ruining her life to the extent that she began to think about quitting. After all, good coders were in high demand, and she had lots of options.

She wasn't sure what to do, but she was sure something had to change.

Sarah knew that she liked working with computers and code more than she liked working with people. People could get messy and intense and emotional. Not her favorite thing to manage. Working with her fellow coders was fine—they got one another— but the whole budget-schedule-management-people thing was not working.

But she was, above all, curious. Why were meetings with coders okay and meetings with finance and management types not okay? Finance people were people, too. It didn't really make sense, so, being a practical person, and a coder who loved data, Sarah decided to find out more about what made her so good at parts of her job, and why the other "messy people parts" were so uncomfortable. She had heard about a test she could take that might yield some information about this quandary and, after checking it out for herself (Sarah was generally skeptical about psychology stuff), she decided to take an assessment called the CliftonStrengths Assessment (by the way, you might know this test by another name, StrengthsFinder).

Know Your Strengths

The CliftonStrengths Assessment is a test that you can take online that teases out what Donald Clifton's research calls your signature strengths. This is not a personality test like the Myers-Briggs test; this assessment digs into what Clifton determined were the thirty-four independently verifiable strengths that are related to workplace achievement and worker satisfaction. In the CliftonStrengths model, a strength

is a talent (what you are born with), plus knowledge (what you have learned about the domain over time), plus skills (the experience and mastery needed to put that knowledge into action). The strengths have funny names like Intellection and WOO (winning others over), but all are correlated to things that are useful at work.

Knowing your signature strengths is useful because the data is clear that people who can practice their signature strengths at work are viewed as more successful. Gallup, the organization that owns the CliftonStrengths Assessment, reports that people who "have the opportunity to do what they do best every day" are six times as likely to be engaged in their jobs and three times as likely to report having an excellent quality of life. These differences can amount to millions of dollars in any large organization.

The data has been correlated to millions of workplaces and are generally considered reliable by folks in the HR and talent management worlds. While we don't often recommend going down the assessments trail, sometimes it is useful to step back and see if you can get more data on what work is a good fit for you.

The CliftonStrengths Assessment helps you identify your signature strengths. If you can then redesign your job to take maximum advantage of your strengths, the data shows that you'll probably be happier and enjoy the contribution you're making—which means you are more likely to find your work meaningful. This can be particularly useful if you're an independent contractor who does lots of different projects in different settings and doesn't have just one job description in one place. If that's you, knowing your strengths in detail can

help you focus your energies productively and direct your efforts creatively in each new project.

After taking the CliftonStrengths Assessment, Sarah discovered that her signature strengths, in order, were *Analytical* (people who are especially talented in the Analytical theme search for reasons and causes; they have the ability to think about all the factors that might affect a situation); *Input* (people who are especially talented in the Input theme have a craving to know more, and they often like to collect and archive all kinds of information); *Achiever* (people who are especially talented in the Achiever theme have a great deal of stamina and work hard, and they take great satisfaction from being busy and productive); and *Deliberative* (people who are especially talented in the Deliberative theme are best described by the serious care they take in making decisions or choices; they anticipate the obstacles).

Sarah also scored for *Connectedness* (people who are especially talented in the Connectedness theme have faith in the links between all things, and they believe there are few coincidences and that almost every event has a reason), which surprised her. She didn't think she was very good at this "connectedness thing" at all. But when she talked to other members of her team about her strengths, they all said that this was obvious. (As part of the CliftonStrengths Assessment, you are supposed to share your results with others at least five times to fully understand how others view you and your strengths. This is an important step, because we don't always have an accurate idea of how we show up to other people in the world.) Trusting the feedback of her colleagues gave Sarah the insight she'd been looking for. She was effective in the people part of managing her software team because she could see the connection between how they worked as a team and how good code got written—and that activated her Connectedness strength sufficiently to more than overcome the challenge of being an introverted team leader. While she understood that schedules and budgets are necessary to run the business, there's nothing about them that directly affects the quality of the software—they are purely administrative tasks that have nothing to do with the coding effort at all. Since the schedules and budgets are "disconnected" for Sarah, her Connectedness wasn't helping compensate. The disconnection and her introverted nature both contributed to her feeling uncomfortable and unhappy in those biweekly management meetings. Was there a way to get rid of the budgets-and-schedules part of her job and do more of the code architecting? That would be a big change. She'd have to knock out a few walls to do it, and she'd need help, too. The hard part was figuring out who could do the scheduling and budgeting—what engineer likes that stuff, anyway?

Then Sarah had an epiphany.

Production engineers.

She knew there was a small group of engineers who spent much of their time doing scheduling—the Production Engineering group. They were the ones who took the finished software and released it to the outside world via download sites and secure firewalls and version numbers and upgrade pricing and all that gritty but very technical stuff necessary to put some software out into the field. They lived and died by scheduling—just schedules that started after the development group was all done. They were good at scheduling, and some of them even liked it. Budgeting was the same sort of thing, so they'd be able to pick that up easily. And Production was always bugging Development, asking, "When will you be done? When is the test version ready? How long until the update fixes can be released?" It never ended. Why not let Production manage Development's scheduling? It was some extra work for them, but then they'd stop asking for Sarah's schedules because they'd already have them. Production attended those biweekly management meetings already, so that wasn't any extra effort.

Maybe this could work.

Sarah took one of the senior production engineers, Seth, out to lunch and ran it by him. Seth thought it would possibly work, but since it required "knocking down the wall" between Development and Production, it would have to be sold to both of their bosses. Seth could back her up, but the proposal had to come from her side.

Sarah decided to remodel her job description and design a role that better used her signature strengths (and those of her colleagues in Production, too). She told her boss that she was preparing a proposal for an efficiency enhancement that would accrue benefits to both the Development and Production groups without additional hiring. He said he'd support her in at least making the proposal and to proceed on the proposal (seldom do good managers not want to hear that their best employees have an idea that improves things). She prepared a fifteen-slide PowerPoint presentation for the key managers in both Development and Production. The first five slides used detailed graphs and statistics to make the case for how effective software team leadership improved code quality and reduced development time. She used the next five slides to explain the business benefits of developing better code faster using a time-to-market metric that was familiar to all of her managers. This showed empathy for her managers' concerns by making her argument in terms that the management valued (she was solving their problem—not hers). She used the last five slides to outline the restructuring of the scheduling and budgeting functions out of Development and into Production Engineering to improve coding and reduce friction between the groups. She was able to include a mockup of a new integrated schedule dashboard that Seth made up for her—and that was an obvious improvement over the current schedule reports. After forty-five minutes of discussion and tough questions, the managers decided to give it a three-month trial run, which of course worked. And the rest is history.

It took some work and creativity (and a few more uncomfortable meetings), but Sarah now has a job that she loves. She successfully knocked out the wall between Development and Production, which allowed her to remodel her role and redesign her work. She is still the coding team lead, with the commensurate salary and responsibilities that go with the job, and she has to go to those biweekly management meetings only once a quarter (and she doesn't have to present anything when she goes, because she sends out a detailed development report in advance). She gets to spend more time on high-level software architecture problems and is now leading a new team of coders developing better debugging tools (Sarah hates bugs). She used her strengths, empathy for her bosses' problems (more good code, faster, with fewer bugs, and better time to market), and even solved a problem for the production engineers (no more hassling people about schedules), and in so doing made them more valuable, too.

And they all lived a little more happily—and isn't that the point?

Strategies #3 & #4—Relocate or Reinvent (aka: The Internal Job Search)

We put these two strategies together because they are really two variations on the same theme, which, simply put, is: Search for a new job inside your existing company. It's similar to searching for a new job outside your existing company—just a whole lot easier to do and less risky to try. If successful, you end up getting a new job, but you never have to quit the old one because your new employer just happens to be the same company you already work for.

The approach is essentially the same in both instances, with a fork in the road before the final steps. In both relocate and reinvent, you are pursuing a new job in a new area—not a direct extension of your existing role (that would be Strategy #2: remodel). In relocate, you are making a sideways move that you can slide into from where you are without extensive preparation or retraining. It's a pretty accessible move. In reinvent, you are really making a big shift—one where your prior experience isn't very transferable and you're going to have to make some serious investment in preparing or retraining to get that job. Reinventing is much harder, but it's still easier to do in the company where they already like and trust you than by jumping into a whole new company as well as a whole new career track.

So, you can see that both relocate and reinvent start out the same—you're starting to get bored or you've identified another area you'd like to work in. You start nosing around and finding out more about some other kinds of jobs and decide you want to make a sideways move into a different kind of work. (At this point, these two approaches are identical.) If it turns out the move you want to make is within arm's reach, then you're relocating. If not and some heavy lifting is required before you're a viable candidate for that very different kind of job, then you're reinventing.

Both relocating and reinventing use the same simple four-step process based on our design mind-sets.

- **Get curious.**
- **Talk to people.**
- **Try stuff.**
- **Tell your story.**

The Tale of Two Accountants

Remember, both relocate and reinvent use the same approach to looking for a different kind of job, but still in your same company. In fact, you won't even know if you're doing a relocate or a reinvent until you've gone well down this redesign path to discover what's required to succeed. We'll illustrate Strategy #3 (relocate) with Cassandra's story, and we'll illustrate Strategy #4 (reinvent) with Oliver's story. Cassandra and Oliver have almost the same story right up until the crucial moment when it becomes clear that Cassandra can relocate but Oliver will have to reinvent. (Just read their stories . . . it'll make sense when we get there.)

Cassandra and Oliver were both in their early thirties and working in the Accounting department of a mid- to large-sized company—Cassandra in a telecommunications manufacturer and Oliver in an insurance company. They each had an undergraduate accounting degree from a good college but had no graduate training. They had both been on the job for about three years and were starting to get bored. They had largely mastered their jobs but were still years from being eligible for a management promotion in their respective finance departments. They each were wondering what to do next and whether or not to pursue a long-term career in finance. They'd both liked accounting well enough in school, and their parents had encouraged them to pursue a stable and reputable job—it doesn't get more stable than accounting. But the truth was neither Cassandra nor Oliver was feeling enthusiastic about doing the finance thing for the next twenty years. What they both noticed was that marketing looked more interesting than accounting.

The marketing people seemed to have more fun (at least there was a lot more laughing during a marketing staff meeting than there was during finance staff meetings). They got to do creative stuff like advertising and public relations and making cool videos. Marketing got to go out to field sales events and even visit customers during new-product rollouts, so they got to travel to interesting cities all the time (accountants never traveled).

Maybe marketing was the way to go. But where to start? They both did the right thing. They each began to *get curious* about marketing and started to *talk to people and try stuff.*

Cassandra's Competitive Advantage

Cassandra was already friendly with the marketing people. She sat right across from their group, and one of her school friends was in that department (that's how she got the interview for a job in the Accounting department in the first place). So her first prototype interview was with her old school pal, Marcie, who gave Cassandra an overview of what marketing did, the difference between Product Marketing and Marketing Communications (whatever that means), and who the easy-to-talk-to people were. Marcie recommended that Cassandra talk to a number of the other marketing group members, and if she liked what she heard, she should go ahead and reach out to Derek, the VP of marketing, who was a pretty approachable guy. So that's what she did. After three pre-work coffee klatches, two post-work wine-bar meet-ups, and a couple of lunches, Cassandra was more attracted to marketing than ever. She took Marcie's advice to heart (it pays to trust reliable helpers) and sent Derek an email asking if he would be willing to give her some career counsel, which Derek gladly agreed to.

Cassandra was a little nervous as she knocked on his office door, but felt better after Derek greeted her warmly, saying, "Hi! I was wondering when you might call. I heard you've been canvassing the group and figured you'd want to talk at some point. What's on your mind?" Cassandra had done a good job of getting curious and talking to people. Now she needed to be ready to *tell her story*—and she was. So she answered, "Well. I've been at the company over three years now and am able to apply my accounting degree effectively in the Finance department, but I've got creative interests that I think the company could benefit from that aren't needed in finance. As you've heard, I've been meeting with your staff, and everything I hear about marketing really excites me. At this point I'm trying to decide if I should make a change and pursue a marketing career. What do you think?" (Notice that Cassandra didn't ask Derek for a job or even ask if he thought she was a good marketer. She just asked for his counsel about a career change—a pretty low-threat request that left Derek lots of room to reply however he wanted to. She didn't try to corner him or get something from him that she didn't yet deserve.)

Derek said, "Well, you've talked to the right people, but you've really not done any marketing, have you?"

"No, I haven't."

"Tell you what," said Derek. "Let me see if I can't find some projects that you could do in the Marketing department that will allow you to take a test-drive. You might want to try this thing you think is so attractive before you mess around with your finance career. You're looking at us from across the hall, and I know it looks like fun, but you don't really know what it's like day in and day out to do our kind of work."

Within a couple of weeks, Derek figured out a project for Cassandra, doing some competitive analysis for the marketing team. She didn't need a marketing background to do the job, and her familiarity with the company's database was a real plus. Derek worked with her Accounting manager to get her a little bit of relief so she could spend a few hours a week working on the project. Which went really well. And at the end of six weeks, Derek had decided that he could make a full-time job out of it and, just like that, Cassandra moved from Finance to Marketing.

The competitive analysis project grew under Cassandra's leadership, and within a few months she made herself indispensable. Cassandra was happily relocated and it only took a few months.

It wasn't quite so easy, however, for Oliver.

Oliver Tries Stuff

Despite following his parents' advice, Oliver had always considered himself a creative guy and secretly wondered if there was a way to have a more creative job. He tried talking to his boss about this, but his boss dismissed his inquiry.

"No one wants a creative accountant, Oliver. Those are the guys that end up in jail."

That was a good point, but his boss didn't get it.

Oliver didn't want to be an accountant anymore. He wanted to try something different.

Oliver was kind of shy, and looking for a brand-new job in a brand-new company seemed scary. So he started to look around his insurance company for other jobs where being a creative person was valued, because it didn't feel so scary to talk to people who he worked with. One place where people seemed to be rewarded for their creativity was marketing, and he had met a few people in that organization who were on the company bowling team. He started prototyping his way forward with a few coffees and a few lunches and discovered that, indeed, marketing jobs were more creative than accounting. But at one of these prototype interviews his bowling partner, Serena, was blunt with him. "Look, Oliver, you are a nice guy, but you don't have the skills or the training you need for the things we do in marketing. There is no way I could recommend you for a job in my group."

WHEN RELOCATE BECOMES REINVENT

Here's the important point of divergence between Oliver's and Cassandra's stories. In Cassandra's case, there was a "marketing" job that was mostly managing a competitive analysis database and supporting the sales force—tasks where her accounting administrative skills were easily transferable. And the person in charge was willing to take a bit of a risk on her (which wasn't really all that risky, because the competitive database was getting no attention at all). Cassandra had a relatively small "ask" for Derek, and she had good support in his department. By contrast, Oliver wanted to do real marketing—branding, new-product messaging, communications—the really creative stuff, for which his background in accounting was no help at all. And the Marketing leadership in that company was more risk-averse. So Oliver's "ask" was big.

The lesson is—be honest with yourself about your situation. Do your homework, get curious, and talk to people, so you know what's really required of the job change you want to make before asking others to give you a shot. When it comes time to tell your story and ask for that new job, you want to be ready to tell a winning story. In this case, the relocate strategy was just not available to Oliver. Oliver was on his way to reinventing himself—or on his way back to accounting.

Now . . . back to Oliver and his bowling buddy, Serena.

●————————————————————————●

Serena's reaction initially discouraged Oliver, but he got up the courage to ask her to list all the things he would need to learn to be a competitive candidate for a marketing job. Armed with that list, Oliver put together a plan. (Oliver is really good with lists and plans.) He realized he would need to completely retrain himself if he wanted a more creative job. After asking around, Oliver decided that he would go back to school (he chose to buy the expertise and the "badge" that came with it) and get an MBA. He found a good program offered at a nearby high-quality university, one designed

for working professionals, with classes held on nights and weekends. He decided to focus on marketing and communications.
He knew it would take him almost three years to complete his
degree—all while working full-time in Accounting—but he was
willing to put in the time if it meant that he could have a more
creative job in the future. And he asked Serena if she would be
willing to be on his unofficial advisory board to help him with this
career transition.

She was flattered to be asked and agreed.

Oliver enrolled in his MBA program and, one year into the program, took an interesting class called Social Media Marketing 101.
He was amazed to discover this data-driven approach to creativity. Here was a type of marketing that was inherently creative but
where his ability to crunch numbers was also valuable. And since
social media's primary target is a younger demographic, learning
to be good at this would be very useful. You see, his company
was starting to realize that their old ways of marketing insurance
weren't reaching an important new audience—the Millennials.
Oliver had to write a paper and build a social media site for the
final exam for the class, so he decided to write about marketing insurance to Millennials. He also built a prototype Facebook
page to test some of his ideas for marketing campaigns aimed at
Millennials.

His Facebook page was just a prototype, but it attracted more
than a thousand likes in just its first few days. He got an A on his
paper and the data he was harvesting (legally) from his Facebook
page showed some very interesting trends.

Oliver was smart enough to leverage his schoolwork into a "try
stuff" project that he could use to advance his candidacy at his
company. He showed his paper and his Facebook data to Serena,

his informal adviser. She was very impressed and asked him to put together a presentation for her management team. "The Millennials are becoming a strategic priority for the company, and, frankly, nothing we've come up with has half as much traction as your Facebook prototype," she said. Bingo—Oliver had just been offered a chance to try stuff in front of the people he hoped one day would make him a marketing job offer. This was his chance.

Oliver worked all night and made a very successful presentation the next day. A few days later, Serena called him up with an offer. "Management has decided to put together a SWAT team to attack the Millennial problem. I'd like you to join as our design and data analyst. And I've worked it out so that you can continue with your MBA while you work with us."

Oliver was ecstatic. He took the job and has never been happier. He gets to be creative when coming up with new ways to market insurance to younger people, and he gets to wire up his social media pages to collect tons of data for analysis. It's really his dream job, for now.

Oliver didn't tell his parents until six months later—after he got his first raise in his new job. They were a bit stunned, but figured if he'd already gotten a raise, he was going to be just fine. They were right. Oliver thrived and never looked back. He was successfully reinvented.

That Grad School Thing

In the reinvent strategy, it is often necessary to retrain yourself for your next step. If you decide to go back to school part-time or full-time, you are taking on a big project. If you decide that grad school is your path to the future, you turn your attention to the task of selecting a graduate school, identifying what degree to get, preparing their admission package, taking the necessary entrance exams, and so on.

It's time-consuming.

It's exciting.

The idea of getting a brand-new master's degree in business or a teaching credential or applying to law school, or whatever it may be, is exciting. But sometimes the focus on "going to grad school" is a way of ignoring why you're unhappy in the first place. Grad school is the solution if and only if you have identified the right problem to solve.

We cautiously recommend this direction—but only after you are really sure that you are ready for a big change, because graduate school is incredibly expensive, it takes a lot of time and preparation to get in, and it usually takes a lot of time and money to complete. And if you do it full-time, there's several years of lost salary to consider.

And it might not work out! We've known more than a few people who went through all the trouble of getting into a good grad school, completing a graduate degree, and then finding out that the new degree wasn't that helpful.

That's a very painful and expensive way to learn.

Going to grad school—whether you do it at night while still working, like Oliver did, or you quit your job and go back to school full-time for one or two years is a big decision. So before you go to grad school (or even start the process of applying to grad school), we suggest you answer an important question.

What Is Grad School For?

As you can probably guess, we have some thoughts on that question. Folks go to grad school to get some combination of these four things:

Expertise. This is mostly what the graduate schools will tell you they're for. They're going to teach you a bunch of stuff that you didn't know before. Different schools focus on different things—implementation, theory, finance, marketing, entrepreneurship, etc.—so it's a good idea to do your research, because each school has a specialty that they are known for and their own approach to teaching (which is called "pedagogy"). You naturally want to pick the one that focuses on your area of interest, teaches the way you like to learn, and has a solid reputation in the field you're pursuing.

A network. Grad school introduces you to people you wouldn't have met before, and this becomes a new community of people that you can network with to help your career. This is a completely legitimate reason all by itself to go to grad school. The top schools have the most powerful networks, and even though you'll never hear them admit it, it's these networks that justify the super-high prices of the most elite schools. The better the school, the more influential the network. (That's why every Supreme Court justice sitting on the bench in 2018 went to either Harvard or Yale for law school [RBG went to Harvard but finished her law degree at Columbia]—if you want a seat on the Supreme Court someday, you have to be in the network.)

A pivot. You get permission to be a different kind of person when you retrain at grad school. This is part of what Oliver wanted (and

Cassandra didn't need). In addition to becoming competent at *doing* marketing, Oliver needed a professional identity that went with that new job. When people in the company heard about him moving to marketing, some would ask, "But . . . aren't you an accountant? What're you doing over in marketing?" Oliver would then tell this story about his new identity: "I started as a finance person, but I've always planned on a broad business career. That's why I got my MBA in marketing. I was collaborating with Serena and the Marketing team throughout my grad studies, so it was just the natural next step for me to move into marketing full-time." You can sometimes pivot without grad school, but the world still believes that having a graduate degree makes you more credible. The degree gives you extra permission—let's call it a "power pivot." Education counts for a lot—perhaps more than it deserves to—but we don't make the rules, we're just trying to help you play by them and win.

A badge. Graduate school gives you a badge so you get to say: *I have an MBA. I have a master's in public health. I have a law degree.* You get the badge, and some badges are made of silver, some of them are gold, some of them are platinum. In some fields it really matters whether your grad school is ranked or not. So if you are going back to school for the "badge," make sure you know how important rankings are and check out their professional placement rate. This is particularly important in professions that are overcrowded and oversubscribed, like law and architecture. Placement rate from lower-tier schools in both professions are 20 percent or less, meaning the 80 percent of these folks who got the badge might not get to use it as a practicing lawyer or architect. And some professions literally require the badge. You can't practice medicine without a medical degree. You can't practice counseling without a psychology degree. You don't need a Ph.D. to teach in a university (neither of us has one), but it's a lot easier to become a professor if you do.

Ultimately, you have to decide whether or not the time and money are worth it to buy a new degree. Just be sure you know how you value each component of what you're getting—the expertise, the network, the pivot, and the badge.

Sometimes people spend all that money just for the badge. Sometimes they spend all that money just for the pivot. Sometimes it's a particular mix of three or four of the elements. It doesn't matter, as long as it's worth it to you. But please have a bunch of prototype conversations, and a few prototype experiences, so that you can be more certain that grad school will make a difference in your future. If it still feels like it's worth it to you, then go for it, choose a good school, and work hard to master the material you need for your new job.

If it's a good fit . . .

Go for it!

Cassandra's Epilogue— When Having More Fun Isn't

Cassandra's story didn't end with getting that new marketing job. The story continued, and not as predicted.

The competitive analysis project grew under Cassandra's leadership, and within a few months she made herself indispensable. After a year, Cassandra and Derek had lunch again, because it was about time for her performance review. Derek asked her how she was doing, fully expecting her to say "fabulous," because she was successful and was on her way to a marketing career without ever having to go to grad school.

Cassandra took a deep breath. "Well, I'm really not that happy. In fact, I'm really anxious most of the time and I'm not sleeping very well."

Cassandra went on to tell Derek that she was struggling with supporting the Sales department. The salespeople always wanted more competitive intelligence on what the other companies that they competed against were doing. And you can never know everything about your competitor, so the salespeople were never completely satisfied. They loved the help they got from her, but they always wanted more. They never stopped calling and asking for help.

So Cassandra went home every night feeling like she wished she could do more for these people, but she didn't know what it was. It was never enough. It drove her crazy.

"I don't know what I'm doing wrong."

"You're not doing anything wrong," said Derek. "Welcome to Marketing. In marketing the customer never loves you enough. You can never know your competitor well enough. You're never, ever done. It's just the nature of the work. It's interesting, it's creative, it's flexible, but we are always dealing with ambiguity. We're never done!"

Cassandra said that she didn't like ambiguity and she really didn't like the feeling of never being done.

"Well, if you'd like to do the kind of work where at the end of the day you know you got the right answer, and you know everything is done, and there's nothing left to worry about, there's a big group around here that does that kind of work. It's called the Finance department. Remember? Maybe the ambiguity that comes along with the fun of being in Marketing isn't worth it to you. What do *you* think?"

Cassandra realized that for her, a little boredom was nothing compared to the satisfaction and peace of mind that came from getting the answer right and being done—really done—by the end of the day. She hated to admit it, but she concluded that she would be better off back in Finance. It took a few months for an opening to come up, and Cassandra had to work extra hours for a while to maintain the competitive database until Derek could replace her, but it all worked out eventually, and everyone lived happily ever after.

Except the salespeople.

But those people are never happy.

Things Change—Like Cassandra and You

So . . . what did Cassandra do wrong? Why did her relocation fail?

She did *nothing* wrong and her relocation was a great *success.* This is crucial to understand.

Cassandra is a living, breathing, growing, changing, ever-evolving, human person. She's not a machine and neither are you. There is no way in the world that Cassandra or Derek or Marcie or the Man in the Moon could have predicted the outcome of Cassandra's move into Marketing. It's the kind of thing that only time and experience will tell. It took a year for it to make sense to Cassandra. In the first four to eight months on the job she was so excited by the newness of everything and the fun of learning so much that she didn't even notice the stress. It was only after ten-plus months on the job, when she was going home for the 237th time leaving another half-dozen salespersons' questions unanswered, that it dawned on her why she hadn't been sleeping well.

Life design is just that—it's design, which means iteration and lots of prototyping. It is good news that we're always growing and changing. And nothing was lost. When Cassandra returned to Finance, she brought with her a much deeper insight into how the company ran. She had a better understanding of how managers in Marketing and other divisions thought about the business. She was actually better at her accounting job because of her experience in Marketing. And she knew herself better now; she was able to reframe her story when things got boring (as they do for all of us now and then) to "Well . . . I sure like sleeping at night!" She knew she could always have coffee with the Sales and Marketing people, which was almost as fun as working with them, and not nearly as stressful. With her new understanding of herself and the business, her old accounting job really was good enough . . . for now.

At some point, it's natural, we all outgrow our jobs. If you are a bright, creative person, and you have a designer's mind-set of curiosity and a bias to action, you will probably grow your skills and abilities faster than the job you're in. That means that every few years or so (sometimes faster, sometimes slower) you might outgrow your job. Then, to keep building your career, it's time to look for the next job. If you are in a healthy organization with an advocate for a boss, the organization will recognize your abilities and collaborate with you to find a new, more challenging role for you. But it doesn't always work that way. Maybe your boss doesn't care or isn't an advocate for you or anyone. If that's the case, you may need to make the first move.

Often, the best first move is to change jobs right where you are. You can employ one of the four strategies we've described, and just as they worked for John, Ann, Sarah, Cassandra, and Oliver, we're confident that at least one of them will very likely help you find a way to revitalize your job situation without quitting.

You Can Redesign Rather Than Resign

But if not . . . if none of these strategies work, it might mean that the time has come to leave and move on to another place. Fortunately, the process of get curious, talk to people, try stuff, and tell your story works for finding a new job outside your company the same way it does to find one inside—it just takes more work and more active networking. To help you with that process, we've got some recommendations in chapter 9. But before seriously starting to look for a new job, you'll have to decide it really is time to quit the one you're in. And an important part of doing that successfully is quitting well.

Try Stuff

1. **Pick one of the design-in-place strategies and write a short, 250-word story that describes a successful redesign of your current job.**

Reframe and Reenlist
Remodel

Relocate

Reinvent

2. Share your story with three friends. Explain that you are prototyping several new ideas for getting a better job, and this is just one of them. Then read them the story—just read it. No "throat-clearing"—no "Uh, this isn't very good, and I'm not sure you are going to like it . . ." Just read it with confidence.

3. Take notes on your friends' reactions, and compare them.

4. Evaluate this story with the gauges below.

5. Follow up with a short reflection on what you've learned about this plan.

6. If, after reflection, you think you are ready to do something, start the process of getting curious, talking to people, trying stuff, and telling the new story about the job or career that you've decided to pursue.

Write Your Story Here

_____

_____

_____

_____

_____

_____

DESIGN IN-PLACE WORKSHEET

Pick one of the design-in place strategies and write a short, 250-word story that describes a successful redesign of your current job.

❑ **Reframe and Re-enlist**
❑ **Remodel**
❑ **Reinvent**
❑ **Relocate**

Write Your Story Here

_____

_____

_____

_____

_____

_____

_____

_____

_____

_____

_____

_____

Evaluate Your Story with These Gauges:

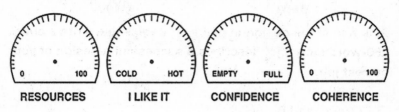

RESOURCES   I LIKE IT   CONFIDENCE   COHERENCE

Write Your Reflection Here:

_____

_____

_____

_____

_____

_____

_____

8
Quitting Well

Everything has its season. Everything changes. Everything ends.

And the data says that you will have many jobs and even multiple careers in your lifetime, which means you're going to be quitting some jobs. And when it comes time to quit your job, it is best to quit well.

Look, there are lots of ways to quit, but in general we have found that they all fall under two typical types:

1. **The bridge burner**
2. **The two-week lame duck**

Bridge burners are a classic archetype—appearing in movies regularly tossing a Molotov cocktail over a shoulder while heading out the door. You can hear their theme song as they roar out of the parking lot—Johnny Paycheck's 1977 hit, "Take This Job and Shove It." It may be a fun song or make a good movie scene, but it's a terrible strategy. Never do this! It might feel good in the moment, but it's a really bad idea in the long term. Never quit in anger, and never leave without giving the company time to figure out what it's going to do once you're gone. You'll thank yourself in the future.

If we're ruining your quitting fantasy of scorching the earth with your righteous indignation speech while coworkers applaud and the jaws of upper management hang open in stunned awe at your eloquence—we're sorry. And don't get us wrong—we understand how tempting the scorched-earth, bridge-burning fantasies are. Every one of us has considered this strategy at least once in our imagination, but let's keep it there where it does no harm (and even in your imagination, beware watching too many bridge-burning reruns).

The **two-week lame duck** is the most popular archetype—used thousands of times every day. We don't have any hard statistics, but we're betting the overwhelming majority of resignations follow this pattern: (1) Worker finally decides to quit. (2) Worker sets the date. (3) Two weeks before the date, worker delivers the following short, safe resignation memo:

TO: My Boss
FROM: Larry
RE: Resignation

I am resigning my position as senior duck plucker to pursue other interests. My resignation is effective two weeks from today's date, making Friday, March 28, my last day of work here at Lucky Duck Enterprises.

I have appreciated working at Lucky Duck and wish you
and the company all the best.

Sincerely,
Larry

Worker punches the clock, barely, for the next two weeks, makes
lots of awkward conversation with coworkers, and then slips away
quietly into oblivion.

Larry resigns this way knowing that "it's customary to give two
weeks' notice" and that resignation letters are best written remembering that less is more. Keep it short. Get away clean. Larry relies
on the fact that everybody knows you won't get much (if anything) done after you announce you're quitting, and nobody really
expects you to. If you're lucky, they'll just tell you to go home and
still pay you for those last two weeks. Or . . . so goes the conven-
tional wisdom.

The two-week-lame-duck approach isn't wrong. It just isn't particularly right. If it's all you can muster due to extenuating circumstances, it's okay, and we certainly won't judge you for doing so. It
probably won't hurt you (like the bridge-burner approach), but it
won't do you much good, either. After all—Larry plucked a few
thousand ducks in his time at Lucky Duck, and he deserves a little
more of a lift into his future from all that effort. That's why we're
going to recommend a third, different way.

3. The generative quitter

Generative Quitting

Just like there is a way to redesign your job, there is a way to design your way out of one. Most people think of quitting as a negative thing, but we think quitting represents an opportunity. It is the turning point between finishing something you've been doing well and starting anew. We therefore suggest reframing quitting as a chance for you to author a great final chapter for your old job en route to writing the first great chapter in your next.

We're going to teach you the power of generative quitting.

Generative quitting can be a great design experience, one that leads to an even better understanding of who you are and what really motivates you. Generative quitting requires the following:

Prerequisites

1. **Try redesign first.**
2. **Ask the boss.**
3. **Choose quitting.**
4. **Find a new job first.**

Generative Quitting Steps

1. **Leave the campsite better than you found it.**
2. **Rev up your network.**
3. **Set up your replacement to win.**
4. **Exit well.**

"Hey!" we hear you say. "What's with all the prerequisites, anyway? I'm ready to quit right now!" If so, we understand—but hear us out. Generative quitters know how important it is to leave a job on good terms, so they're attentive to those prerequisites. Doing the prerequisites well makes the always tough task of quitting well a lot more productive.

Try Redesign First

If you have gotten to the place where you've just had it and you want to quit *today,* you might have jumped right to this chapter and skipped over everything else. If so, we ask you to take a look at chapter 7 ("Don't Resign, Redesign!") and try out the ideas there. Please consider that there may be big advantages in "changing jobs" right where you are.

Even if the redesign doesn't pan out, the time you've spent trying is never wasted. After applying your design thinking process to the problem, you'll have learned a great deal about yourself and about your company (and therefore about your entire industry), and you'll have a better story to tell as you start your new job search.

Ask the Boss

Maybe it really is time to leave—you're unhappy and bored, and you have tried to make it work where you are but it didn't pan out. Maybe you're not sleeping well because your nagging boss is texting you at 9:00 at night with action items and work never seems to go away. Then what should you do?

Let's assume that you have tried one or two of the designing-in-place strategies from chapter 7 and they didn't work. There's one more thing we'd like you to try—ask your boss one simple question and see what happens.

Sam is a young engineer at one of those big Silicon Valley tech companies that everyone wants to work for—you know which ones we're talking about. He really enjoyed his first few years at the company, designing and implementing testing strategies for the company's software products. But then things got bad. Really bad. Suddenly, Sam's boss was on him almost every day. It seemed like Sam couldn't do anything right—nothing pleased his increasingly picky and critical boss. After months and months of this, Sam figured the only thing to do was to quit, and he was already drafting his letter of resignation when, at the eleventh hour, he reached out to Bill. As a former student, he decided to play one of his "office hours for life" cards.

After Sam explained his plan to quit, Bill said, "I know this sounds crazy, but why don't you set up a meeting with your boss and ask him why he is so unhappy with your performance? It never hurts to ask, and you've decided to quit anyway. His feedback might be useful."

Sam didn't like this suggestion at first. He thought he'd rather have a double root canal with no Novocain than have an honest conversation with his boss, but he gathered up his courage and set up the one-on-one.

Sam took a deep breath and asked a very simple question (this is the question we think you should ask): "What am I doing wrong?"

His boss sat there for a moment, looking stunned. Then he said, "There's nothing wrong with what you are doing, Sam. In fact, you are one of the most productive engineers in the group. It's not you, it's me. I'm going through some tough stuff at home."

Sam's boss then told Sam how his marriage was breaking up, and about the nasty divorce that was unavoidable, and how unhappy he was because he hadn't been able to see his kids in a month. He finished by saying, "I'm sorry that I've been unloading on you. You don't deserve it. But right now, I don't have the bandwidth to manage you or anyone else. Just go and do whatever you think we need—I'll sign off on any project you bring me."

Sam listened to this with a renewed sense of empathy for his boss. He also went home and put together a proposal to automate some of his most difficult experiments, which his boss then rubber-stamped.

Six months later, his boss quit. Sam is now a senior engineer in his group and happier than ever. He has a lot of autonomy where he works and enjoys mastering the technical challenges of his job. And to think that he was just one meeting away from making a pretty big mistake.

The point is, you never know what's really going on, what's really motivating people, until you ask. So before you quit, have that conversation with your boss. Ask one simple question.

"What am I doing wrong?"

And then just listen. Do not get defensive and do not argue—listen with as much empathy for your boss as you can muster (we know this is hard). And then maybe do the same thing with your boss's boss. Who knows what you'll discover?

Choose Quitting

Once again, you might be asking, "What? I've already decided to quit. What's this 'choosing' thing about?"

Good question.

What we mean is—you choose quitting. Don't let quitting choose you. Make quitting *your positive, generative choice.* Too many people act like quitting happened to them, as if it were the last resort ("It was the last straw"), an involuntary outcome ("I had no other alternative"), an injustice ("It wasn't fair"), or fate ("It was just one of those things").

That sounds like letting quitting choose you.

If and when you know you need to leave, then the time has come for you to choose to quit. Reframe quitting as a choice. You choose to quit. Positive psychology and self-determination theory all agree: What you choose to do in life is what gives your life meaning and purpose. So make it a point to quit with a purpose.

Find a New Job First

There are two good reasons to find a new job before you quit: (1) it improves your chance of landing that new job, and (2) it increases financial stability.

1. **Employers respond four times more often, give out twice as many interviews, and extend three times as many offers to employed folks versus unemployed applicants. Employed people are more attractive than unemployed people. Period. It may not be fair, but it has a certain logic to it. A prospective employer can easily wonder, "Hmmm . . . what do all those other companies that haven't hired you yet know about you that I don't know?" The best way to avoid the misperception that you're unemployed because you're a bad employee is to not be unemployed. This isn't always possible, and it's not fatal**

if you can't do it, but land that new job before quitting.
Sure, finding a new job is a huge project. We get that,
which is why the next chapter is dedicated to just that
subject, but let's finish inventing a better way to quit first.

2. **Don't forget about the money. Being unemployed is**
   expensive. You do not know how long it will take to find
   the new job (three to six months is the rule of thumb
   in most labor markets), and being unemployed for that
   long is both costly and scary. So we recommend finding
   the new job before leaving the old.

We know how hard this can be to arrange. Between the two of us,
we've probably looked for new jobs while still doing the old one
twenty times. We know that it is hard to work full-time at your
current job and work almost full-time *at the same time* looking for
a new job. Oh—and it's a bit tricky doing a job search without
your employer finding out that you're looking around (i.e., you're
on your way to quitting). But it is still the best strategy we know
to make sure that, when you quit, you have set yourself up for
future success.

Okay. Now you are ready to quit and quit well.

Leave the Campsite
Better Than You Found It

When backpacking in the woods, all good campers know the rule
"Leave the campsite better than you found it." It's a good rule for
life and work, too. Deciding to make things better at work before
you leave does a lot of good. It helps your colleagues, who have to

pick up the pieces, succeed. It honors your employer's trust in you. It will probably improve your references from your employer. And, most important, you leave knowing that you did the right thing (and weren't just "phoning it in") before you left. For all those reasons and more, this is a good idea. If you do it, you'll stand out from the crowd.

Bill's Campsite Maintenance

Bill had had a great experience—an incredibly demanding experience, but a great one—working at Apple. But after six years on the job, despite his efforts at renewal, the work had lost its appeal. During his drive one glorious spring Monday morning, after a weekend that felt way too short, Bill had one of those unmistakable "aha" moments. A voice came to him seemingly out of nowhere and said, "If you're really unhappy at work, you can just quit." He was so startled by this idea (and the voice) that he almost drove off the side of the road.

Bill had the sudden realization that he had been thinking like a prisoner—he was thinking that he *had* to stay at Apple, and he had lost his autonomy somewhere along the way. He realized that if he was unhappy, which he was, he could do something about it.

And, just like that, he suddenly felt free again. And he started generatively quitting.

First (as we recommend) he tried to reinvent himself at Apple, which ended up not working. He activated his professional network and started talking to people, trying stuff, and quietly looking for new opportunities elsewhere. And he looked around his campsite and got busy cleaning up.

One thing he most wanted to make sure of was that his team

would be in good shape after he left. Bill got to work behind the scenes. He had two key people promoted—they were deserving and overdue. He orchestrated giving the next big laptop program to a project leader he trusted and respected. This took months to accomplish, but it was worth it. He really cared about the people he worked with, and Bill knew that if he could be helpful to their careers at Apple, it would work out best for everyone.

Bill also used that time to pursue outside opportunities discreetly and, eventually, Bill's informal networks started to surface job opportunities, two of which looked particularly interesting. One was with one of the first e-book start-ups, and one was with a brand-new product design consultancy. Bill felt pretty sure one of these would be his next job.

When a job Bill wanted was offered to someone else, he knew he'd reached a decision point.

He had worked on eleven laptops during his seven years at Apple.

He didn't want to do number twelve. Bill was headed to that design consultancy.

He wrote a polite resignation letter, thanking everyone for a great ride, sent it to his boss, and went home. When he walked out on his last day three weeks later, he felt great about what he was leaving behind as well as where he was headed.

Moving from the "driving-to-work epiphany" that spring Monday morning to his resignation had taken almost a year. It was truly Bill's year of quitting well.

Rev Up Your Network

Radical collaboration, the "asking for help" mind-set, is a critical mind-set for any designer, but it is especially important when you are quitting well. You should do everything you can to preserve and expand your network of friends and colleagues, both inside and outside where you work, before you leave. For all the reasons we've mentioned before, your network of teammates and colleagues at your current job are a gold mine of future referrals and job possibilities. Now, before you quit, is a great time to reach out and reinforce those connections.

Get to know that interesting person who works the front of the house in your restaurant, that field salesperson who is always the top monthly performer, that assistant head cashier who was kind enough to let you schedule around your son's soccer championship. Make the connections tangible and touch base; a handwritten note, thanking someone for their time or being helpful, is always appreciated (handwritten notes are such a lost art). A lunch, on you, is appropriate for more important connections, and you can always schedule your prototype "exit interviews" over a coffee. The more people you reach out to and connect with, the better.

During the weeks before changing jobs, before you announce that you're quitting, there might be some people who you want to tell about your job change. Be careful, there is a risk that someone will slip and your boss will find out about your plan to quit before you want him to. Your "I'm about to leave" information is highly confidential and should be doled out on a need-to-know basis, and as close to the final event as possible. If you don't really need to tell someone, don't. But bringing someone into your confidence can really reinforce your relationship, so do this discreetly and strategically.

Set Up Your Replacement to Win

This is a companion step to leaving the campsite better than you found it. Your campsite cleanup is focused on making life better after you go for the people you've been working with during your tenure at the company—your friends and colleagues. There's another person you can help—and help in a very big and unexpected way.

Your replacement.

The person taking the job you're about to vacate.

This setup involves two things: getting rid of any messes that you don't want lying around (with your name on them!) so that the new person has a good clean start, and documenting the key insights, procedures, and contacts necessary to do your job well. If you're attending to taking care of your campsite, you've already got the first task well in hand. That leaves just the second task— writing the Quick Reference Manual for your job.

This sounds harder than it is. You're not writing a 128-page manual, you're just documenting, in one convenient place, the insider knowledge you've collected on the way to being successful in your job. This includes things like:

- **Regular meetings, activities, and reports the job demands**
- **Reliable, helpful people with special knowledge to solve certain kinds of special problems**
- **Any pressing issues that you're dealing with right now**

- **Old problems that were solved but might reawaken if not checked now and then**
- **If you had people working for you, a short summary of the strengths of each of your direct reports, so that their new boss starts with a positive impression of her new staff**

Dave once wrote a manual for his job before he quit. It was easy; it ended up being about twenty pages and took six hours to write. He turned that manual in to his boss at the same time he submitted his resignation letter. His boss was absolutely flabbergasted. "Wow! I've never seen anything like this before. That was the best quit I've ever seen. You should write a book about quitting!"

Dave settled on a chapter.

The next time you quit—write a Quick Reference Manual to being you and you'll blow your boss away (and expect the person who takes your old job to call and thank you for it).

Exit Well

Movie producers will tell you that the two most important moments in a film are the climax and the conclusion. When you quit, you are writing the screenplay of the final scene of the movie of your job. It is going to be one of the strongest memories that your company and the people in it have of you. Be sure it's a great scene that you want people to remember.

Leave them laughing and wanting you back.

You are in control of your exit narrative—your quitting story. And you'll probably tell that story at least twice: once in your resignation letter, and the version you tell in person. When the time comes and you've gone public with your quitting, people will want to know why you are leaving. You want to tell a consistent and positive story. Do not dwell on negatives (everyone knows about them, anyway), do not focus on the past, and resist the temptation to "even the score." Be clear and concise and emphasize the positives about your future challenges.

Bad bridge-burner example: "I'm leaving because Dan, my boss, is a micromanager and the company has no long-term strategy. I'm tired of working on projects that keep getting canceled because the top brass can't get their act together. And Dan's a jerk—did I mention that?"

Good generative-quitter example: "I'm leaving because I have an opportunity to take my career to the next level and learn new and exciting things. I love this company, and I'm sad to be leaving my great colleagues here, but it's time for me to move on to my next challenge."

It's not hard to do this right. Give yourself a good script and, most important, stick to it. You'll be glad you did.

Good Quitters Unite!

So, to recap . . .

Don't quit unless you really have to.

If you are going to quit—quit generatively. We're all going to be quitters at some point in our lives, so let's learn to quit well.

Now that you have a plan for quitting well, it's time to remind ourselves of the designer's way of finding that new job we talked about in prerequisite 4. Let's zoom in on designing our job search so that it is efficient and successful.

Try Stuff

#1: IMAGINING YOUR QUIT

This is a structured imagination exercise that will help you to figure out what it will feel like when you quit, and help you understand what you like and don't like about your current job. Beyond that, it may ultimately help you decide if you want to quit or not.

1. Imagine that, having exhausted all other possibilities, you are going to quit your job.
2. Create a job description that includes everything you do—include the stuff that you are supposed to do and stuff that you actually do. Make it a comprehensive list of all your responsibilities.
3. Now review those responsibilities, and see which ones could potentially be delegated to someone else. Cross those out.
4. Review the remaining responsibilities, and see which ones you do not enjoy doing. Cross those out, too.
5. Review what's left on your list—the items that are left are the responsibilities and tasks that are part of your

job description that you enjoy. This is your core job description.

6. Make a list of the new and valuable things you would like to do, if you had the time, training, and support. This is the stuff that would be either helpful to your organization or related to your learning something new, or both.

7. Recompile the list—this is your new core job description. It is designed around your current skills and your emerging new interests. It shouldn't fit the "job" you currently have; it's the one you want.

8. It shouldn't be a fantasy job description.

9. Once you've completed this imaginary job redesign, wait a day or so and then come back and read it. Is it consistent, does it describe a job that makes sense? Could someone with your skills and abilities be expected to be good at this job?

10. Now imagine that you are able to find the job you've just described. Really imagine it, and inhabit what it feels like to quit your current job for this one. There is no risk, it's just in your imagination. Then imagine going through the steps you'd have to do to make this new job real.

11. List those steps.

Here's why this imagination exercise works. Adopting the role of the "quitter who moves on to the better job," even in your imagination, allows you to free yourself from the constraints that control the reality of your current job, These are most likely bogging down your imagination. Imagining quitting and moving opens up your creativity and, assuming you like some of the ideas in your new job description, it suggests prototypes that you could try, even in your current job.

Prototypes like:

Brainstorming with some of your current colleagues about taking on those responsibilities that you delegated away in this new job description.

Having a conversation with your boss about the things you do not enjoy doing. Imagine sitting down with him or her and brainstorming about how to increase your efficiency by *not* doing these things.

How could you prototype learning some of those new things you want to learn, things that would make you happier and might make your boss happier with you, too?

In the end, by imagining this possible future you will have learned something about how you react, physically and emotionally, to this new job possibility. And you have a chance to experience any regret or second thoughts about leaving the job you have, before you actually do it. You might learn something from that experience, too.

We recommend going through this imaginary redesign before you actually quit. It is a refreshing way to reboot your creativity and redesign whatever you're doing, without the real world constraining your solution. And you will almost always learn something about yourself.

#2 THE "QUITTING WELL" PLANNER

After you decide to quit, and before you actually leave your job, make a plan to quit well. As described above, a good, generative "quit" has four steps, as described below.

Fill in the template to organize your quitting strategy. As your "quit" unfolds (quitting is a dynamic situation and things can change fast), feel free to modify your plan. The thing to remember is that there are important tasks to accomplish and important relationships to maintain. You'll want to be systematic in managing your quitting project.

Leave the Campsite Better Than You Found It

Make a list the people you work with and who work for you (if any). Figure out how to make sure they are positively affected by your departure. Now is the time to go to their boss and praise their accomplishments. Be selfless and give away any political or social capital you have—it doesn't come with you to your next job.

Employee _____ Positive Outcome ____

Employee _____ Positive Outcome ____

Employee _____ Positive Outcome ____

Employee _____ Positive Outcome ____

Rev Up Your Network

Make a list of all your good relationships at work; touch base before you go.

_____	Touch Base _____
_____	Touch Base _____
_____	Touch Base _____

Make a list of the people you want to meet before you leave, and schedule a coffee.

_____	Coffee _____
_____	Coffee _____
_____	Coffee _____

Set Up Your Replacement to Win

Outline your Quick Reference Manual for the person taking your job after you leave. Consider the following lists and sections, and add or subtract as needed.

1. Regular meetings, activities, and reports (include examples, templates, schedules)
2. List key colleagues and helpers (names, roles, email, phone).
3. List current key issues, problems to be addressed (one page each, with room for notes).
4. List old problems that could resurface if not maintained,

including what to look for and what, if any, maintenance
is required to keep them solved and stable.

5. **Procedures for regular functions of the job**
   o Reference company documents if available.
   o Write summary procedures for key actions not
     documented elsewhere.

6. **Personnel summary of each of your direct reports (if
   any)**—including what makes them a great employee,
   and especially any pending promotions or recognitions
   left undone and/or career development projects you
   were working on, etc. (look out for their futures—you
   won't be there to finish what you started with them)

Exit Well: Write a Positive "Story" About Your Departure

Write a short (less than 100 words) story about your departure, one that is easy to memorize, that you will tell people
once your resignation becomes public.

Make sure you include these three elements:

- Something positive about the new opportunity for you
  (do not mention the positives about the new company—
  nobody wants to hear about the "greener grass"; make it
  personal, not universal)
- Something positive about your old position—come on,
  there must have been something
- Something positive about the people you are leaving
  behind—this should be easy

_____

_____

_____

_____

_____

_____

Armed with your plan, you can start the quitting process. It may not take a year, like it took Bill to leave Apple, but plan on spending 2–6 months on this project. Take your time and do the quitting process well. And, although you are now mentally a short-timer in your current job, remember that you are playing a very long career game. You want to always be building your professional reputation and network, both of which travel with you wherever you go.

9

Moving On

Finding a new job can be stressful. It can feel difficult. It can feel somewhere on par with getting an elective root canal.

We get it.

We *really* get it.

Look, we don't mean to shamelessly direct you to our first book, but if your next job is in a new industry, or is a different role, or if it's been a really long time since you've last gone looking for a job, then this job search may be a bigger project that deserves some extra preparation. In that case, we encourage you to grab a copy of *Designing Your Life*, with a particular eye on chapter 7, "How Not to Get a Job," and chapter 8, "Designing Your Dream Job." If you think that your next job is not a job but self-employment, that's a special case, and we talk about getting started on your own in chapter 10 of this book.

However, if you think you know the sort of job you have in mind, know the kinds of companies in your area that are a likely fit, and have the right experience, qualifications, and contacts in your field, then we've got what you need right here in this chapter. We're going to leverage what you know about yourself and what you know about the current job market and use it to launch your external search.

It's All About the Story

Here's a simple but profound reframe: The best way to get a job is *not* to ask for a job, it's to ask for the story. Ask for (lots and lots of) stories, and you'll find a job.

This counsel is at the heart of our redesign strategies relocate and reinvent from chapter 7—it all starts with *get curious* and *talk to people*. The most effective way we know of to pursue and land new job opportunities starts with prototype conversations, rooted in sincere curiosity, with professionals in your area of career interest.

The next step in finding a job is for you to spend another one, two, or three months having lots of interesting conversations with lots of interesting people—most of whom aren't currently hiring—so that you can connect into the conversation about hidden jobs, somewhere along the way.

In *Designing Your Life*, we told the job-search story of Kurt. Since we last wrote about Kurt, he's moved twice and gone through two more job searches—all successfully using our approach.

The Standard Model of Job Searching

Kurt's first big job search happened when he and his new wife relocated to Atlanta. Kurt had just completed four years in the Stanford Design Program—two getting his master's and two more in a postgraduate fellowship. And that was his second master's degree, on top of one he already had from Yale in sustainable architecture. After he and his wife, Sandy, discovered their first baby was on the way, they decided to move near the grandparents in Atlanta. Kurt was finally ready to harvest the value of all those shiny, prestigious degrees to get the career he would love that would also pay the bills and provide for his new family. Kurt arrived in Georgia serious about landing a job, fast. Kurt found job postings on job boards that fit his background like a glove. He submitted thirty-eight job applications along with his prestigious degrees, impressive résumé, and thirty-eight individually crafted, thoughtful cover letters.

You'd think, with his background, he should have more job offers than he could count, but it didn't turn out that way. Out of his thirty-eight applications, Kurt received terse rejection emails from eight companies and never heard anything at all from the other thirty. Eight no's and thirty nothings. No interviews, no offers, no follow-up calls. And this is a guy educated at Yale and Stanford.

Kurt failed at what we call the "standard model of job searching." He looked for jobs listed on the Internet or corporate websites, read the job descriptions and assumed they accurately described the available jobs, decided he was a good fit, and submitted a résumé and cover letter, and waited for the hiring manager to call. And waited.

And waited.

Still waiting.

The problem is that 52 percent of employers admitted that they respond to less than half of the candidates who apply. And the hit rate for landing a job with the standard model is about 5 percent. It was a lot of work for Kurt, with zero return.

This standard model fails so much of the time because it is a model based on a number of mistaken ideas. One is that someone is reading your cover letter. Not so—most large companies use what is called "talent management" software and your résumé is scanned and indexed by key words. No human ever reads it. If your résumé and cover letter don't have those key words in them, you are invisible in the talent database. Another is that the job description on the Internet is accurate, and that's mostly not true. Job descriptions are at best shorthand for what is really needed to be successful on a job, and are not always written by the people doing the hiring. And finally, for the jobs listed on the Internet, jobs that get thousands of qualified candidates, the odds are stacked in favor of the employer. They most likely get hundreds of qualified résumés in the first few hours (or if you are an Apple or Amazon, in the first few minutes) of the posting going live. There's no need to look at the rest of the résumés that arrive late to the game, because there are plenty of good candidates in that first batch. You have a very small chance of being found in this stampede of résumés.

Cracking the Hidden Job Market

In the United States only 20 percent of all the jobs available are ever made public. In most job markets, four out of five jobs are not even visible using the standard model of job hunting. And most of these invisible jobs are the good ones, the creative ones, and the ones worth competing for.

So how can you break into this hidden job market? Well, it's tough but not impossible. The hidden job market is visible only to people who are already connected to the network of professional relationships in which those jobs reside. This is a reason that we strongly suggest you mine your network at your current job before trying an external search. When you look for a new job inside your current company, you're already an insider, with access to the hidden job market. It's an insider's game and you have a natural advantage.

When you start an external job search, it's hard to get inside that network because you are an unknown job-seeker. But it's quite possible to crack that network with our reframe of curiosity and story-seeking. As a sincerely curious person and someone not looking for a job, you can become an insider through connections built by getting the story. Then, once you become part of the "job community" conversation (and, remember, *interested is interesting*), things start to happen. Those "locals" in the community that you've been getting the story from start opening up access to their previously hidden job opportunities.

That's how it works.

And it doesn't work (or works less than 5 percent of the time) the other way around.

Kurt Gets Hired

Kurt was disheartened by his lack of success with the standard model of job finding. He decided it was time to apply design thinking to his job search. Kurt stopped applying for jobs and began to *get curious and talk to people*—he started engaging in prototype conversations. Kurt's a pretty good networker, and in the next few months he had fifty-six prototype conversations with people he was genuinely interested in meeting. Those fifty-six conversations resulted in seven different high-quality job offers and one dream job (the real kind, not the fantasy kind)—which he took. He ended up in a great job where he had flexible hours, a short commute, decent money, and work that he found meaningful in the field of environmentally sustainable design. And he was given access to the opportunities that produced those seven offers *not* by asking for a job but by asking for people's life stories—fifty-six times.

When you're out there "getting the story," you are just a curious person who's talking to interesting people doing interesting things in a field of work you're interested in. You are *not* a job-seeker (yet), which is why you are such an easy person to talk to. While conducting these conversations, it is critical that you really are *not* after the job—you're *just* after the story. If you "smell" like a job-seeker in disguise you'll be found out and the process won't work. So really lean in to your curiosity (and never bring a résumé to a prototype conversation).

"But wait a minute," you say. "You just told me how Kurt got seven offers out of his fifty-six conversations. How'd that happen? How does just getting the story turn into getting the job?" Good question.

And it is surprisingly simple.

From "Get the Story" to "Get the Offer"

Most of the time the person you have been in conversation with is the one who gets you from where you are to where you want to be. From "get the story" to "get the offer."

"Kurt, you seem very interested in what we do here, and from what you've said so far it sounds like you have talents we could use. Have you ever thought of working someplace like this?"

More than half the time, when the approach we're recommending results in an offer—they start it. You don't have to.

If for some reason they don't start it for you, and you have completed seven to ten prototype conversations, and you have found an organization that you are really interested in, you can ask one question that will convert the conversation from their story to your offer. "The more I learn about American Environmental and the more people I meet here, the more fascinating your organization becomes. I wonder, Allen, what steps would be involved in exploring how someone like me might become a part of this organization?"

That's it. As soon as you ask "What steps would be involved in exploring how someone like me might become a part of this organization?" Allen knows it's time to shift gears and start thinking about you as a candidate.

Note that you don't say, "Wow—this place is great! Do you have any openings?" That's going way too fast, and the answer to that question is probably "No." The *what would be involved in exploring how* question is open-ended (not yes or no) and invites possibilities far beyond jobs that might be immediately available. And hopefully you have already established a connection and earned some regard with our hypothetical Allen, so he's going to give you a candid but supportive reply. In some cases, Allen may even say, "No, we don't have any opportunities around here, but I think you might be a great fit in one of our partner companies. Have you met anyone at Green Space yet? I think you'd like what they're doing."

It happens. All the time.

By the way, in six of the seven places that Kurt received offers, he didn't have to ask about openings. He just got their stories and they flipped the conversation and asked him. All but one of the offers he got were for unlisted jobs—they were part of the hidden job market. The one job that was listed was the one he ended up taking. But the listing wasn't posted publicly until after he'd already scheduled a conversation with the CEO, which went really well, so by the time it was posted, he was already the top candidate.

Oh, and there was one sweet moment toward the end of Kurt's search. The final interview at the company where he landed a great job was with the five-person board of directors. Their first question was "Do you think you can be effective in establishing partner relationships within the sustainable architecture community here? After all, you've just moved to Georgia and you don't know anyone in the business community here." Looking around the table, Kurt had the happy surprise of recognizing that he'd already had coffee and knew the "story" of three of the five board members. He answered, "Well, I've already successfully established a relationship with three of you. I'd be happy to keep doing that kind of effective outreach on behalf of this organization." So, yes, he nailed the interview. But before any of that, he'd had lots of conversations.

After a few years in Atlanta, Kurt and Sandy and their little girl moved again, this time near Indianapolis. Because he wanted to focus on fatherhood, Kurt decided not to look for a full-time job, but to join the gig economy and try his hand at consulting. Kurt employed the ideas you'll find in chapter 10 to build a business working for himself and it worked great. He was able to charge pretty good consulting dollars doing new and interesting projects, and he was able to stay as busy as he wanted.

Not much more than a year later, Kurt and Sandy moved again—this time to Chicago. After settling in, Kurt was ready for a full-time job again. So he started yet another search by, you guessed it, talking to people. Kurt was getting pretty good at this by now, so he got a jump on it and started reaching out to people in Chicago while he was still in Indianapolis. Sandy asked people at her new university if they'd be willing to talk to Kurt and connect him to people with interesting stories in the area. Sandy's new colleagues were happy to help. All Kurt needed was those first few connections to get started on cracking into the hidden Chicago job market. And Kurt's target had changed—his work in Atlanta had taught him that environmentally sound architecture and urban development require collaboration from lots of different parties, and he discovered he was really good at bringing different parties together and doing "radical collaboration." During his stint as a consultant, he worked with lots of entrepreneurial companies (who needed help but couldn't afford him full-time), and he had come to really appreciate the creativity of entrepreneurs. So he was looking for something that combined those two new interests. His Chicago interviews took him to a group that was running an internship program for future entrepreneurs doing social enterprises, many of which were directed at the kinds of cool design and environmentally progressive ideals that he held so dearly. He suggested that what they needed was someone who could do an unusual combination of things: teach, inspire, and motivate young people; administer lots of details and activities; and radically collaborate with future social entrepreneurs. It turned out, Kurt suggested, that he was exactly the oddball they were looking for.

About three months later (five months after his first emails were sent from Indianapolis), he landed the offer to be the operations manager of an Entrepreneur Internship Program sponsored by a local Chicago investment group. The job involved recruiting participants, managing relationships with partner organizations, some teaching, and lots of field-event management. It was radical design and collaboration all over the place. And here's the interesting part. He *never* would have wanted this kind of job three or four years earlier when he was starting out. Now a job that put together this wacky collection of his signature strengths (teaching coordinating, mediating, marketing, etc.) was exactly the right one—and he was thrilled.

And along this job journey, Kurt had been growing one particular skill that proved to be more powerful than he realized.

He got really good at telling his story.

Get Ready, Get Curious, and Get Out There

There's no reason Kurt's story can't be your story. It deserves to be everybody's story. So get out there and have a great time designing yourself into a terrific new job. Getting curious, talking to people, trying stuff, and telling everyone you meet your story.

Unless.

Unless your next job isn't a job.

If the next chapter of your career adventure isn't a *job*—it's being your own boss—then your next chapter is our next chapter.

Try Stuff

- Give yourself a long weekend and do something you really like doing to recharge your batteries and get set to start a whole new season of job searching. Get your head wrapped about taking at least three and up to six to nine months for this project. Pace yourself—this is not a sprint.

- Make a Take It with Me inventory, listing all the assets you've gained during your employment in your current work. Don't forget to list all types of things: learnings, peak experiences, hard challenges, people, relationships, personal growth, accomplishments, future goal clarity, credibility building, etc.

- Read and search and click your way all around your locale and your area of career interest to find out what's happening, what companies are leading, and who's doing what.

- Reach out to your network for referrals to "get the story" meetings, prototype conversations about relevant topics that are current in your field and of sincere interest to you. And scan LinkedIn for people you'd like to have coffee with, and do not ask them for a job! They will be blown away that you think they are interesting.

- Then start having those conversations and enjoy yourself! Make the learning its own game and its own reward.
- Repeat the process until it works and you find a new job worth taking.
- And throughout the process, keep doing great work in your current job. Finish strong to start strong.

10

Being Your Own Boss

Dysfunctional Belief: *The only way to have a career is for someone to hire me, and to work for a company, in a job I can tolerate.*

Reframe: *One way to have an amazing career, with lots of autonomy, and have a job I love is to invent it!*

When you think like a designer you are flexible, nimble, and ready to adapt to change.

Get ready.

The times.

They are a-changing.

Thomas is a student at the local community college who recently began driving for a ride-sharing service. He is looking to make a little extra money to help with his student budget. Sharon, a midcareer marketing executive, started giving marketing advice to help out a friend who is doing a start-up. She liked this kind of skills-specific consulting so much she decided to take on a couple of other clients on the side. She enjoys helping, and the extra income is a nice benefit, too. George, an electrical engineer, was laid off from a company where he'd worked for seventeen years in what they called a "right-sizing" (it didn't seem "right" to George).

Although there are a lot of jobs out there for someone with his engineering background, George is having trouble finding a new job that looks interesting. However, during one of his interviews at a big tech firm, the hiring manager asked if George would be willing to take on a project that the company needed done in a hurry, working as a consultant. George is intrigued with the technical nature of the problem and, without really thinking it through, said "Yes." In a bit of a panic, George went to the Internet, grabbed a work-for-hire consulting agreement, and cooked up a proposal for the project. The company said yes, and before he knew it, George had a consultant's badge and was showing up for his new gig at the big tech firm, Monday through Friday.

Thomas, Sharon, and George are all part of an army of part-time and full-time people who work as consultants in order to have more freedom and control of their careers. They set their own hours, work when they want to, and are their own boss. In this chapter we will explore this new way of working and give you some ideas and design tools tailored for setting up shop, running your own business, and maybe even inventing the job you love.

We'll start by reframing these gigs, side jobs, and consulting engagements as "prototyping for money." We will show you ways to build a simple business plan that can help you maximize your consulting income while giving you more time off and freedom to do the work that you find meaningful. Our goal is to help you design a work life, project by project, that really works for you.

We are firm believers in the words of Alan Kay, a technology pundit and a former Apple fellow, who said, "The best way to predict the future is to invent it." In this chapter we show you how.

> **Dysfunctional Belief:** *I don't have a real job—I'm just doing temporary consulting—and this isn't the career I thought I'd have.*
> **Reframe:** *I'm not doing temporary work; I'm prototyping alternative ways of working and being my own boss, for money. Prototyping is a low-risk way to get curious, try stuff, and take control of my work life.*

Prototyping for Money

When you become a life designer, you don't just accept the default reality of what's happening to you. You build your way forward.

Sure, the economy is changing, and some of those changes involve automation and eliminating jobs. Other jobs are being outsourced or changed from full-time to project-based work. It's happening, it's not stoppable, so it's a gravity problem.

But you, friend, are not a victim in this new economy.

As we said, when you think like a designer, you are flexible and nimble. With any gravity problem, you start with Accept and embrace the emerging realities of a more fragmented workplace and adapt your design strategy to the reality at hand.

The upside in this scenario is that it has never been more acceptable to change jobs frequently, and to work outside the normal 9:00 to 5:00 constraints of a regular job. The key to success in this new, rapidly changing economy is developing a portfolio of jobs you like, ones that will outlast the assault of AI and automation. That way you can build a well-lived, joyful life, while enjoying all the freedom and benefits of this new way of working.

Throughout this book we have proposed reframing the dysfunctional beliefs about jobs and work that keep you stuck. We think these reframes are the key to getting you unstuck and moving again, and moving in the right direction.

We like to reframe:

From a fixed mind-set —➤ to a growth mind-set
   From a disengaged worker —➤ to the designer of your life and career
   From a temporary worker with no security —➤ to a consultant with a long-term plan

When you move from a fixed mind-set to a growth mind-set, you realize that there are more possibilities for your life and your work than you originally thought.

When you move from one of Gallup's 69 percent of disengaged workers, disenchanted with work, to the designer of your life and career, you realize that the power to change your circumstances is often in your hands.

When you apply design thinking to the idea of temporary work, in what some now call the gig economy, you end up creating a consulting lifestyle that is potentially better than your old straight job. You start to think and act like an entrepreneur who's in charge of your work, your career, and your life design. This approach can give you challenging and interesting work, freedom and autonomy that feels great, more time with family and friends, and a life that really works for you.

Sneaking Up On Your Future

If you want to see what it feels like to "live in the future you invent" and become a consultant or start a business to be in charge of your work destiny, our advice is simple.

Prototype the change you're looking for!

We keep saying that bias to action and prototyping, two of the six mind-sets of a designer, constitute the DYL way of sneaking up on your future, getting off the couch, and doing something. We recommend building a simple, fast prototype of what it's like to be a consultant. The hope is that you can do this on the side, like Sharon, the accidental marketing consultant, did, so that you have a stable income from your current job to build on, and a little more time to explore options. Or, if you are in a situation like George, where you suddenly find yourself a consultant by necessity, our prototyping strategy will work, too, but there is a little more urgency in the situation, so you will want to scale your consulting business quickly. All the more reason to have a design strategy for getting a couple of paying prototypes "in the bank." And the future *is* already here—someone in the world is already doing the consulting you want to do. So let's get curious and go talk to them.

Here's a process for building your first consulting prototype. And remember, prototypes are supposed to be simple to build and ask interesting questions. In this first prototype, we are asking the question "What does it feel like to be a consultant?" To get an answer quickly, we will use someone else's sales and marketing platform to find your first project.

- Start with curiosity—about the work you might do, what skills you can offer the world, and about consulting and what's involved in getting started. Brainstorm a list of things that you know how to do, things that might be "consultable."
- Let your curiosity drive the next step—setting up prototype conversations. Talk to other consultants who are similar to you and ask them for their stories. Ask where they list their services, how they find clients, and how they get paid—do they ever have clients that don't pay, etc. Find out how they feel about their consulting practice; ask for the pros and cons. You will find that most people like talking about themselves and their work, but be clear that all you're asking for are their work stories. Make sure that they know that you are not asking for project leads—that would feel like you're hustling in on their business. You are just having a conversation about their favorite subject, themselves.
- Now narrow down the options for the "consultable skills" you brainstormed. Pick one version of your "consulting story," one that contains your "offer" and why working with you is unique and compelling. Write it down, make it a good story, and keep it short—no more than 250 words. Run it by your friends and fellow consultants. Do people understand your story? Do they understand what your service is, and what you're promising to deliver? Repeat and refine your story until you think it communicates, quickly, the services you offer as a consultant.
- It takes a lot of work to market and sell consulting services. We will get to that in the next prototype; this

time around we are going to keep it simple. Set yourself up on one of the many digital platforms where clients post projects. These platforms collect a lot of clients in one place, so you don't have to cold-call folks or advertise your services yet. You can look over the projects they post and see if there are any that are a fit for you. (Try Freelancer.com and Upwork.com for general consulting projects in all categories, Toptal.com for software projects, and even your local Craigslist for projects of all sizes.) These sites allow you to start fast and build up a reputation quickly; they supercharge your prototype. Build your identity on one of these sites, post the story of your offering, and get going.

- Bid on one simple, small project, doing something you already know how to do and something you are genuinely good at. Since this is your first consulting project, and you have no reviews on the site yet, you might have to bid a few times before you are selected.

- Once you've locked in the project, spend extra time on it, even more than your bid, to make sure that you nail it. This prototype is about learning and building your professional reputation, not making money. Reputation is everything in consulting, so you want to overdeliver on your first project to make sure that you get a good review from your first client. Once the project is complete and the reviews are in, it's time to reflect.

The purpose of this prototype was to ask the question "What does it feel like to be a consultant?" So step back and ask yourself, *How did that go?* Reflect on the experience, read your client's review and their rating of your service, and reflect on your own performance. Ask yourself, *What did I like about the project? What didn't I like? Do I agree with my client's feedback? How could I have done the project better, faster, with less effort, so that I can make more dollars per hour next time?*

Assuming that you liked the experience, or at least didn't hate it, try it again. Maybe pick another easy project just for the practice. Or pick a larger, more involved engagement to see what it's like to manage your client through multiple phases of a bigger project. Make sure you are producing high-quality work, the kind of work you would expect from a professional consultant, and that you are overdelivering on the project.

Once you have a few positive reviews from a few clients, you're ready to move to the next step. While working on projects that come from these large aggregator sites is relatively easy, it's hard to charge premium rates because of the quality of the clients (folks looking for cheap consulting) and the intense competition for project work. At some point you want to manage your own marketing and sales efforts so that you can differentiate your services and make more money. Here's how you do that:

- **Now that you have a few projects under your belt, refine your story and come up with a better way to tell people about what you do, and what makes your service or product delightful and extraordinary. Again, keep it simple and powerful, no more than 250 words.**
- **Build a prototype Facebook or LinkedIn page, or, better yet, your own simple website, and tell your new story digitally. Buy a couple hundred dollars' worth of targeted ads that describe your services to the specific audience**

that you think wants to hire you. See how many visitors to your page or site you get, and how many of these visitors give you their email and contact information. Follow up on every inquiry and see how many you can convert into a proposal. Then measure how many proposals turn into actual consulting work. These are important metrics—and don't get discouraged if you have trouble getting all the way through what people call this "sales funnel" to real consulting projects. It probably takes ten "impressions" (someone who saw your targeted ad) to get one inquiry and ten inquiries to get to one proposal. You should probably be able to convert about 50 percent of your proposals to real work—that's why targeting your advertising is so powerful. But it takes a lot of sales activities to generate those consulting dollars. That's what makes sites that aggregate consulting projects so successful—they do that up-front sales work for you. But they take a percentage of your bid as a commission and you'll never become a premium-priced consultant on one of those sites. They are mostly for rookies.

- Prototype your story (your "marketing message") and your service offerings (what you do and deliver for your clients) one or two more times—do some A/B testing (pick two very different marketing messages) to see which version gets you the most visitors to your page or site, and which message leads to more conversions to proposals.

- Every time you win a project, you have set a new bar for your hourly or project rate. You now have hard evidence that the right kind of client will pay a certain amount for your service. Your goal is to get enough projects in the pipeline that you can increase your rate each time you make a proposal. That way, all of the new business you acquire is worth more than the old business.

- After a few months of these activities, and a few more successful projects, stop and reflect on the process and your results, and decide if you want to do it again.

Another one of the mind-sets of a designer that comes into play now is *awareness*. Assuming that you've enjoyed your consulting experience so far, and you got some positive data back from your prototypes, you're ready to dive a little deeper into the self-employment economy. Let's take a look at what we'll call the "workflow" of that business, and what a solid business plan looks like if you want to thrive in this new way of working.

Ride the Workflow

If you're going to be your own boss with your own consulting practice, you need a plan.

A business plan.

Now we can hear your objections loud and clear.

That's too hard.

I didn't go to business school!

I don't have the money.

I don't know how to do that.

Wait, what?

Your first business plan doesn't have to be overly complicated. Here's a super-simple business plan template that anyone can master. It's just six steps:

1. Go back and figure out what you are good at (empathy for *you*) and what the world needs (empathy for your potential *clients*), and ask the questions "Is there a sweet spot between what clients need and what I know how to do? If so, can I address this sweet spot with my consulting offering?"

2. Decide what will distinguish your special version of "getting the job done." Is it getting the job done fast, or with high precision, or with high reliability, or with lots of creativity? Figure out what will make your product or service stand out from the rest of the consulting crowd.

3. Set up a workflow (see page 265) that is repeatable, scalable, and measurable (you'll want to know if you are getting better).

4. Accept that to charge a premium for your service, you have to get good at sales and marketing; that's how you will build a sustainable business. Try hard to optimize the rest of your workflow so that you are efficient at delivering your service.

5. Once you get good at the workflow of consulting, and have developed a stable of repeat clients and have lots of great reviews and referrals, you can start raising your rates.

6. Once you get really good at your business, see if there are parts of your workflow that you can hire out to "gig workers" who charge less than you. Outsource these

nonessential activities, and mark up these services, generally 10 percent to 30 percent, and build this cost into your next proposal. Outsourcing the nonessential allows you to take on more work, multiply the value of your hours, and make more money.

All consulting businesses have a *common workflow.* The basic workflow of these businesses has seven steps (and an eighth step if you want to keep it going—lather, rinse, repeat) and it looks like this:

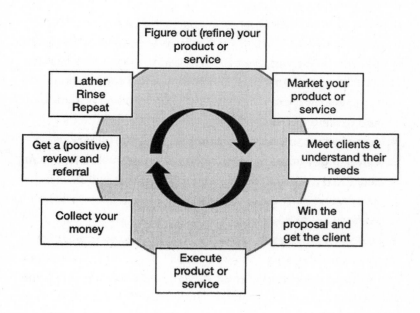

This cycle represents the workflow of everything from ride-sharing to personal coaching to freelance design services and beyond. And this cycle points out that, as a consultant, it is not enough to be good at your service or product offering. You'll need to wear a few hats. For instance, you'll need to figure out how to attract clients (wearing the marketing hat), you'll need to be good at understanding your client's needs (wearing the design researcher's hat), you'll need to collect your money (wearing the chief financial officer's hat), and you'll need to be great at getting reviews and referrals (wearing the customer service hat). All of this is in addition to providing your own special version of the product or service you started with.

Let's use an example to illustrate this workflow. Let's say you have decided to start a new life-coaching practice, on the side at first, but you are hoping to go full-time as soon as possible. You will need to make an initial investment, and it can cost thousands of dollars and take months of training to get your life-coach certification from a recognized institution. But with a good training and certification, you can charge a lot for your coaching session, typically between $50 and $150 for a fifty-minute session, by phone or in person. Sometimes the school that certified you will help you find your first clients, to start you might list yourself on a "life-coaching directory" (an aggregator of clients that will charge you a sales commission), but eventually most of your clients will come from your own marketing and, we hope, referrals.

To get this ball rolling you need to do a lot of personal marketing and outreach, maybe through social networks like Facebook and LinkedIn. Once you meet a prospective client you'll probably have to spend some time with them, pro bono, to convince them that your service will be valuable. Then the process begins of understanding their needs and designing a coaching program that works for them. They might stay with you for a few weeks or a few months, but at some point you will have "fixed" their problem (or they will have run out of time or money) and they become an ex-client. All along, you will bill them for your time and gently prod them to pay you. The hope is that this leads to a good review on Yelp and, even better, your hard work leads to a referral and a new client.

Life coaching (or being a consulting interior designer, a landscape architect, an engineer, a personal assistant, etc.) is a job where you really are an entrepreneur, and you thrive based on your own initiative. You succeed based on your marketing savvy, your empathy for your clients, and your ability to turn current clients into referral sources. You are still your own boss, you set your own work schedule, and because it takes skill and training to do this job well, you can make a lot of money for your time. The better you get at differentiating your service, the more referrals you have, the more you can charge for each session. There's a big difference between making $50 a session and $300 and, although where you work is a factor (coaches are cheaper in some cities than others), the biggest difference in your hourly rate is your reputation and professional referral network.

How do you get to charge the highest price for your time? It's all about telling your story.

Most people who are new at being their own boss make the same mistake.

They think it is all about "doing the job."

It's really not. It is about telling your story, again and again. It is about marketing, marketing, and marketing—to get the next job, and the next job, and the next job. So it's time to accept that telling your story, which is all that marketing is really, is part of being a successful "boss."

Be Extraordinary

Average folks make average money.

Who wants to be average?

At anything?

The data indicates that the average self-employed worker makes less money than they would if they had a full-time job. If doing a little consulting on the side is about having a second income, and maximizing money isn't critical, being average might be okay with you. Or, if you don't want to take the time to be creative and design a differentiated product or service, then you might be content to make an average return on your work.

Assuming you think you are talented (and you are) and deserve to be paid a little bit more for your skills than everyone else (you certainly do), you need to design a way to be paid a premium for your work. That's going to take some empathy for your clients, some mind mapping (if you are solo) or brainstorming (if you have a team of folks who like to be helpful) to come up with new ideas, and a lot of prototyping to see what works best for your clients. Everyone can do this, and every job can be approached with a creative design in mind.

The truth is: People who make extraordinary offers end up with extraordinary clients.

Let us say that again: People who make extraordinary offers end up with extraordinary clients.

And when you have designed your customers' experience to be extraordinary and delightful, you find yourself working with people who are happy to work with you.

Some examples:

Ahmad is a ride-sharing driver who has designed five custom

music playlists with different client "personas" in mind, including a Bollywood soundtrack that he uses to introduce people to the music he loves to listen to. He has developed an uncanny empathy for his riders and loves it when he successfully matches the playlist to the personality. A virtual dance party in his car ensues. He provides his clients with a ride and more—free mineral water and spicy candy from his hometown in Mumbai, and the biggest smile you have ever seen. Oh, and he wears an old chauffeur's cap and has a dashboard covered with bobblehead dolls to up the campy atmosphere of his ride.

The results? Amazing reviews, great tips, and several offers of full-time employment. He is one of the highest-paid drivers in his region.

Cindy is a personal trainer who comes to your house with all of the equipment she needs for your training, and who always looks fresh and ready to go, like you are the first client of the day. Cindy takes very specific photographs of your form, and compares them from workout to workout to optimize your progress. She takes meticulous notes on every aspect of your exercise and can show you, on your private personal page on her customized website, the data on how much leaner, stronger, and fitter you've become. And Cindy always brings some vitamin water and a new fitness wearable or step tracker for you to try, for free, to maintain your motivation between sessions.

Tom, a graduate of the ArtCenter College of Design and a fine art photographer, is still waiting to become famous for his amazing images. In the meantime, Tom loves helping people learn about photography and their cameras. A while back, Tom noticed that a lot of people buy expensive, full-featured digital single-lens reflex cameras (DSLRs), but they can't figure out how to use them. They default to operate them in "point and shoot" mode, losing out on the creative potential these amazing pieces of technology offer. In response, Tom started his own DSLR school under the name PhotoTrainer. He designed a series of classes to teach people how to master their DSLRs and, more important, how to think of these cameras as an extension of their personal creativity. Tom is an endearing and patient teacher, and in his classes he is careful to emphasize each student's creative potential. His beginner class inspired a second class on photo composition and another one, an advanced class on taking great portraits—each designed in response to what his students said they needed. Tom even does one-on-one mentoring, helping his students discover what he calls their own "visual photographic vocabulary." Tom's offering is unique, but he's a photographer, not an HTML guy, so he hired a Web design specialist to build and update his custom website where he does all his own marketing. Tom is still waiting to be a famous fine art photographer, but in the meantime he's more than paying the bills and having a great time helping people develop their creative confidence.

These self-employed consultants know how to make their services delightful. Cindy isn't just a personal trainer; she's a data scientist maximizing the efficiency of your workout and a specialist in cutting-edge fitness tech. Tom doesn't just teach you how your camera works; he helps you rediscover your inner artist and visual creativity. Each of them, through word-of-mouth referrals, has more clients than they can handle. This allows them to raise their rates every time a new client signs up, and this maximizes their income per hour. And once this happens, they have more freedom—freedom to take every first and third Friday of the month off, freedom to work with only their "best" clients and thereby maximize everyone's happiness, and freedom to create even more compelling service offerings (anyone up for a free Apple Watch?).

The Customer's Journey Map

How do designers at companies like Apple and Snapchat come up with amazing services that delight us and make us happy customers? And how can you be like Ahmad, Cindy, and Tom and design amazing experiences for your prospective clients, services that will create loyal customers and great reviews and referrals? Sounds like it's time to introduce you to a design tool that will help you figure out how to maximize your customer engagement and make your service brilliant. It's time to learn to use a tool called a "journey map."

A journey map describes the entire experience of finding and experiencing a product or service, and maps out the customer's journey over time. With a journey map you can identify points of friction that can be designed out. In addition to eliminating friction, a good journey map identifies places where you can change the game and delight your customers, we call these "magic moments." The result of this delightfully designed journey is a happy, repeat customer, and that leads to a profitable engagement for everyone involved.

Journey maps come in all shapes and sizes and no two maps are alike, but regardless of their format, all journey maps capture the customer's experience of discovering and using a product or service. If you want to dive deeper into the subject, Google "journey map" or go to UXMastery.com, a user-experience design site for more details and examples. But if you just want to get started with this new tool, we suggest using our simplified template for creating your customer's journey.

Our simple journey map visualizes the journey of the customer on a timeline, divided into three columns. The "Before" column describes how your clients find out about you, the "During" column is about the experience of your product or service while it's happening, and the "After" column is about the service and support you provide after the client's job is complete.

In addition, our simplified journey map has three rows. "Activities" are listed on the top row—a detailed list of all of the activities that occur before, during, and after your service or experience. The middle row is labeled "Emotions," and it charts the emotional roller coaster of your client. This is sometimes called the Empathy row, and it's all about mapping how your client feels during the experience of working through their product or service jour-

Client	Before	During	After
Activities			
Emotions			
Magic Moments			

ney. The bottom row is called "Magic Moments," and it contains sketches and pictures of moments of delight that you've designed into your customer's experience. These are the moments you can turn into magic and win a customer for life.

For example, when Cindy, our personal trainer, was thinking about designing her consulting service for women, she made a journey map for Debora, one of her first customers, that looked like this:

Customer Notes:
Mid-40s tech executive, three children and a full-time job. Was an athlete in college but hasn't exercised regularly in 10 years. She would like to lose some weight and get fit. Would also like to increase aerobic capacity and flexibility. Particular emphasis on stomach and hips. Can only meet first thing in the morning, and after work on Tues. and Thurs.

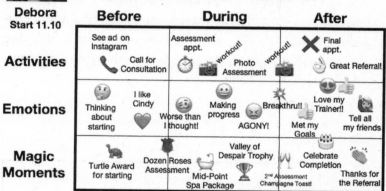

You can see how she mapped the whole process of working with her. It starts with a potential client seeing her ad on Instagram, then there is a phone consultation, that critical first assessment appointment, then weekly fitness sessions, and photo assessments, and finally the client, empowered with their new fitness habit, ends their engagement. Cindy takes specific notes on the map of her client's goals. She also designs high-value magic moments that make training with her fun and productive. For instance, every new client gets a dozen roses for their first session, and a spa coupon after they hit their first milestone. Cindy is also very aware that working out is a tough habit to sustain. Every client goes through what Cindy calls the "Valley of Despair," where workouts are agony, and they need a little extra encouragement, and she's designed a moment to recognize that. And finally, when they have met their goals and established a fitness regime, clients leave. That's no problem—Cindy brings them a miniature cake with candles to celebrate their accomplishment. Does she always get an amazing review and several referrals? Of course she does.

That's the way a journey map works. Once you've designed your client's personal journey with your service, you can start prototyping the "magic moments" that you've designed into your map. Take these moments one at a time and make sure you survey your client each step of the way so that you can measure their satisfaction with your service. You are trying to increase client conversion, client satisfaction, and referral rates—and the best way to do that is to really understand their experience.

Delighting your clients is a never-ending design process, but it's fun to do. And as you get better and better at understanding your clients, new needs will emerge that will lead to new product or service offerings—it's a creative and potentially lucrative cycle that will keep your job from getting stale. Living a life of creative prototyping, and working with people who you like and admire—that sure sounds like the blueprint for a job well designed. And a well-lived, joyful life.

And Now the Good News

McKinsey, the famous business consulting firm, did a study on the future of work. In it, they hypothesize that automation, artificial intelligence, and turning everything into software will swallow up a lot of jobs. They predict a great deal of disruption. However, they noted that there will be more, not less, work for designers and anyone who applies a creative mind-set to their work. Evidently, these "creative jobs" are difficult, if not impossible, to automate.

Capabilities such as creativity and sensing emotions are core to the human experience and . . . difficult to automate. [Our] study suggests that there is the . . . potential to generate a greater amount of meaningful work. This could occur as automation replaces more routine or repetitive tasks, allowing employees to focus more on tasks that utilize creativity and emotion. Financial advisors, for example, might spend less time analyzing clients' financial situations, and more time understanding their needs and explaining creative options. Interior designers could spend less time taking measurements, developing illustrations, and ordering materials, and more time developing innovative design concepts based on clients' desires.

The conclusion of the McKinsey study is that the core things that make us human, like empathy and creativity, are going to be more and more valuable in the future. Being creative and having good social and emotional interpersonal skills are at the heart of the new creative economy, and the consultants and entrepreneurs who will succeed will be masters of these soft skills.

So it turns out that if you listen to McKinsey (and many CEOs do), practicing the mind-sets of a designer sets you up for success in the future economy. In the end, it is our human creativity that will save us all.

Dylan's words have never been truer.

The times.

They are a-changing.

So let's all accept what is, join the party, and put the forces driving those changes to work for us by thinking and acting like life designers capable of imagining and building a future that works for everybody and a work life that allows us to be happy.

Try Stuff

Using the template on page 277, which you can also download from our website (www.designingyourwork.life), or by copying the format shown here, make a journey map of your consulting idea, and the experience you want to design for your potential client. Include elements in all three rows—the experiences, the feelings, and the magic moments. You might want to turn your paper sidewise, or get a large piece of paper for this—these maps tend to get long. Add as much detail as you can and make sure you map the Before, During, and After of the service or experience. And look for magic moments along the journey that can make your offering remarkable!

Client	Before	During	After
Activities			
Emotions			
Magic Moments			

11

All Disruption Is Personal

Dani is a young single mom living in the Mission District of San Francisco with twin boys, working hard to support her family by herself. To make it even more challenging, the pandemic closed the local elementary school, and now her boys are home 24/7. They have to share a laptop to do their online school lessons, and the Internet is good on some days and not so good on others. So in addition to doing her job as a claims adjuster for a major national insurance agency, a job she can easily do from her kitchen table, Dani is a part-time fourth-grade teacher, part-time IT manager, and full-time overwhelmed.

Derek is a senior at Stanford. As a young Black man, he knows what it's like to be pulled over by the campus police as he's coming home late from a study session, just for "driving while Black." Derek's grandparents marched with Martin Luther King Jr. in the sixties, and his parents raised him to be a proud Black man, so as a freshman he requested to live in Ujamaa (Swahili for "extended family"), the Black theme house on campus. But when Derek saw the video of the murder of George Floyd, something inside him broke. The callous indifference of the police officer kneeling on Floyd's neck until he was dead was too much to take. That night Derek and some friends organized an online meeting of all the student groups on campus, and everyone agreed that they had to do something. They instantly formed a Stanford chapter of the Black Lives Matter movement and connected via Instagram with their national leadership. But they wanted to do more. In the past, it would have been easy to organize a protest and probably take over Building 10, the president's office. They had done it before—but now, with students spread out literally all over the world, what could they do to make their voices heard? That night Derek called his dad, who was also outraged. They both felt overwhelmed and helpless. What could they do from their bedrooms to stop the killing of Black people by the police in America?

Regina is a young climate activist working for the World Wildlife Fund. It is meaningful work, work she is called to do, and during the pandemic she Zooms into office meetings every day with a sense of purpose. But lately she's finding herself experiencing an increasing sense of dread. Catastrophic climate events are happening all over the globe at an alarming rate. Massive fires in the Australian outback are unprecedented, as are the devastating and record-breaking fires in Northern and Southern California. There were so many tropical storms and hurricanes in the Caribbean in 2020 that the World Meteorological Organization ran out of names. And the storms are getting bigger and bigger. There are so-called hundred-year floods in India and China, followed by even bigger floods in the next season. Ironically, there are unprecedented droughts around the world as well. Regina's dread is amplified when she reads about climate change deniers claiming it is all a hoax. Regina is working hard at the WWF to make positive changes for wildlife and the planet, but she can't sleep at night worrying that it isn't going to be enough. She is beginning to feel permanently overwhelmed and depressed.

Ben is a young congressional aide, working for a Democrat from a liberal district in California. Like a lot of people in his generation, he's liberal on some issues, conservative on others, and for the most part can't really see much difference in the two parties. Nevertheless, he is trying to make a difference and he's willing to work for not too much money to change the system from within. And it's pretty cool to be in the cloakroom with the Democratic caucus before a big vote—he's literally backstage, watching democracy in action. Ben loves to talk politics with anyone who will listen. But lately he's noticed that the discussions quickly get out of control. His uncle Steve, a very conservative Republican, is a case in point. Every conversation turns into a shouting match. Ben is frustrated; it seems that the country is so polarized and people are so invested in their own bubbles of information that he can't have a civil conversation with anyone. "How are we going to solve the problems in America if we can't even agree on facts? And how can we debate the important issues, the way I was taught in high school civics, if every conversation falls apart in the end?"

There is disruption and overwhelm everywhere.

For everyone.

The global pandemic, brought on by the COVID-19 virus, rocked the world, but it wasn't the only disruption.

The year 2020 also brought about the recognition that there is a lot of unfinished labor when it comes to universal civil rights—the Black Lives Matter movement is but one reaction to the crisis.

The climate grows more and more unstable everywhere in the world. Floods and massive storms hit some regions hard. In others, baked earth, drought, and the subsequent collapse of agriculture and the famine that follows is the big issue. When an impressive-beyond-her-years fifteen-year-old climate activist, Greta Thunberg, became a more compelling spokesperson for the cause than our hesitant global leaders, you knew there was a problem.

Divisive politics, Internet bubbles, and echo chambers are fracturing our ability to have a real and civil conversation about hard problems and making it seemingly impossible to come together to find solutions that work for everyone.

Just listing all of these disruptions is overwhelming and exhausting.

And unprecedented.

We know that the word *unprecedented* gets thrown around a lot. Unprecedented lockdowns, unprecedented unrest in our cities, unprecedented storms and fires, unprecedented political challenges. It all feels so, well, unprecedented. But in many ways, it also feels like more of the same. The year 2020 unambiguously ushered in what futurists call a multicrisis tipping point, with so many natural and man-made systems stressed beyond breaking and falling like dominoes, with one crisis leading to another. What's next, we joke, tornadoes of fire? (Had them in California.) Locusts? (This year saw the worst year for locusts in Africa since 2003.) Murder hornets? (They're here.) The universe exploding? (Almost—the Advanced LIGO gravity wave detector discovered the massive collision of two black holes that sent shock waves rippling across time and space.)

The pandemic made it obvious that, in times of rapid disruption, having a plan and sticking to it doesn't work. Were you planning that large church wedding in June? Sorry, couldn't happen. That company sales off-site in July—nope. Even those hard-to-get reservations at that special restaurant—first inside, then outside, then—sorry, it went out of business.

Disruption is everywhere and disruption is always personal.

That's why these last chapters of the book focus on you—the individual, the mom, the dad, the worker, and the boss. Our scale of change is YOU, whether you are a gig worker, an office worker, a stay-at-home homeschooler, a manager, or someone who used to occupy a C-suite that doesn't really exist any longer.

We are not going to focus on corporate restructuring, organizational redesign, compensation strategies for hybrid workers, or other weighty big-picture issues. We'll leave those subjects to the business consultants and the tenured faculty in the Economics Department. That's their expertise, not ours. We are the human-centered design guys, and we'll focus on the impact all this change is having and is going to have on you—the human in the equation.

And so many humans in the equation are lost and hurting.

Disruption is hard, the losses are real, and we respect the pain and sacrifice in everyone's situation. If you lost a loved one to the pandemic, our hearts go out to you in your loss and grief. So many people have been lost to this disease—it's almost too much to bear, and words are inadequate.

We also acknowledge that the changes of 2020 and 2021 affect people differently, so we can't generalize their impact. If you work in some industries, like hotels and tourism, or work in a restaurant or own one, you probably lost your job or your business. If you have a factory job or a food-processing job that requires you to show up and work your shift, COVID or not, then you risked your life just going to work.

On the other hand, if you work for a streaming service like Netflix or Zoom, or a tech titan like Apple or Facebook, your business has never been better. More people at home, streaming, commenting, and "liking" on their devices, has meant more eyeballs, more screen time, and more people buying new screens.

The data shows that the effects of the pandemic hit low-income families and the elderly the most. And that grocery clerks and workers cutting up chickens at that big poultry plant in Iowa would be declared essential workers and find themselves on the front line of the crisis?

What has been hard for people is not just that the world has changed and changed quickly, it's that on some level, we know it's never going to be the same again.

That's not change—it's disruption.

Things Will Never Be the Same Again

Disruptions are changes—big changes. While all change requires some adaptation, they don't all rearrange your life. Finally moving from a manual shift to an automatic transmission, because now there are kids in the car with you, is a regular change—life goes on. Having kids in the first place and no longer being just the two of you is a disruption—your life will never be the same again.

Getting so frustrated with polarized politics that you re-register as an independent because all the parties make you nuts is a big change, but you're still the same person (unless you were a professional politician and now your constituency is sending you hate mail). Deciding that the country of your birth just isn't your country anymore and that you should move permanently overseas to another culture and language is a disruption.

Getting a really bad case of bronchitis, which means you have to skip a family holiday dinner lest you infect your aging aunt, is a change, but you'll be back for the birthday celebration in two months and all will be forgotten. A disruption is not being able to hug anyone other than your immediate family for a year and having to wear a mask whenever you're in a public space, especially indoors.

Anything that makes it feel like you're a very different person or you're now living in a very different world is a disruption. Disruptions can be personal, regional, or global. Dave had all three in 2020. In March, Dave's wife, Claudia, received a diagnosis of terminal cancer. The diagnosis completely altered how the two of them lived for the next nine months until Claudia died in December—which then permanently altered Dave's life. In August, the firestorms that hit Northern California came within a mile of Dave's house. His house survived, but close friends lost their homes, became fire refugees, and some abandoned their land, never to return. And Dave, like everyone else around the globe, went through the novel coronavirus pandemic. So in all senses—personally, regionally, and globally—Dave's life will never be the same after 2020.

Responding to these different types of disruptions varies because community matters. Are you going through this alone or just in your family? Is everyone in town going through it together? Or is everyone on planet Earth going through it with you? Those are pretty different experiences, but they all share the realization that things will never be the same again.

Each of you reading this has your own current and past disruptions—those things after which your life will never be the same again. But we have tools to design your way through the experience. We don't have all the answers. No one does—disruptions are too big for a one-size-fits-all response, and despite being a shared experience, disruptions hit each unique human uniquely. But we do have some ideas to share that have worked for others and may help you as well.

Our conclusion as we moved beyond 2020 and its disruptions is that not only is disruption the new normal, but the occurrence of disruption is on the rise as well. As the world has shrunk and resources are ever more constrained, many systems are in overload. Climate change, income inequality, racism, artificial intelligence, global populism and nationalism, the availability of clean water, the shift from fossil fuels to renewable energy, and more, all tell us that the incidence of big change—disruptive change—is accelerating. Once upon a time a person might live an entire life and never see a regional or global disruption, and that stability would help her greatly in handling the unavoidable personal disruptions of the births and deaths of those she loved. But those days are over. In today's world, life-altering disruptions are a reliable and proliferating feature for us all. Because of the scale of change that disruptions bring and the typically long period of time between the arrival and the resolution of that change, disruptions require special design tools.

Which is why we call it Disruption Design. In today's reality, if you want to build a well-lived and joyful life and thrive at work, you need to be able to recognize a disruption and design your way through it.

Disruption Design is a new core competency for modern life.

Bad News—Good News

The bad news (as if predicting more disruptions wasn't bad enough) is that Disruption Design isn't just one thing. Disruptions aren't all created equal. Designing for life after the 2020 pandemic takes a different response than if, for instance, there were a sudden and pervasive worldwide shortage of clean water. The good news is that regardless of what the disruption is, the mind-set of a Disruption Designer is the same (which is the same as the mind-set of any good human-centered designer—it just demands a huge level of *acceptance* to embrace a massive, unwanted, and challenging change). And the overall process of Disruption Design is the same for all true disruptions.

The first step of the Disruption Design process involves realizing where we are—a very tricky place we call the Waiting Room.

Now Where Are We?

The first order of business in the Waiting Room is a strategic reframe.

In mid-2020 as we started listening to lots of people describe their struggles in responding to the COVID-19 pandemic, we started to pick up some consistent refrains.

I just CAN'T WAIT for this thing to be over, so I can get BACK TO NORMAL life again!
I am SO DONE with this! When are we going to get things RESTARTED?!

Many of us felt like the world had just stopped, that our lives were on hold, and collectively we were thrown into the Waiting Room—a place where we had to sit out the pandemic until the world started back up again.

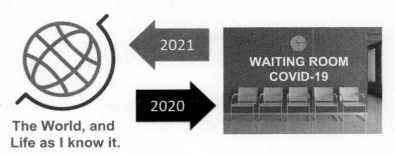

2021

2020

WAITING ROOM COVID-19

The World, and Life as I know it.

The Waiting Room is the natural place to go when an emergency occurs. When you hear the sirens, you pull the car over *and you wait until the trouble passes you by.* Then a little while later, when it's safe again, you get back out on the road and continue on your way—just a little delayed. What happens in the Waiting Room is one simple thing—waiting. No changes. No reassessing your situation. No adjusting of plans. No jettisoning of out-of-date ideas or dysfunctional beliefs. No growth. Just a ticking clock awaiting the restart of normalcy. There are lots of times in life when the Waiting Room is a totally appropriate place to be, but it's a disaster during a disruption.

Remember that our definition of a disruption is a change after which you recognize that *things will never be the same again.* After a disruption, there is no going back. The Old World isn't on hold. It's gone. The next place we're all going is the New World. Naturally, what we all want when big change arrives is to move from the Old World into the New World as quickly and painlessly as we can. We want to get across that line—and fast.

Old World   New World

The only problem is—it doesn't work like that. It's not a two-step process with the new following closely on the heels of the old.

It's a three-step process, and the middle phase—the gap in between the old and new worlds—is the one we want to focus on.

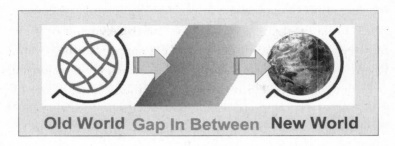

Old World **Gap In Between** **New World**

As designers, we know it's crucial to frame our problem well. We want to be working on the right problem, and we want to frame it realistically and actionably. So our answer to the question posed in this chapter, "Where are we?" is very important to get right. Now where should we look for insight on how best to think about this confusing gap that we're in during a disruption?

Well, when in doubt, designers look to Design Thinking and Design Thinking has at its core one infallible tenet: Just Be Human. The original, technical name of Design Thinking is Human-Centered Design. It's all about using a human approach to making things that humans can use effectively.

The fundamental truth is that if you get the human part right, you can't go wrong. Design Thinking's tenet that we just be human prompts us to remember that human beings have been dealing with disruptions for a very long time. Disruption is not new—it may feel new—but humans have been working hard on how to handle disruption since the first human stepped out of the cave. Now, more than ever, is a good time to tap into both ancient wisdom and modern theory about how life works when huge change is upon us.

There are any number of models for the three-phase process that humans experience when going through major change. Many ancient cultures and wisdom traditions recognize some form of the evolutionary growth cycle of life, death, and rebirth. Developmental psychology talks about dependence, separation, and independence (or childhood, adolescence, and maturity) in becoming an adult.

Here's how we suggest a Disruption Designer might think about it. Design always starts "here." This is so important that we had this reminder embossed on the cover of our first book:

And as we stated before, the "HERE" most people feel they are in after a disruption is the Waiting Room. It's the natural human response. It's where we all begin.

While it's the place we all begin, it's not the place we have to stay, and it's definitely not a good place for designers. But it's not all bad. When you're waiting, you feel like you have an appointment with the future. You feel like something new is coming your way—and that's all good. But let's face it, nobody likes to wait. The Waiting Room is a place where you're losing ground on the project of transitioning into the future that is starting to form. The Waiting Room is a place where expectations get misaligned and biases calcify, making your entry into the New World harder than ever. The first step of Disruption Design is to get out of the Waiting Room by reframing it into the Acceptance Zone.

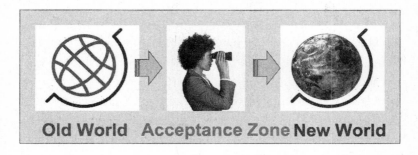

Old World   Acceptance Zone   New World

The Acceptance Zone is quite different from the Waiting Room. It may not be the place you asked to be, but once you recognize that you're in a disruption and things will never be the same again, you *want* to get into the Acceptance Zone, because that's the only place from which you can start taking action and design your safe landing on the future shores of the New World.

This reframe is critical, and it's the key strategic reframe in Disruption Design. It's also simple because all it takes is a shift in your mind-set. All you have to do is accept the fact that a big change is under way, your Old World is ending, and the New World hasn't arrived yet.

In the Acceptance Zone, we don't really know what's going on. We don't know what happened to the way things were. And we don't know when or how things will shift into a new normal. But we accept where we are. The exciting thing is that the Acceptance Zone is brimming with both the not-quite-yet-visible raw material of the coming new reality and a sense of anticipation, almost of time itself being on tiptoe, looking for the new world to emerge.

The Acceptance Zone is home territory for a Disruption Designer—and you have to get into it in order to design your way out of it. Don't take it personally. It has nothing to do with you and nothing to do with the nature of the disruption that's put you there. It doesn't matter if your partner died or your neighborhood burned to the ground or the coronavirus altered the work world forever—the first and necessary stop on your trip to the future is the Acceptance Zone because you're a human being.

And we hate it. We don't want to be here. It's scary. It takes some courage to do this. No wonder many people never make it out of the Waiting Room.

Change is hard. Letting go of familiar things that are ending—especially when the ending is not of our choosing—is very hard. If we have to go through that, then at least let's get on to the new thing as soon as we can and get back to living more happily. Who wants to wander around in the confusion of the Acceptance Zone, not knowing what the future may hold or even where we're going to try to land in it? Once we've accepted that we're in one of those big life-will-never-be-the-same-again disruptive changes, the last thing we want is to be stuck in between—in nowhere-land. "Let's

GO!" we want to shout, and we want to get out of there as fast as our legs and the Internet will carry us.

But we can't. And if we successfully fool ourselves into believing that we can skip the Acceptance Zone and jump immediately to the New World, we'll very likely fail and have to go back and start over again, but this time from an even harder starting place with even more losses to get over.

So we're not going to do that. We are going to acknowledge that (1) we're in a disruption and (2) the disruption tossed us into the Waiting Room, and (3) *we don't have to be stuck there*. We can reframe our situation, enter the Acceptance Zone, and use Disruption Design to navigate our way through. To pull off that reframe, we need to have the right kind of acceptance—we need to have generative acceptance.

Disruption Design Goal #1: Generative Acceptance

While acceptance is simple, it isn't always easy. There are three kinds of acceptance:

- **Oppressive acceptance**
- **Suppressive acceptance**
- **Generative acceptance**

We want to practice generative acceptance, so we need to be able to recognize the other forms, which, while popular, aren't too helpful.

Oppressive acceptance is what the hapless victims do. *Oh NO!*

My world is ending!! I can't believe they're doing this to me. This always happens—why me? I'm screwed. Now what do I do? It's easy to get overwhelmed by disruption. When we recognize that it's the beginning of the end of the way we understood things to work, our first inclination is to wonder how things work now. But there is no answer to that question yet, so we're at risk of being overwhelmed by it. We've been accustomed to understanding things and feeling on top of situations. And when that's gone, we feel at sea. The victims' fear is perhaps understandable, but by overstating the problem and perceiving themselves as incapacitated, victims get stuck.

Suppressive acceptance is what the stoic heroes do. *Well, looks like a big storm brewing here—but no worries, I've got this. I can take it. You just gotta tough these things out, ya know? Fortunately, I've got the toughness to do just that.*

This approach is just the flip side of the coin from the victim. By understating the problem, the heroes rush in where fools fear to tread and are quickly vanquished by the scale of the situation, if not crushed by it. Failed heroes can be badly stuck and are usually confused and angry—which won't help them to design their way forward.

Both the victim and the hero are avoiding reality by misperceiving it.

Generative acceptance is what the Disruption Designers do. A designer takes things just as they are and knows how to design forward. *Whoa, this is a really big change. It sure looks like it's going to disrupt things. I'm not positive where this will all lead, but now's the time to start being observant and adaptable while things settle down. I wonder what things will be most affected and how?*

The mind-set of a Disruption Designer starts with acceptance and moves quickly to curiosity. "I wonder . . ." is a great place to be in the Acceptance Zone. Curiosity gets you engaged and looking for what's hidden. It keeps you moving but doesn't try to resolve things prematurely. And keeping engaged and moving are just what the Acceptance Zone calls for. Our first goal is to enter it (by acceptance) and cross it (by staying engaged through active curiosity). Recognizing the Acceptance Zone as being full of the future and offering you some time to get ready for it is a huge reframe that is the first goal of Disruption Design.

Where Grief Meets Growth

The endings that come with a disruption include losses—often big losses—and that means part of the ending process is grief. Elisabeth Kübler-Ross's work became the standard for understanding the process of grief, which goes, nonsequentially, through five stages of experience: denial, anger, bargaining, depression, and acceptance.

When we talk about the life design process, we illustrate it as follows, in six steps, with Step 0 being Acceptance.

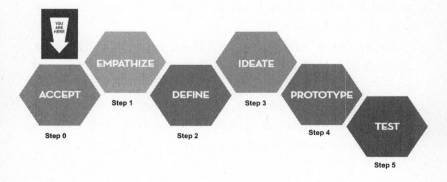

Acceptance is always the presumptive start of design because you can't solve a problem you're not willing to have. The traditional illustration of the product design process starts with Step 1, Empathy, and just assumes Acceptance. However, Acceptance is often such a demanding step when doing life design, and one so often skipped over, that we show it explicitly as Step 0. It's where everything begins.

We think it important to note that *grief ends where design begins—in acceptance.*

In a disruption, grieving is a necessity. Coming out of the 2020 pandemic, the entire world was grieving the loss of people, relationships, places, traditions, jobs, and careers. The losses were huge, and to move on from such losses, grief is an unavoidable part of the experience.

But where do we go as our grieving comes to an end? In fact, how does one ever get done with grief? Dave's wife died only eight weeks before this chapter was first written. At that time, Dave was pretty sure he was never going to get over it, but he was hopeful, even confident, that he would get past it and become fully alive again.

A powerful catalyst to getting past (if not entirely over) your losses is to start building your way forward into a new well-lived and joyful version of your life. We can grieve our way up to design, then design our way beyond grief.

David Kessler, Elisabeth Kübler-Ross's longtime collaborator, updated their work after Elisabeth died to include a sixth stage of grief: Finding Meaning.

Kessler recognized that getting to acceptance was necessary but not sufficient. People had to make meaning from their losses in order to move on well—and that meaning-making typically took root in how they went forward, integrating the lessons of those losses into their future selves.

Kessler was interviewed on *PBS NewsHour* in January 2021, shortly after President Biden had presided over the national memorial remembering the then more than 400,000 Americans and 2 million global citizens who died in the prior year from COVID-19. Kessler was speaking about the challenge of recovery and the scale of grief being experienced worldwide. As he spoke of how to move forward and make new meaning, he acknowledged to the viewers that indeed the pandemic was a huge cause of traumatic stress, so as we start to exit the pandemic, whole populations will be experiencing some degree of post-traumatic stress. As a way to deal with that, he reminded us to not forget that by processing our grief as generatively as possible, we can go beyond acceptance in making a new life and experience post-traumatic growth. A key goal of this book is to offer you some ideas and tools that can make that choice easier.

Whether you're reading this chapter during the latter days of the pandemic or years later during perhaps your own or a new global disruption, it is our sincere hope for you that you can work your way through the ending of the grief process and as you enter generative acceptance begin to design your way forward to a new and meaningful experience of your life and your membership in the human family. If the pandemic taught us anything, it is that we really are all in this together and that we need each other.

The Acceptance Zone is also a good place to keep setting the bar low and clearing it with small, energizing design efforts that keep you going and growing and avoid getting stuck in the Waiting Room.

Disruption Design Goal #2:
Be a Wayfinder to Be Future Ready

There are two strategies for how to get from *here* to *there*: navigation and wayfinding. They're very different, and it's critically important to pick the right strategy that will be effective for your situation.

Navigation means developing an optimal route based on precise information about where you are (Point A), where you're going (Point B), and all the terrain in between. When you've got this information available, it's terrific! Navigating is what your cell phone does using GPS information from satellites and map data from huge Internet databases. We use navigation all the time in all kinds of situations. It works to get to that new restaurant, and it works to plan how to complete your training to become a certified long-haul semi truck driver. Being able to navigate to just about anyplace is so common now that it's the default way we think about getting anywhere.

But it doesn't always work because you don't always know where you are or where you're going, and you sure don't have any data about the space in between. A lot of life is like this, and disruptions are definitely like this. When you're in the Acceptance Zone of change and transition and the New World hasn't arrived yet (what we call "the next normal" following the pandemic)—navigation isn't available. If you relocated to the Midwest to reduce your cost of living when your company made your job 100 percent online, there is no obviously best four-step route to reinventing your family's lifestyle and friend network. If you quit your job to home-school your kids rather than have them watch screens four hours a day, there is no shortcut or fast lane to figuring out just what kind of teaching is the best combination for both you and your kids. If you try turning on your Life GPS in the Acceptance Zone, you'll find you're not getting any location signal and there are no maps available. When that happens, wayfinding is not just the best thing you can do—it's the *only* thing you can do.

Wayfinding means making the best guess you can about which direction to try (not which destination to arrive at), then venturing forward for a bit, then stopping and taking note of where you are and what you can see from this new vantage point. Download six different third-grade curriculum packages, pick one lesson from each one, and give them a try. Then pick the one that seemed most effective and try customizing it for your kids' specific needs. Then do it again and again, and repeat until you finally either arrive at a good destination (homeschool is actually working!) or get enough information to allow you to navigate the rest of the way (the curriculum company connected you to a local mentor and she's now coaching you on a clear plan to success).

D esigners are usually wayfinding because they're trying to invent something no one's ever done before. Well-informed solutions and pathways just aren't available. Accordingly, designers never fall prey to the myth of efficiency.

The myth of efficiency is that whenever you find yourself doubling back over old ground or moving in any direction other than a straight line, you're wasting time and energy, and you're doing it all wrong. That myth is rooted in the false presumption that an optimal pathway is an efficient pathway—and of course the most efficient path is a straight line.

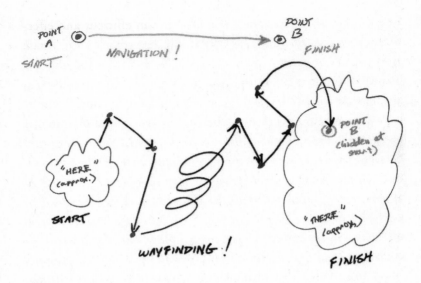

Here's the critical insight. When you find yourself in unknown territory (shown as the general vicinity labeled *here* above) and you're going to an as-yet-unidentified destination somewhere over *there*, a wayfinding route like the one above is *in fact the shortest distance between the start and the finish of that journey.* Really! That long squiggle is what the shortest distance looks like when you're wayfinding. It's the shortest distance measured in units of human discovery and prototype iteration—not miles.

You have to take it one step at a time. At the end of each step, you know things you could never have known before taking that step. And that incremental experience and insight is utterly critical to making forward progress. Yes, of course it will appear inefficient in retrospect—at least compared to straight-line navigation—but that's irrelevant. The only place a straight-line pathway ever existed in the wayfinding journey like the one shown above was in a false image in your head. The eight-step process shown here, including the loop-de-loops and the reversals, is an efficient and effective approach. Each small step eventually gets you closer to where you're going.

It's important not to attempt to navigate when wayfinding is appropriate. Imagine if the designer on the homeschooling journey above fooled herself into thinking she could land *there* in one jump, so she ventured out on the same trajectory shown on her first leg (trying the first "award-winning" curriculum she bought), but she just kept using that same material over and over, lesson after lesson, regardless of how it worked for her kids—hoping to get all the way to the destination of happy homeschooled kids in one giant leap. If she'd done that, she'd have been massively off course, making getting to the right place horribly more difficult. By taking one step (try one lesson out), then stopping and immediately applying her learning and adjusting her path (maybe her kids need less reading and more hands-on projects), she will get where she wants to go in the shortest time.

Be a wayfinder when the situation warrants it—and if there was ever a place that warranted it, it's the Acceptance Zone!

Designing in the Acceptance Zone

In the Acceptance Zone, what are we wayfinding our way toward if the New World isn't clear yet? How do we take any productive steps at all? You let the endings from the Old World direct your curiosity (sounds like, "Hmmm, I wonder how new employee orientation will work now?") and you build your way forward using the simple four-step process we've outlined in detail in chapter 7: get curious, talk to people, try stuff, and tell your story.

What's different in the Acceptance Zone is you're not doing that process to design a new solution for your future work life. You're doing it to transition through the Acceptance Zone and to make yourself future-ready when you've gotten across it and the New World is starting to take shape.

As the pandemic was unfolding, it was clear that work was hugely impacted for just about everyone. Many people lost their jobs, and everyone's work changed—mostly in dramatic ways, as people were sent home and those who did come to work came to a very different place and process. Many millions went from being in the room to using Zoom, and collaboration and social life were transformed. Meanwhile, we were all learning more about epidemiology, disease transmission, and sanitation than we ever wanted to know. Those were all hints about what was worth wayfinding about while the world sorted itself out—while we were transitioning across the Acceptance Zone.

Those changes were, and are, invitations to get curious. You can learn more about how online communities are built. You can experiment with different ways to do your job that being remote permits. Lose your job? You can do a remote job shadow visit with all your friends who are still working and find out what their work and world are like. You can try out lots of different ways to learn more about COVID and understand what is and isn't working for you as a learner, then compare that to others' experience—all in order to get smarter and more savvy about how information moves, who is doing a good job of inviting people to know, and who is doing new things and who's not. You can pay close attention to how your employer is adjusting the work process and see if you can identify how the bosses are thinking and how priorities are shifting.

In the Acceptance Zone, you don't yet know where things will end up, but you do know what's most likely to change. Once you recognize that you're in a disruption and accept that things will never be the same again, you already know what many of those never-to-be-the-same-again things are. That's where you start—by getting curious about those things that are undergoing change. They are the indicators of the future, so just follow them with your engaged designer curiosity. Keep repeating that process and you'll be among the most future-ready people and among the first to recognize when Acceptance Zone is coming to an end and what's on the other side.

That's exactly what we did through most of 2020. By the beginning of 2021, we could begin to see how the post-pandemic world was going to operate and what work design ideas would be most helpful.

The next chapters are the result of that effort. In them we provide the particular design ideas and tools needed to make the most of the new constraints and opportunities in the world of 2021 and beyond. These are not just transition tools. These are new core tools for a future—the next normal—that will be with us for a long, long time to come. The tools described in the first ten chapters of this edition all still apply as the workplace issues and challenges they address continue in the new world, too. What follows are the extra tools to build a work life in which you can thrive and change as the next normal settles in and finally becomes just normal.

At least until the next disruption.

13

Disruption Design

So here we are, and no one can predict with certainty how the changes brought on by the global pandemic will affect you, your work, your family, and your lifestyle. As we said, we are in the midst of a lot of uncertainty and ambiguity—and that's okay, because designers know how to deal with ambiguity. After all, we are always designing into the unknowable future and coming up with products and services new to the world. So the mind-sets we emphasize and tools we'll teach you in this chapter apply to the time of pandemic and they are equally useful in any period of rapid and unpredictable change.

Most of us understand that our jobs can change at any time, pandemic or not. Globalization is rapidly redistributing jobs, and often we have no choice but to deal with the changes as they occur. New jobs that hardly existed ten years ago, in fields like AI and machine learning, are creating opportunities for some and eliminating jobs for others. The rising cost of labor and the need for companies to constantly increase their productivity are relentless forces that drive change in every industry. We've talked about the importance of the Waiting Room reframe, and of adopting a creative and open mind-set when approaching Disruption Design. If there is a silver lining in any of the COVID disruption, it is that while in the Acceptance Zone, we have all been forced to learn new ways of working, new ways of collaborating, and new ways of creating project teams and corporate cultures. All of this is going to prove useful as we move toward the post-pandemic future.

The mantra throughout this book has been "set the bar low and clear it." We believe that the key to success is taking small, proactive steps toward any change you want to make. You don't adopt a new mind-set overnight; adopting a new mind-set, like curiosity or bias to action, will have some starts and stops. You'll use a tool for a while, like the new time management tool in this chapter, and then fall out of practice. What's important is your intention to make the change and your persistence and your grit when it comes to the changing.

In times of high stress, when a lot of change is thrust upon you quickly, you need to prioritize your efforts. Pick your problems carefully—you can't respond to everything with equal force. Again, this advice applies not only during a global disruption but whenever some big change happens, like the birth of a child, a layoff at work, the death of a loved one—any time things beyond your control substantially and irreversibly change your world. We all need some crisis management tools to prepare ourselves for what happens next.

That's why it is even more important to pick problems that are real. Problem-finding is the first step in design thinking, and finding the best problems—the most urgent or important ones to work on—is even more critical when the forces of the world seem to be spinning out of control. Now is the time to get good at the Art of Reframing techniques in chapter 3 and find the MAPs (Minimum Actionable Problem) and the BDOs (Best Doable Option) in your world.

Apply your best efforts, keep the bar low, and make sure your problems are workable and in their simplest form for now. No one needs to borrow trouble, not now and not ever, so prioritizing your problems and your responses is a pretty good way to deal with the current and future reality.

The New Key Issues

As we survey the future of work and how that might affect your lifestyle, we predict that you need to be thinking about:

- **Transitioning to Hybrid Work**—managing the good and the bad of sometimes working from home.
- **Embracing a Big Shift to Being Trusted** and the accountability that comes with it.
- **Upping Your Communication Game** to make sure your contribution is recognized.
- **Remodeling Your Job**, both the place you do it in and the way you do it.
- **Building Your Design Team.** Now more than ever, you need a team, and collaboration with your players, supporters, and intimates is a generative and fun form of radical collaboration.

As you might imagine, we have a point of view and a tool or two to address all five issues.

The Office Is Mostly Over

We've talked to CEOs, COOs, big business owners, small business owners and everyone in between, and the consensus is, we are not going back to the "normal" office any time soon. If you work in a traditional office, with cubicles and a lobby and break rooms and the VP's office in the corner with big windows—well, that way of warehousing workers is pretty much over. Even before the events of 2020, most companies were allowing some of their knowledge workers to work from home, maybe a few days a week, or maybe just once in a while.

We are not sure that there will be an office to go back to, at least not one the size it was before. We spoke with the head of design and innovation at one of the largest office furniture and cubicle manufacturers in the world. It turns out that fitting out an office, even with really expensive stuff, is only 5 percent of the cost; 95 percent is the cost of the lease. In the near future, companies carrying the cost of these expensive leases will have to justify that cost to their shareholders. It hasn't escaped the attention of the bean counters in big organizations that with everyone working from home, they can save a truckload of money if they just shut the office down and get out of their leases. Some big tech companies are preparing for this new future by offering cash incentives for workers to move a certain distance *away* from corporate headquarters.

Remember when airlines used to print a boarding pass for you? Then one day they realized that they could save a lot of money (some estimate as much as a billion dollars industry-wide) if they made you use your paper and your ink to print your own. Well, the same thing is going to happen to the modern office.

You are going to provide one for your employer.

In fact, Pinterest, the Internet start-up that went public in 2019, paid $90 million to get out of a lease on a brand-new world headquarters in San Francisco, saying they didn't think that they would be needing nearly that much space in the future. This is just the start of a not-so-distant future trend. Even if your company wants to return to the office full-time, the financial realities of keeping up with the competition means they probably won't. Market analysts will downgrade the stock of any company whose CEO insists on having her big corner office and all her employees sitting in cubicles where she can watch over them again. It is not likely that we will return to that version of normal.

The chances are that companies that employ mostly office workers are never going to go back to the old way of "officing." More likely they will downsize their spaces significantly, set up a protocol for signing up for an office once or twice a week, and let their newly trustworthy employees work from home as much as they'd like. Many companies we've talked to are planning on going to a 3/2 workweek—three days working from home, two days in the office—or even a 4/1. And that's going to work out better for everyone, so you might as well get used to it and start optimizing your home office. More on that subject in a bit.

And if you think that's just fine for the knowledge workers, but those of you who work hands-on will still go to your "offices," think again. Manufacturing companies, where people need to be physically present at work to make something, are using the pandemic as an excuse to accelerate their move to fully robotic factories. This was happening anyway, so the pandemic is just speeding things up. Robots don't get sick (they also don't need health insurance, don't form unions, and don't go on strike—but that's a different story). Robots can work through pandemics without interruption. Obviously, if you see this coming in your industry, it will represent a major disruption for you, the manufacturing worker, and another good reason to start thinking creatively about redesigning your job and your skill set.

Workforce Transformation

One of the extreme versions of what people are calling the Great Internet Diaspora is the work-from-anywhere trend. Some folks, particularly younger workers who don't need to worry about mortgages and schools for the kids just yet, have decided to make remote work a real lifestyle choice. They are moving to Hawaii or Bali for the surfing and snorkeling, or summering in Yosemite and spending the winter at their favorite ski resort in Canada. Countries like Barbados, Bermuda, and Estonia are offering pandemic worker visas that allow you to stay in their country as long as you want if you can prove you have a remote job.

If you fit this demographic, the temptation to redesign everything (what we called the Wild Card Odyssey Plan in *Designing Your Life*) is pretty strong. You get to pick a wicked-cool "office" location somewhere in paradise, your company doesn't have to pay for your expensive office space and furniture, and Estonia gets the benefit of someone spending that fat tech paycheck in their local grocery store. Everybody wins. A Silicon Valley start-up called Kibbo started buying up Sprinter van campers to support a completely mobile community of digital nomads, who roam the countryside and check in every once in a while at Kibbo clubhouses, complete with fast Internet and community kitchens. It's a modern take on Kampgrounds of America, better known as KOA, enabled by the work-from-anywhere trend and ubiquitous global high-speed Internet.

What's next? Man-made islands floating outside the territorial waters of the United States, home to "digital pirate" communities of gig workers partying and pounding away on their laptops? Sounds like the next big start-up idea to us, and we give it to you, free of charge.

If you are not willing to live in a camper, or if you opt to work from home because of the mortgage and the kids' school, you are in some ways going back to a version of village life in the early 1900s, where the baker lived over her bakery and the cobbler lived over his store. Before the Industrial Revolution, before folks moved to industrial centers to work in factories, working "from home" was the way everybody did it. After the pandemic, it's back to the future: many of us are "living over the shop" again. This is having positive results for lots of people, but it comes with one really big downside.

On the plus side, people are realizing that without a commute, they can get the same amount of work done in less time or be even more productive with the extra time not spent in bumper-to-bumper commuter traffic. This is also allowing the average worker to manage their time spent working differently. If you need to make the kids breakfast and start later on some days, you can manage it. If you want to run some errands in the middle of the day, just turn off your camera and go do it. Arranging for a package to be delivered midday? No problem, you're home all day anyway. Because you're now a trusted employee, you don't need to ask for permission to move your schedule around. This freedom to design your day and manage your time to fit your lifestyle is even better when schools and day-care centers are functioning normally.

The downside is that this work-from-anywhere lifestyle is leading to a new kind of overwhelm—we call it the "no boundaries" overwhelm. When work is just down the hall in the spare bedroom or at the kitchen table in your studio apartment, there are no physical or mental boundaries between work and life. We used to rely on moving around, changing it up, to mark the different periods of the day. Now that's all gone. It's hard to know when one thing ends and the other thing begins.

Bill had a pretty sweet routine before the pandemic. He lives in a San Francisco neighborhood called the Dogpatch (no one knows why it's called that), and every morning he'd kiss his wife goodbye, walk four blocks to La Stazione, his local coffee shop, get his latte and muffin, and walk to the train station. Forty minutes later he was at the Stanford campus and would walk to his office to start his day.

It was really clear when Bill was at work and when he was at home. There were getting-ready times, commuting times, and winding-down times built into the rhythm of his day. In the middle of the pandemic, all of those time markers and physical markers were gone, for Bill and for everyone. The transitions between work and not-work disappeared. This led to a blurring of time and space, and a lack of physical mobility that is unhealthy.

There is some evidence that this is leading to an increase in depression and a sense of overwhelm that is definitely not healthy. Since this hybrid workstyle is probably going to be the new normal, we are going to have to be more intentional if we are going to take charge of our mental and physical health.

Daily Experience Redesign

Doctors and psychologists agree that we need to break up our workday with some physical exercise, a variety of different kinds of cognitive tasks, and some social contact. This is critical for our health. Once you become a hybrid worker, you need to take responsibility for making sure you get all three. You will need to be very intentional about time management if you want to succeed at this autonomy thing. Designers design experiences all the time (think of standing in line at Disneyland), and this new no-boundaries situation calls for a healthy dose of experience design.

Look at your daily schedule, on paper or online, and mark it up to identify four experiences: starting and stopping moments, uninterrupted work time, social time, and physical movement time.

Here's an actual example of Bill's schedule for a typical week during spring quarter at Stanford, marked up as suggested above:

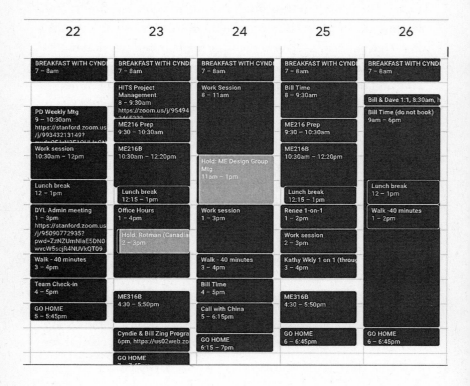

Notice that Bill always schedules breakfast, in all-capital letters, with his wife, Cynthia, and he always has a calendar entry for GO HOME. These are his **Starting** and **Stopping** moments. He's also designed a little social and physical ritual around "going to work." He kisses his wife, says, "Bye, honey, I'm off to work," and then heads downstairs to the spare bedroom/office and closes the door. Now he is "at work." He designed something similar around "coming home." He shuts down his Mac, closes the door to the bedroom, walks upstairs from his office, kisses his wife, and says, "Hi, honey, I'm home," and then changes into a more comfortable T-shirt and pants. In this experience design, Bill makes sure that **Starting** and **Stopping** moments are designed in—he has bookended "work" with a social ritual, kissing his wife, and a physical ritual, going down and up the stairs and changing his clothes. These moments in the experience mark the starting and stopping points of his day.

This playacting seemed a little silly the first week he did it, but now it's actually something he and Cynthia look forward to. It helps her start and stop her workday, too.

Those designed moments set up the boundaries of his day in an intentional way. The same is true for his daily schedule. He makes sure that he takes a break, even a short one, for lunch. He sometimes schedules a video call with his brother or sister while he's eating, just to check in and socialize when they might also have some free time. He always takes a forty-minute brisk walk up one of San Francisco's famous hills. In forty minutes he can get in about 5,000 steps if he keeps up the pace, which he tracks on his iPhone. He schedules this in the midafternoon to perk him up after a lot of morning meetings. His amazing assistant Renée also books what she calls "Bill Time"—which is the time he actually gets to do some writing, or grades assignments, or makes up new lectures. You must schedule this time—the trendy term is *deep work*—but it's really just scheduled time where no interruptions are allowed. Otherwise, the only uninterrupted time you get will be at night, after "work" is supposed to be over.

Remember, note the rhythm of your day. We have a tool for tracking your energy in our first book. But a little basic time management, paying special attention to your starting and stopping moments, is critical if you want to thrive while having the freedom to work from home.

What About the Kids?

We mentioned that many studies have shown that the health impact of the pandemic has unfairly burdened the working class, women, and people of color. The pandemic put a spotlight on income and healthcare inequalities in America and made us confront the reality that not everyone has the same privilege when it comes to designing their lives. This is especially true for young mothers and fathers who have the task of child care and work and might not have the support of a spouse or family nearby.

Dani, the young woman we mentioned earlier, is one of those moms. For Dani, time management tools like the one above are everything. She has to manage down to the minute if she's going to get through the day, much less the week. Luckily she has a good job that was remote anyway, so she doesn't have to worry about a paycheck. For Dani and other caregivers like her, this is a season of *designed overwhelm*. Keeping in mind the "set the bar low" method, we suggest that the goal is simply not to get too far behind, to deal with the major stuff first and let everything else go. Once the kids are back in school, things will get better. Until then, she can exercise her agency and control by designing in as much kid time and social time as she can. Studies have shown that even when you have limited resources, feeling like you have the ability to make choices and ration your resources responsibly makes all the difference in the world. Making good choices under difficult constraints—that's our definition of control.

That and a nice glass of wine after the kids go to bed.

The Big Shift to Trust

Let's be honest, before 2020 one of the reasons work from home was limited to just a few high-level employees was that bosses and managers felt they needed to "supervise" their workers. That really meant they wanted them in the office where they could be watched. It was all about trust, and there wasn't much of it. As we wrote in the Introduction, 69 percent of U.S. workers and 85 percent of global workers report that they are disengaged or actively disengaged at work. We think this lack of trust may play a part, because when you treat people this way, as though you do not trust them, they disengage.

However, since the pandemic, bosses have been forced to trust their employees to get the job done, without relying on their supervision. The results have been an across-the-board improvement in productivity. Most folks have found working from home really works for them. These newly productive and empowered employees are going to demand to be trusted in the future and are going to want the flexibility that comes with a hybrid office schedule. The people we've talked to who have found a way to work from home that works for them say they do not want to go back to the office five days a week, every week. They want more trust and flexibility designing their days, and after this disruption, they will demand it.

Now if you are a paramedic, a grocery clerk, a manufacturing assembly worker, or a frontline medical worker, these changes will not impact you very much. But if even some of these hybrid work predictions come true, almost every worker who doesn't need to be physically present to do his or her job will be able to work remotely for some portion of the workweek. That means that we are entering an era of more (forced) trust, where you automatically get more agency and more control over how your day works for you. And the process of redesigning your job for this new reality isn't a one-and-done thing; it will be dynamic and will change as your daily schedule evolves.

The hybrid workstyle comes with more accountability and responsibility. Your boss may still be deciding what he wants you to do, but you are now more in charge of the how than ever before. This is a new opportunity to design a productive and enjoyable work life, and that's all good! Remember, once you start down the path of working from home, out from under the supervision of your manager, you become a more autonomous worker, and autonomy is one of the positive elements in the ARC (autonomy, relatedness, competence) of your career. Your manager has to learn to trust you—he or she has no other choice. Be worthy of that trust, be more accountable, and you will reap the freedom to design your workweek in the way that works for you.

The Accountability Model

When you move from the supervision model (some would call it the micromanagement model) to the accountability model, you get more personal autonomy, which is great, but the change has consequences that you want to be ready for.

As the system shifts more toward accountability, you'll need to make your work product more visible. You want to make sure that project deadlines are clear (that's your responsibility, not your manager's), and you need to schedule your time efficiently so that you deliver to the deadline 100 percent of the time. And if something comes up and you know you can't make a deadline or a milestone, you need to fess up in advance, before the deadline arrives.

The truth is, most deadlines can be renegotiated if there is a good reason to do so, and the key is to handle it before you let people down. You need to address problems head on and be transparent. You need to communicate more now than ever, and make sure that everyone on your team knows you are getting the job done. Above all, you want to be perceived as predictable—you never surprise your team or your boss with a problem. That's what accountability looks like.

In the new hybrid workforce model, everything needs to be more intentional, and that's probably a good thing. Expectations will have to be made more clear and two-way communication and feedback will have to be more explicit in a remote work scenario.

That's a good change. And workers will be rewarded for what they produce, not just for "face time" with the boss (pun intended). In fact, useless video meetings, where nothing gets done, will become less and less tolerated as "video fatigue" and effective time management becomes more important and more visible. When there's no one around to watch you while you work, *what* you do becomes much more important than how you do it.

This means that leaders will shift from managing you (which never really worked anyway) to managing results, the output and deliverables that make a project a success. By the way, high-performance leaders have been managing this way already. Now all managers and leaders will follow suit because that's what the situation demands.

In the new world of accountability, it's all about deliverables, and these show up in one of two forms—writing, mostly emails and status reports nowadays, and presentations.

Design Better Deliverables

To communicate effectively, you probably need to amp up your writing skills. A huge percentage of your work product will be documented in emails and status reports. Writing a short and to-the-point email is a skill that few possess, so if you get good at this, you'll be noticed. Crafting an email or a clear memo subject line helps busy people figure out which documents need to be opened now and which can be held for later. Keeping your emails short and to the point, with a clear takeaway or request for action, is important and a gift to anyone with an overloaded inbox (and that's everyone). If your work group uses modern digital team management software like Slack, Microsoft Teams, or whichever new collaboration platform your company adopted last week, you need to spend the time it takes to become a power user.

Your boss will notice.

If you are not sure that your grammar and punctuation are up to snuff, go immediately to the bookstore (pick a local one, please) and purchase a copy of *The Elements of Style* by William Strunk Jr. and E. B. White. First published in its full form in 1935, it is the writer's reference for all things grammatical. Read it—no, memorize it. Your writing will improve immensely.

Death by PowerPoint

While the day-to-day of business communication is mostly done by emails, the important stuff, the big milestones and project decisions, happens in meetings. This generally means someone is making a presentation with "slides." This is where an investment in your business presentation skills, if you are willing to do it, will pay off a hundred times over.

There is a good reason that the phrase "death by PowerPoint" is ubiquitous in the work world. Most presentations are dreadful. They are always too long, poorly organized, badly designed, boring, and just plain ugly. Trust us, we know. Research academics make some of the worst slide presentations ever seen. When we attend technical conferences, we are assaulted by unreadable fonts, terrible graphics, way too many words on a slide, and diagrams that are often indecipherable. Add a droning voice-over, a presenter reading each and every word on every slide, and you can't help but put your audience to sleep.

You don't want to be that person.

Look, if you have the chance to present your work or your team's work, you have an obligation to make your presentation understandable, engaging, and effective. If you are going to take even ten minutes of everyone's precious time to present something, you better make it worth it. You need to design your presentation with care and attention, just as you design anything that represents you as a creative person.

As Bill teaches his students, a presentation is always a performance. When you are a presenter, you are onstage, and you are responsible for making your time onstage memorable. In general, people remember what they see, not what they hear, so your graphics and your body language are more important than your words. And people can remember only three things—so organize your performance around the three most important takeaways.

Every good presentation also tells a story. French-Swiss filmmaker Jean-Luc Godard famously said, "A story should have a beginning, a middle, and an end, but not necessarily in that order." So to keep it interesting, be willing to mix it up.

Christopher Booker, in his book *The Seven Basic Plots: Why We Tell Stories*, claimed that there are only seven plots, and these are the backbone of all human stories:

1. **Overcoming the Monster (*Little Red Riding Hood*, *Jaws*)**
2. **Rags to Riches (*Cinderella*, *David Copperfield*, *Rocky*)**
3. **The Quest (*The Odyssey*, *Star Wars*, *The Lord of the Rings*)**
4. **Voyage and Return (*Alice's Adventures in Wonderland*, *Gulliver's Travels*)**
5. **Comedy (Shakespeare's comedies, *The Hangover 1*, *2*, and *3*)**
6. **Tragedy (*Hamlet*, *Romeo and Juliet*)**
7. **Rebirth (*A Christmas Carol*, *Groundhog Day*)**

Whether he's right or not is not the point. These seven plots make great presentations.

As an exercise, Bill has his students construct a simple presentation about something they are working on, twelve to fifteen slides in all, using the default Calibri PowerPoint font, with no graphics or pictures. They then give a five-minute presentation with this deck to the whole class, live.

The results are predictably boring.

Then he asks them to redesign the presentation around a story, using one of the seven basic plots. They must reduce the number of slides by 30 percent and the number of words by 50 percent. This is critical—you don't want the audience reading slides, you want them paying attention to you, the presenter. The students must also isolate and define the three takeaways from the presentation. He asks them to be specific in the fonts they choose and in the graphic layout of their slides. They should substitute meaningful charts and images in place of the words where a picture can tell the story better, a critical step if they are going to cut the number of words in the presentation by half.

He also requires them to practice the presentation five times in front of a mirror, concentrating on their body language and nonverbal expression. Making a video is even better, so they can review and critique their own performance.

Then they must give the presentation to a friend or colleague and ask the friend to write down the three key points that were stressed in the presentation. If the friend fails to name the three key points, they must redesign the presentation and try again.

Then after that redesign, they give their presentation to the class live, and the results are predictably fantastic.

The project "overcame the monster" of a big hairy technical problem and is now back on schedule and headed for success.

The simple idea for redesigning the "buy" button has resulted in a "rags to riches" success story as more people click through to the shopping cart.

We're not there yet, but let me tell you about the fascinating journey our project is on! We've tried many things and been to many places, our "Quest" is a good one, and we are certain to arrive one day at the solution that everyone loves. Here are some highlights . . .

Nowadays Bill rarely has to sit through a boring presentation, at least from his students, and they leave his program ready to communicate their ideas effectively and with style. They know how to design their presentation, communicate with confident body language, and convince audiences (and bosses) that they are doing great work.

In our new work lives, we should all be doing the same.

Relentless Remodeling

Both during the Acceptance Zone period in any disruption, and again afterward as the next normal starts to settle in, take the opportunity to remodel your job. Job remodeling is Strategy #2 in our redesign strategies described in chapter 7. Recall that you can do both cosmetic remodels (changing the slipcover on the couch, hanging up new art) and structural remodels (turning the rear window into glass doors for better yard access). Either way, what you're looking for in a remodel is a small and easy way to execute change that really breathes new life into your job for you—and preferably one that won't require your manager's approval or a new expense budget (free is always easier).

Chances are that even while you are in the Acceptance Zone, the changes brought about by a disruption are littered with remodel possibilities. One of Dave's part-time jobs is with Praxis Labs, a social entrepreneur incubator based in New York. Dave's primary role was to mentor Entrepreneurs in Residence (EIRs)—serial entrepreneurs who were between start-ups—deciding what they wanted to do next. The program was centered on three in-person retreats a year where the whole cohort of EIRs gathered for two to four days. Dave loved the job, in no small part because it took him and Claudia to New York (their favorite city on earth) four to six times a year. But the job was seriously impacted by the pandemic.

People couldn't travel and the New York office was emptied out. Praxis started redirecting its efforts to new programs that could be delivered online. The new programs grew surprisingly fast, and the EIR program was mothballed. On the surface, it looked like Dave was out of a job. But he chose to reframe it as a remodel by applying some curiosity. He asked the company leadership what the best parts of the EIR program were, the ones that they were sad to see go. What assets were built for the EIRs that they wanted to keep? Then he talked with the team leaders of the growing programs to see if their constituencies could use any of those assets or had similar needs. Sure enough, some of them did. Dave volunteered to rework some of those assets and to prototype online engagements for them. He got some takers and was able to keep his role in the company, just redirected to a new set of users. He was doing the same thing, but facing a different direction. It wasn't much harder than putting the couch on the opposite side of the living room. In addition to preserving Dave's job, this remodel kept him connected to that whole community and allowed him to work a lot more with first-time founders, where his experience was valued.

So look around your current job—notice the changes—and see if you can get curious and reframe those changes into an easily implemented job remodel. It will definitely improve your quality of life, it will better position you for the future once you get across the Acceptance Zone, and it might just save your job from being disrupted out of existence.

And we recommend remodeling your job not just in response to a disruption, but *relentlessly!*

We're making a distinction between a big remodel, a high-value remodel—like the one Dave pulled off at Praxis—and little remodels, preferably lots of them. In other words, we don't want you knocking down walls every time—that's exhausting and expensive—but you can rearrange the furniture, swap out the throw pillows, and get a similar sense of a whole new space.

The goal is to help you get across the Acceptance Zone not just in one piece, but in great shape and ready to engage the new beginnings. One of the difficulties of the Acceptance Zone is that while we're in it, we tend to feel helpless. We don't really know what's going on (and during a big disruption, neither does anyone else), and we don't know when the next normal is going to happen. It can be pretty discouraging, especially if it goes on for a long time.

All the more reason to engage in Disruption Design and actively curate your curiosity by talking to people, trying stuff, and telling your story—not only to prepare for the New World but to experientially remind yourself that you are not powerless and you can *and will* design your way forward.

While researching this revised edition, we noticed over and over again that people were just getting weary. About every four to six weeks we'd start hearing people saying, "I'm just *so over this!*" Ambiguity is always hard. Ambiguity dragging on and on is utterly draining, and drained is not a good mind-set for a designer. In fact, you always have *some* agency over your situation and you always can design something that could be just a little bit better.

That's what we mean by *relentless* job remodeling—little changes that you make frequently, over and over and over again. It's all about exercising your personal agency to remind yourself of the power you have to change things. And while you won't get everything you want or all the power you might like, you can still focus on utilizing the power you do have. Relentless remodeling, no matter how small, is energizing and generative.

One week it might be starting work ninety minutes earlier than usual so you get a better chance of catching people in other time zones live on the phone. You might change your calendar app on your phone to one with a better to-do list manager, or maybe try one of those meditation apps, spending ten minutes a day to get centered. You could start curating different art prints to use for your Zoom video backdrop, and see who comments on which ones to perhaps find an online art appreciation buddy. Myriad small changes can have positive impacts on your daily work experience. This is the "set the bar really, really low and clear it frequently" program.

No remodel is too small.

Once you try this, you'll quickly discover that it's not hard to do and is pretty addictive, which is a good thing. You'll improve your mood, reinforce your confidence, keep your mind limber, and have more opportunities to be noticed—all of which will improve your performance and your future opportunity in the next normal. We actually hope that you get so enamored of relentless remodeling that as a dedicated work designer you will make it a permanent practice.

When Remodeling Isn't a Metaphor

While you're relentlessly remodeling your workstyle, and since you are likely to be working from home at least some part of the week now and in the future, make a little investment in your workspace. Temporary measures, implemented when you thought this pandemic thing was going to blow over in a few weeks, need to be redesigned.

For instance, when the lockdown first hit Stanford and Bill had to start teaching from home, he put his laptop on the ironing board because he could adjust its height. (Getting your keyboard slightly below normal table height, with your forearms in a neutral or slightly lower position, is critical to avoiding back problems and carpal tunnel injuries.) Of course that wasn't a long-term solution, and neither is working from the kitchen table. A barstool around the island in the kitchen—not workable long term. That dining room chair repurposed with a card-table desk—not going to cut it.

So now, along with your other new responsibilities, you are the "facilities manager" of your home office. You need to design a simple workspace that is comfortable, somewhat private, and good for your body. Your most important investment is a good office chair. A well-designed office chair, like the Aeron from Herman Miller, can be found secondhand online and is worth its weight in chiropractor bills (and with all of the office downsizing that is going on, there should be plenty of great chairs available cheap for the next few years).

Finding a spot that isn't heavily trafficked and doesn't have a lot of background noise is also a good idea, because those video calls are easier when no one is bothering you (and you aren't bothering your housemates). Of course, if you can repurpose the guest bedroom to be a semi-permanent office, that's even better. A consideration of ergonomics, which according to *Merriam-Webster's Collegiate Dictionary* is "an applied science concerned with designing and arranging things people use so that the people and things interact most efficiently and safely," is important, for both your physical and your mental health. (It's a lot easier to be depressed when you've screwed up your back sitting in a bad chair for eight to ten hours a day.) There's lots of information about healthy workspace design on the Internet—research and then design a space that works for you. And bonus points for designing a great background, real or virtual, so that you look professional on all those video calls. And of course, Zoom cats are always welcome!

It is also time to invest, if you can, in a better Internet connection. (Add another title to your home business card—IT manager.) Cable systems generally deliver faster and more reliable Internet than phone line or DSL systems. If you are in an urban area, you should investigate getting a fiber-optic link directly to your home. Bill got one: it gives him almost gigabit speed up and down (fiber is symmetrical) and he never loses the connection. It is reasonable to request that your employer pick up some of the cost of this improved service. After all, you are doing it so that you can work more efficiently and effectively for your company. Frozen video calls and dropped connections are not just frustrating, they can really have an impact on the quality of an important meeting. If you are often in a customer-facing role, the quality of your Internet connection now reflects on the professionalism of your company. If you can upgrade, it's certainly more than worth it.

Reinvention on Steroids

For many (too many) people, the 2020 pandemic did not merely change or disrupt their work life —it ended it. They lost not just their jobs but their entire industry. The restaurant, travel, and hotel industries—just about anything that involved lots of people getting together in one place—were dealt a devastating blow. Some faced a permanent disruption. It's estimated that a third of the restaurants in New York City that closed during the pandemic will never return. Not to mention the loss of so many live entertainment venues and associated jobs—comedy clubs, theaters, sporting events, and speaking conferences. The performers, athletes, and speakers depend on those events for income, as do the places and staff that host them.

The hard truth is that many of the jobs lost during 2020 and beyond will never return. Disruptions on the scale of the 2020 pandemic permanently impact or even eliminate whole sectors of the economy. If you find yourself in a situation where not only will what you used to do never be the same again, it won't even *be* again, then you're facing a Reinvention on steroids.

Reinvention is Redesign Strategy #4 from chapter 7. It's the hardest, slowest, and most costly of the four strategies (Reframe and Reenlist, Remodel, Relocate, and Reinvent), but when the situation demands it, it's the only one that works. Normally, when people do a reinvention of their work, they do it in the same industry. They move from actuarial analysis to social media marketing, but they make that move while staying in the life insurance industry, where they have contacts and credible references. They may jump from accounting to event management, but they do it in the college and university sector, where people recognize where they've worked before. If your reinvention is being driven by a disruption impacting not merely your job but your entire economic sector, you're going to have to pull off that reinvention by crossing both job functions and industry markets.

Anna had run housekeeping operations in a large hotel. She'd worked in the hotel business for over a dozen years, starting in her teens. College wasn't her thing, so she just went to work as soon as she got out of high school. She didn't have a degree, but she sure had drive. It took no time at all for her bosses to recognize that she was reliable, dependable, teachable, and also cheerful. And who doesn't love a great worker who's a delight to be around? She was quickly put forward for roles in which all her competitors had college degrees. She didn't get every promotion, but once someone gave her a chance at a leadership role and she nailed it, her career went great. She was running a large operation and had dozens of people working for her when the pandemic clobbered the hotel. They cut back and hoped to ride it out, and Anna was kept on. For a while. Then it got so bad they let 90 percent of the staff go, including all the people in Anna's department. She went on unemployment benefits for the first time in her life.

Now what? Even if hotels made a comeback, she didn't want to be in that high-risk situation again. And the competition for the few jobs potentially available would be so cutthroat, she wasn't sure she even wanted to work in one of those places again. She needed to reinvent herself.

What Anna had to do was take a whole new look at her skill set and what she'd accomplished in the past and identify it in generic terms, not hotel and hospitality terms. She didn't just run the work scheduling of over twenty-five janitorial employees, she resource allocated a large, flex-scheduled workforce. She didn't just come up with a largely pictorial training manual for new non-English-speaking groundskeepers, she developed and successfully deployed a graphical user interface (GUI) based workflow process and onboarding system.

Anna figured out the essential work processes and tools and competencies that she'd developed over the years and found a way to describe them in terms anyone would understand without defining her as a hotel person. Then she had to get someone to listen to her new and improved story.

On Steroids Means Do It Twice

The special challenge of cracking into a whole new sector is figuring out which sector to approach and finding people to talk to who will give you a chance to try stuff and tell your story. The goal of trying to find a new job in a new sector where you have no contacts is just out of reach in one step. So the first goal isn't to get a job.

Set the bar lower.

The first goal is to find an interesting sector and craft your new story. The second goal is to then crack into that sector and use that story to network your way to a new job.

- **Goal #1: Find one or two interesting new sectors. All you're doing now is finding places that might be good**

target industries or economic sectors for you to shift into. Start by thinking about all the different kinds of work and economic activity where your generically reworded skills may be useful. Hopefully that is a list of four to six areas. Then shorten that list down to the top two that you think look interesting.

Anna thought about where scheduling a large hourly workforce and constantly having to train new people on workflow procedures might be useful. She made a list:

- **Construction**
- **Farming**
- **Landscaping and landscape maintenance**
- **Delivery services (an industry that exploded after 2020)**
- **Call centers**
- **Home healthcare and hospice services**

As Anna looked over the list, she felt most attracted to construction (her uncle was a carpenter and she always liked the guys he worked with), and home healthcare and hospice services (such industries are growing, and she'd been really impressed with the hospice staff who helped out when her grandmother died).

Her first step was to actively network to everyone she knew in search of personal referrals to anyone who worked in either of those fields. She used exactly the technique described in chapter 9, "Moving On." The only difference was she really wasn't looking for a job at all yet—she was just being curious about these industries and wanting to learn more about them. She remembered to ask every contact for other contacts and ended every live inquiry with the power question: "Thanks so much for your time. I have just one last question. If you were me, what would you do next?"

That approach got her eight conversations, three in construction, three in home healthcare, and two in hospice. After those conversations, she had a much better idea about how things worked in those fields. She now had enough information to do some online research about how those industries were growing, what challenges they were facing, and how roles that she might be a fit for were changing. When she put that research together with her conversation notes, she was able to start imagining what she could do in those fields and what further questions she had about them.

Then she went back to the people she'd met for a follow-up conversation focused on specific topics of interest in their field. She approached the general manager of a concrete contractor to discuss the increasing use of decorative and custom concrete for indoor applications and the effect that this was having on their business. She reconnected with the operations manager of a hospice group to discuss the recent influx of for-profit hospice providers and the impact of that development on the traditional nonprofits. The quality and relevance of Anna's questions got her those follow-up conversations, which led to more networking and more conversations. All still just exploring these industries and types of businesses—*not looking for a job.*

Now Anna was well enough informed to articulate effectively and meaningfully how she could contribute to these kinds of organizations. She was able to craft substantive examples from her hotel work that would translate credibly in ways people would understand and believe. One person she'd met along the way at the concrete company had said, "Anna, I really like the way you think. Feel free to call me back anytime." And one of the hospice nurses she'd spoken to had said, "By the way, the scheduling process around here is a nightmare. I hear they're considering a total overhaul, so I'm not really sure that what I'm describing about it will be true much longer."

Anna went back to both of them. She asked the concrete person who in their company could use her skills and would he refer her to that individual? She asked the hospice employee, "Who is leading the scheduling overhaul project, and would you introduce me?" because she knew that new systems often mean new jobs and openness to new people with new ways of thinking and doing things.

That's when she started her second round of getting curious, talking to people, trying stuff, and telling her story. But this time she was asking for a much more focused story (remember, the best way to get a job is ask for the story), and when the time was right to tell her story, she had a great one ready to present about how she could contribute in a job role that she knew they needed. Her techniques worked, and eventually she got two offers, one with a construction company and one in healthcare. She decided to go with the construction company because it got her outside more often and she liked the variety of personalities on the crews.

So she implemented the four steps of the Reinvention strategy (get curious, talk to people, try stuff, and tell your story) twice, always using the story-based networking approach to Moving On, and was able to land a new job in a new field that had a very good shot at being the start of a new career. It took about 50 percent longer than finding a new job in the hotel industry used to take her, but her patience, persistence, focus, and cheerful curiosity paid off.

Designing her way forward worked for Anna, and it can work for you, too.

Design Team—Beyond Ideation to Load Sharing

In our first book we talked about the importance of building a design team to support your professional work and your life journey. We reframed this as "You live and design your life in collaboration with others," and we talked about three kinds of teammates: Players, Supporters, and Intimates.

Players are the active participants in your life design projects—in particular your ongoing work-related redesign projects and prototypes. In this new work reality, they are also probably hybrid or remote players, and it will take a special effort to get to know and trust them.

Supporters are those go-to people you can count on to care about your life. They are the people close enough to you that you rely on their encouragement to keep you going. They are particularly good folks to bounce ideas off of and your go-to source for high-quality feedback. Most of these were probably remote during the pandemic and may also be remote if your career trajectory has you moving around a lot, so keeping your connections alive will take some managing on your part.

Intimates include your immediate and extended family members and your closest friends. These are likely the people most directly affected by changes in your life design. They are the most influential people in your life, and you'll want to communicate with them a lot. Hopefully, many of your intimates are in your bubble and you have direct contact with them. This makes them even more important for your well-being. Be kind to them, because they are experiencing stress and a lack of connection, too.

A healthy team is more than two people and not more than six, including you. We recommended in the first book, and we still agree, that one extra-large pizza should be able to feed your whole team. Optimally your team would be three to five people.

A design team is essential when you are in the ideation phase of your life design. Being able to assemble people who know you and your story for a quick brainstorming session is a real asset, one you want to nurture. But in a post-COVID world, your design team is even more important when it comes to helping you out and sharing the load. Networking, staying connected, and moving the ball forward on your design path take a lot of time and a lot of what psychologists call emotional labor. Your design team can unload a little of that labor by stepping in on tasks that need doing. For instance, networking always goes a little smoother when someone on your team sends a "warm introduction" to a potential prototype interview candidate. Even when you set the bar low and you're doing your best to clear it, having someone on your team hold you accountable makes it twice as likely that you'll accomplish your goal. You get the idea—

having a design team you can count on will provide you with the support that you need (that we *all* need) to thrive. Don't be afraid to ask for what you need—that's why you're on a team. And pay it forward by offering to help out your teammates when you can.

Checking In

Having a design team with some players, supporters, and a few intimates that you can open up to is critical during times of high stress and high change. It is even more important when you are isolated by circumstances from your teammates. The pandemic emphasized our isolation, but we have seen the same high-stress change/isolation circumstance occur when folks join a start-up or lose a job or suddenly have to care for a sick family member. In times like this, a team is your lifeline, and you will be glad you invested the time to build one. Your work (indeed, your life) is a marathon, not a sprint, and you need the support of your creative team to be successful and to thrive.

At the Life Design Lab and on every teaching team that Bill and Dave are part of, every meeting, even short ten-minute stand-ups, starts with a check-in on the personal stuff that has happened since the last meeting. Monday-morning meetings are always a little longer because people have their weekends to talk about. Research at Google has shown that teams perform best when they have psychological safety. This means that teammates believe they can take risks on a team without feeling insecure or embarrassed.

The way you create psychological safety is though sharing, without judgment and with affirmation, what's important to you on a human level.

We always use a prompt for the check-in, just to help people get started. Some good prompts are:

- **What was the highlight of (your day, yesterday, your weekend)?**
- **What was one thing you learned recently?**
- **Give us three words that describe how you are feeling today.**

You get the idea; the prompt is something specific, not too personal, and *not* about work.

Reframing Community

As we pointed out in our first book, healthy communities are always about something. Communities come together around a shared interest or affiliation. Dave is part of a strong community of people who are trying to live out their faith in all aspects of their lives. Bill belongs to a men's group, a community that has been gathering for at least thirty years (twenty-seven years with Bill) to support one another in becoming better fathers and more authentic men. Bill's men's group pivoted to online video chats because of the pandemic; surprisingly, something wonderful happened. Several men who had dropped out of the group because they had moved away could attend meetings again. Old special voices were back in the mix, and the group is far richer for it. The men are careful to always check in with one another before they start their meeting because there's no "milling-around time," like there was when they met in person. But overall, with renewed intention, their community is stronger than ever. He doubts that they will want to go back to in-person meetings, not if it means half of his community can't make it.

Like you, Bill and Dave belong to many different communities. Each group needs care and feeding, especially when the only way to get together is virtual. Both expanded their definition of community to include a new digital component. Dave can now meet with colleagues in New York with ease, and Bill is holding office hours with students who graduated years ago.

Yes, we all got isolated in many ways and from many communities, but by reframing our idea of what community looks like, we can design our way forward and build virtual communities that can keep us connected in all the ways that matter most.

And this reframe of community is also a reframe of family.

A silver lining in all of this chaos is that families have found new ways of communicating, with video and multiperson voice calls, and are having more get-togethers this way than ever before. Bill's three adult children used to call once in a (long) while. Now Bill's family has planned a video call once a week to check in, and most of the time everyone shows up. Many families have found that the digital domain is fertile ground for reconnecting in more meaningful ways.

So what does virtual community and video chatting with family have to do with job Disruption Design? Now more than ever, we realize that work and life are not separate things. You will show up to get the job done better when you are emotionally supported and connected, having a community and a team you can count on.

You have to be a whole healthy person before you can be a good teammate. That means that now you are bringing your whole self to the job.

You really are the Human in the Room, and we'll explore what that means in the next chapter.

Try Stuff

Rituals

Take out your calendar and make the following modifications and observations:

Design in a ritual for "going to work" and one for "coming home." Put them on your calendar and make a point of designing in a social and physical action at each starting and stopping moment of the day.

In addition to starting and stopping moments, mark up the following on your current calendar: meeting times, uninterrupted working times, socializing times (this can be with colleagues or with family and friends), and physical movement and exercise times.

If you don't schedule it, it will not happen!

Note where you are out of balance, especially with physical movement and exercise, and then make one or two small adjustments to your schedule and see how it feels. Remember to set the bar low and change small things you can measure, like steps, at first. If logging 5,000 steps is too big a goal, try 2,000—that's about a twenty-minute walk at a medium pace.

Keep making small changes in your schedule until you like the rhythm of your days and you're getting most of your tasks done without working late. Or if you schedule some personal time or time with the kids in the middle of the day—no problem. You can shift those working hours to after the kids go to bed—a quiet time in most households that can be very productive deep work time. In any case, take advantage of your new freedom to schedule a work life that meets your needs, week by week.

Presentations

Take out an old presentation and examine its structure. It's probably just a list of bullet points, maybe tied together by some logical sequence, but not organized as a story. That's okay—that's your starting point. Now take about thirty minutes and redesign it around these design principles:

- **Every presentation tells a story. Which of the seven plots would be the best to organize the information in this presentation?**
- **What are the three major points that I want to get across to my audience? What do I want to make sure they take away and remember?**
- **How are those three points emphasized and made clear? Do I have a last slide that repeats the takeaway points?**
- **I need to reduce the number of slides by 30 percent and the number of words by 50 percent. Where can I condense and clarify my three main points, and what can**

I eliminate that is not necessary? Can I replace a bunch of words with an image, a chart, or a graphic that I can speak to, and also cut down on my audience reading my slides?

- What is the arc of my story—the beginning, the middle, and the end, and maybe not in that order?
- How do my slides "look"? Are they intentionally designed? Are my graphics and pictures high-resolution and clean? Have I used an appropriate font? (Hint—if you don't want to learn about fonts, and that is a deep, deep rabbit hole, just pick Helvetica. It comes on almost every computer. It's clean, clear, and communicates well. Use bold for the titles, regular for everything else, color for emphasis. It's the all-purpose solution when you don't have the time to choose.)

Then practice this new presentation five times and film yourself at least one time and watch it with a friend. See if they can pick out the three main points. If not, redesign it and try again. You will be amazed at how much more impact your presentations have if you follow these design principles. And how much more attention people pay to your ideas.

This is all about making sure that you get recognition for your contribution. When it comes to office politics, as defined in chapter 6, that's the most important thing.

14

The Humans in the Room

All of us, in times of disruption and accelerating change, have faced the unknown and wondered how we were going to cope. We have asked ourselves: How do I deal with this new abnormal normal?

This is an important question, and we all have to answer it one way or another.

Another crucial question that many of us need to answer is: How do I help *us* deal with all this?

In this collective question, *us* is that group of people you work with or who perhaps work for you. Most of us work in an organization of some kind. Whether it's three of us in a software start-up, or 200,000 of us working at the University of California, or 378 of us in a hospital, or a dozen of us at our furnace repair service—how we work has been disrupted in ways that are just as critical to how you have been disrupted.

As we wrote earlier, we are not trying to write the definitive corporate reorganization book. Lots of people better suited to it are working on that. Nevertheless, there are a few things we've seen that may be helpful for different settings. So whether you're a small business owner, a corporate manager, a team leader, or just a person who drew the short straw and is in charge of the crew this afternoon, here are some Disruption Design ideas we hope you find useful.

Because you aren't the only human in the room. Everyone you now work with is bringing their whole selves to work—and all the humans in the room are struggling in one way or another.

The Leadership Challenge

The watertight compartmentalization of work life and personal life, where everyone could act at work as though they were just their role ("I'm the head of HR"; "I'm the quality engineer who does the stats on the project"; "I'm the fourth-grade teacher") is over. We are all revealed on video to be fully three-dimensional human beings with kids and pets and messy bedrooms. And that changes a lot of things for both staff members and leaders.

Organizations that have moved or will move to a hybrid worker model are now facing a challenge that calls for new leadership. How do you create a positive corporate culture, with engaged workers who like working together on project teams, when most workers get to see each other in person only a few days a week or month? How do you manage the messy reality that you are having meetings with your employees and you are all Zooming into one another's homes where you may be seeing maybe more about one another's personal lives than you really wanted to? And certainly more than you are used to.

We call this new work phenomenon the Human in the Room—and while it may be disconcerting at first, we are going to argue that this may be one element of the hybrid workstyle that's going to change the shape of organizational leadership for the better. And it works both ways. Your employees can see into your home, too. Lifestyle, indications of income level, and family situations are now online and being shared. Everybody now knows what they used to guess at. Your employees are talking about it, too—office gossip doesn't get disrupted. For the first time in the history of the modern workplace, we are now all revealed to be something more than our job. We are all revealed to be humans.

Our thesis has always been that good work design starts with good life design. People want a life with a job in it, not the other way around. Now that everyone's homes and private real-time situations are part of our visual and emotional workspace, we can't help but see the whole human being, and your cats and dogs and kids and moms and granddads are all in the room with us. When we started seeing news anchors on television not only broadcast from home, but broadcast from home with the cat on the couch behind them or their kids breaking in on screen, we knew the game had shifted.

Becoming more human at work doesn't necessarily change the work itself or change the content of the work-related conversation. The reports filed by the reporters pictured above weren't different than they used to be, but both their coworkers and their viewers feel differently about them as people now. It's that change in who we see others at work to be (be it peers, employees, bosses, or customers) that invites an opportunity to lead differently—to lead more humanly—and if that doesn't quite make sense yet, to certainly lead with more humanity and compassion for the humans in the room.

Zoom Out to Zoom In

This sudden leap in our shared humanness at work provides a great opportunity to augment the conversation that leaders have with their staff. If that's handled well, we think it's going to result in a more engaged workforce all around.

We are not suggesting you make a big shift and start adding a lot of touchy-feely stuff to every business and work conversation. That would be disingenuous and inappropriate. We do suggest you start with some small moves with big dividends. Start with just increased personalization in the transitions into and out of conversations. While the reports given by those reporters didn't change, when they wrapped up, the anchor's segue had a new personal touch to it: "Thanks for that great report, Lisa, we'll see you tomorrow—after you've had a chance to snuggle with that darling cat."

That sort of thing does make a difference and is easily done. Just don't overdo it. Zoom-based meetings include more overt transition facilitation than in-person meetings because we don't have access to the same body language and eye contact cues online as when we're together. That means the meeting leader more often directs who speaks next and the topic. The increase in transitions creates lots of little chances to add the human touch. There is great power in doing segues and transitions with both business effectiveness (the well-run and organized meeting) and personal attentiveness (the more human meeting).

Once you've gotten comfortable with using a more human touch, you can up your game. This next opportunity is largely focused on one-on-one conversations. In those conversations, try Zooming Out—opening the conversation briefly to a broader scope that includes things beyond work.

While drafting this chapter, Dave had to get some documents notarized at his insurance agent's office. Dave knew that his agent had a family of five living in a pretty compact two-bedroom apartment, in which running a business and parenting three kids trying to go to online school all at the same time was really tough. While the agent was getting his logbook out, Dave asked, "So how's it going at home? Everyone still on top of each other?" His agent's shoulders relaxed a bit as he said it was going okay, but boy, after ten months of closed schools and offices, it was pretty claustrophobic and everyone was pretty tired.

It wasn't the kind of question that would have made sense a year before, but that was before everything changed. When we're all in something together—in a pandemic disruption or any kind of disruption—there's an increased opportunity for expressing our shared humanity. Allowing for that simple connection and human recognition improves trust and authenticity. That Zoom Out (asking how the family is doing) allows the Zoom In (getting the business taken care of) to work better and feel more meaningful to everyone because it allows work to be more a part of an undivided life rather than an isolated and disconnected activity.

And you can go one step further with Zoom Out to Zoom In, if it fits you, your situation, and your employee. For this step, you actually have a "how's life?" conversation with the employee, not just a transitional comment.

Managers can *care about* the whole (work and personal) lives of employees and *care about* their home-office hybrid situations without having to *take care of* those things. Some aspects are beyond the job responsibilities, and you don't have to know the gory details to know how it's going. Leaders can treat staff as humans who have a job, not merely as workers. That's zooming out to see a bigger picture beyond the job. You can even structure this conversation formally, if (and only if) doing so is aligned with your leadership role and is compatible with your organizational culture and is desired by the employee (opt-in only). You can invite employees to do the Compass exercise from *Designing Your Life*, which is included at the end of this chapter. If that's too heavy a lift, you can start with the Good Work Journal (GWJ) we shared in chapter 1 of this book, which is not threatening at all and does catalyze an increase in personal engagement and satisfaction. When they write up their Compass essays or GWJ, they do *not* have to turn them in, as it's really none of your business. But you can ask them where they're experiencing alignment at work with their ideas and how you may be able to better support them in experiencing coherency or engagement in their role. If you suspect that conversation is too personal to share with the boss, that's no problem. Just have the whole team do the exercise and let people share their insights and challenges privately in pairs or triads—all confidentially and without turning in their writing or requiring reports on their conversations.

It's okay for workplace leadership to *facilitate* employees' experience of getting clearer on how to build their engagement, coherency, and meaning-making at work without intervening into their values or violating their privacy. You can provide tools and processes that help them to figure it out without having to know or judge the specifics.

This opportunity has always been there, but it became substantially more available after 2020 for two reasons. First, the hybrid work model and the prevalence of video meetings softened the ground for these conversations significantly, and second, the heightened experience of vulnerability that the pandemic forced on everyone increased both the desire for and readiness to pursue more integration and coherency in life and work.

Whether we intended to invite the human into the room or not, we're all human.

And we're all in the room.

Great leaders recognize this and adapt for the benefit of all.

Assets, Not Artifacts

How do you project your leadership and authority without the corner office and the big desk? Many of the artifacts that leaders have historically relied on to create their professional persona—the big desk, the clothes, the corner office, the fully equipped shop or kitchen, the big car, the posturing or body language—just don't work anymore. These things aren't all gone all the time, but their previous power to create an image has been seriously deflated. Nobody is noticing what car you drove up to a Zoom meeting in, and they can't see your new shoes or the view out your window, either.

So what do you rely on? You shift from artifacts like appearance or office size to assets like how well you run a meeting, how effectively you are managing from a distance, and what your performance and deliverables look like. In the last chapter we discussed moving from managing you to managing deliverables. That shift applies to the leaders doing the managing just as much, if not more, as it applies to the workers being managed. Bosses will be held accountable not only for bossing well, but for getting their own things done and delivering on time.

For example, Silicon Valley is renowned for working crazy hours. One expression of that culture in many companies was people regularly showing up to meetings five to eight minutes late—especially the boss. After all, he's so important that he's working even crazier hours than you are and can just barely squeeze in your meeting because of all that important work being super busy. Going to the virtual work environment ended that nonsense overnight. Zoom meetings start on time and end on time. Period. We are all already spending way more time on Zoom than we want, so we're sure not going to sit around waiting for you. And since you don't have to drive anywhere or wait for an elevator, there's no excuse for it.

The same goes for being ready for that meeting once you arrive on time. You've got to have a clear agenda, know what you're doing, be ready to facilitate the discussion, and engage with all the participants effectively. All that was important before, but the expectations took a huge jump after the pandemic, and those raised expectations aren't going back down again.

Ever.

Artifacts of importance are over.

And now it's all about those assets.

Leadership assets include the following types of things. If you have few of these at hand and have been overrelying on sheer power or charm (or even a fancy car and fancier shoes), stock up on these items:

- **Production assets**
  - **Sales**
  - **Reports**
  - **Plans and budgets**
  - **Programs**
  - **Products and services**
- **Process assets**
  - **Workflows**
  - **Procedures**

- ○ **Paths of promotion and professional growth**
- ○ **Communications (in person, in print, online)**
- • **Human assets**
  - ○ **Approachability**
  - ○ **Candor, sincerity, authenticity**
  - ○ **Reliability**
  - ○ **Confidentiality**
  - ○ **Compassion (with appropriate boundaries)**
  - ○ **Availability and rapport**
  - ○ **Trustworthiness**
  - ○ **Emotional intelligence, self-control**

All these assets are critical, and it's time to make a thorough inventory and start stocking up on what you need.

Easier Than Ever

While you're taking stock of your assets, it's also a good time to reframe networking and community. As we talked to leaders in many different organizations, and especially those working in organizations of over a hundred people, we consistently heard questions about how to respond to changes in networking and community formation brought on by the pandemic and the new hybrid work reality.

The bottom line is that some things will be easier in your new work life, and other things will be harder.

Let's tackle the *easier* first.

While getting together at a mixer event or a big conference is hard, if not impossible, getting together one-on-one is easier than ever. One-on-one conversations, both formal (scheduled) and informal (unscheduled and serendipitous) have always been a backbone of getting work done. The tailored personal interaction and focused attention of a person-to-person conversation is peerless. One-on-ones can occur between bosses and employees, peer colleagues, work acquaintances, casual collaborators, and every other imaginable combination. And historically they've been hard to come by because people are busy and are usually in the wrong place to meet up.

Those days are over, and it's one of the gifts in these difficult times.

Everyone, or very nearly everyone, is now frequently if not constantly at home and online. They aren't commuting or on the seventeenth floor or "away." They're sitting in front of a computer and just one browser tab away from virtually every other person on earth. And most of those people are a lot lonelier, both personally and professionally, than they've ever been and are glad of some interesting or worthwhile human contact.

So it has never before been as easy to successfully engage with someone directly. People's schedules have never been more available, and never before have they been more inclined to talk to you than now.

So talk to them!

If you're a manager like most managers we knew up until 2020, then finding time and availability to do one-to-ones with your staff was a continual struggle and terribly expensive. Redeploy some of that commute time and too-long meetings time that hybrid work has given back to you in regular one-to-ones. Research has made very clear that the single highest correlate to having a positive experience in college is having direct and regular interaction with a faculty member or staffer who cared about you and your work. That's an observation about people, not universities, and it applies in the work world just the same as it does in colleges. People work harder and are more engaged when working for a boss who cares, and nothing—N-O-T-H-I-N-G—demonstrates caring more than time spent one-on-one. Grab that chance.

Whether you're a manager or not, take this golden opportunity to up your one-on-one interactions. Make a commitment to reaching out to colleagues not only when you have a problem needing a solution, but also when you have curiosity about their work. Make "get curious and talk to people" work for you.

And while you'll usually need to schedule these interactions in advance, you can still get the bumped-into-her-in-the-lunchroom serendipitous conversation. It won't literally be by accident like in the old days, but it can be unscheduled. Here's how—make a phone call and convert it to an impromptu video meetup.

It's still considered inappropriate in most work cultures to attempt an unscheduled video call by just video dialing someone. But in most work cultures, it is okay to make an unscheduled phone call, if done respectfully and graciously. If you make an unscheduled call and you reach someone live, you of course announce yourself and your intent for a conversation, then ask, "Joan, I think this may be about a fifteen-minute conversation—does now work for you?" If yes, great. If no, try to book the conversation later. If you get a yes, then you can up the play: "Hey, if you're online now, how about we do this on video?" And if they are, you quickly send them the video link you already just happen to have ready or call them back on their preferred platform. At most that redialing takes two minutes, and by making it a video call instead of a phone call, you have a much more personal interaction and leave a much more powerful and memorable impression.

If making an unscheduled call feels too forward or confrontational for you, that's okay—don't try things that you can't do authentically. But if you're on the fence, give it a few tries before you dismiss the idea. When we were all in the office or on the job site all the time, no one was ever "not doing anything." But in the hybrid work environment, the workday is often not continuous. There are small breaks throughout the day or quiet periods when we may be busy but are not in fact totally uninterruptible. The hybrid environment means your chances of catching someone in an available moment are greatly improved. Be courteous and respectful of people's time and don't overrun your requested time—but do go for it and you'll be surprised how often you succeed.

Harder Than Ever

The explosion of remote work may have resulted in direct meetings getting easier, but on the flip side of that, onboarding new staff and building company community and culture is much harder. The reason is simple. Remote communications technology works great for sustaining and exercising relationships that are in place between people who know each other already, but it works much less well in facilitating the creation of new relationships and integrating new people into existing networks of relationships. Something unique happens when we're all actually together in one place, something that doesn't happen online, and that unique something is an important contributor to community and culture formation.

Onboarding is the process of getting a new employee established as a contributing team member of the organization. It involves getting the legal and accounting paperwork done; providing them with the tools and information needed for their role; educating them about the company's policies, products, and services; and most important, making sure they are connected and related to their coworkers so as to be able to effectively collaborate. It's that last critical step that the hybrid work model has changed. The other steps can be done electronically or remotely quite adequately, but we've been forming relationships and communities in person since the Stone Age, and doing so remotely is different and harder. Effective staffing is one of the single most important functions of any successful enterprise. If you can't successfully bring new people on board and get them integrated into the collaboration community of your enterprise, you've got a huge problem.

The challenge faced by someone new trying to crack into a well-established network is described fairly accurately by the Mark Knopfler song that says, "Sometimes you're the windshield / Sometimes you're the bug." If you're the new person, the existing network is that impenetrable windshield and you feel like the bug about to go splat when you hit it. Back when we all went to the office or the lab or the campus or the construction site together every day all day long, it was simpler.

Once upon a time on your first day, the boss would introduce you around to everyone and openly remind people of your role and the importance of bringing you into the fold. "Annette, be sure that Eloise here meets everyone on the product launch team. After all, she'll be writing the documents that our customers first read, so she really needs to understand what we're trying to accomplish here." If you've got a good boss, some time during that first week you'll be handed off to a network mediator who will be responsible for making sure you get properly connected. It sounds something like, "Now, Eloise, I want you to meet Haran. Haran is your go-to guy for getting connected. Haran knows everybody, and everybody trusts him. Whenever you're unsure who to ask for help or whose work your work may impact, ask Haran—he'll know."

That way of getting people integrated into the team was heavily dependent on being together. The smartest thing you could do after that introduction was take a walk around the building with Haran and just listen in on the twelve different conversations he'd have with people he'd "bump into" over the course of an hour or two.

But that doesn't work on Zoom.

We need to adapt to our new environment.

And the best way to manage the hard task of onboarding and integrating new team members is to use breakouts to break in.

Breaking Out to Break In

While remote, online communications may make midsize to large-sized group interactions (anything over six people) seem *less* personal, they actually can make small group interactions (three to six people) *more* intimate. We've seen this firsthand in our Stanford courses and online professional workshops, where we teach sixty to over a hundred people at a time online and make extensive use of video breakout rooms for small group interactions. We've heard the same report from managers and leaders in for-profit corporations, nonprofit NGOs, service organizations—virtually every work context you can name.

In an online small group setting, every face in the gallery gets equal visibility. When someone is speaking, that person has the floor uncontested. This changes the group dynamic in a dramatic way. The boisterous extrovert is less domineering and the reticent introvert is less easily dismissed. Small group video meetings level the playing field in a way that creates a real advantage for someone new to the team. In a small group breakout room, a new employee can quickly get up-close-and-personal exposure to important colleagues, and will have a chance to make a strong impression and truly be seen in ways that would have taken months to orchestrate in the old system.

Both managers of new employees and new employees themselves can take action to leverage this opportunity. Managers can be sure to incorporate activities that require going into "breakout rooms" of three to six people during their large group online events. The more the better. During a two-hour class with sixty students or clients, we will likely go into breakouts of the magic three to six people, many different times, for anywhere from seven to twenty minutes at a time. Establishing a good rhythm back and forth between the plenary group and breakout groups during any meeting of an hour or more will do wonders to help build community in the workplace.

And if you're the new employee and your managers don't do this, you can do it for yourself. When you attend an online meeting, pay close attention to what issues are being brought to the surface and whose point of view on those issues may impact your work. Very quickly following such a meeting, identify what small groups of people it would be helpful for you to debrief with further to address follow-up considerations, and invite them to a short meeting to coordinate. Keep it to just three to six people, so you have a chance to connect personally, and keep the meeting short—twenty minutes or less to address a very specific question or action item—so that you've got a much better chance of getting their attention.

By using breakouts this way to make quick but strong personal connections, you'll be able to break in more successfully and establish yourself (or your new employee) effectively as a highly functioning member of the community.

Gathering for Good Reasons

What organizational leaders told us about their reaction to the remote-intensive, new hybrid working model was overwhelmingly positive. They were thrilled that we can effectively collaborate and get the job done regardless of where people are and without the huge facilities costs required to have everyone working in the same place at the same time.

"*But,*" they maintained, "we can't do everything remotely. It just doesn't work. Something is lost along the way when we aren't together, and we can't afford that loss without serious impact to our business."

CEO after consultant after manager after small business owner told us they were trying to figure out the answer to this question: *What is it that we do that we* really *need to be together for in person?*

The short answer is: It depends.

What is clear is that being together does matter. Sometimes. Just when it matters and to whom varies according to the enterprise, its tasks, and its organizational structure. There is no one right answer to when it's critical to get people face-to-face. What is critical is that the organization's leaders figure this out and support it.

It may be for ideation—allowing people to leapfrog off one another's ideas and experience the dynamic of a high-performing team hitting a state of flow and coming up with the killer ideas that make all the difference.

It may be for celebration—getting the group together to acknowledge and celebrate the hard work, specific contributions, and important outcomes delivered by various teams and individuals. And in so doing, ensuring that people get what they really want beyond a paycheck—recognition and regard in the presence of their peers and their bosses.

It may be for communication and alignment—periodically having everyone in the room and getting fully informed on the current status of projects and pending priorities, including an open floor for questions, concerns, and pushback. Hosting such a "town hall" experience in person ensures that alliances work and interdependencies don't catch us by surprise.

It may be for customer acknowledgment—bringing together providers and buyers or users of products or services in order to see and touch the lives that are actually affected by what workers do day in and day out.

There are countless good reasons to make the effort to gather in person, and you can probably already guess how we suggest you find out for your organization what your good reasons may be. It's four steps: Get Curious. Talk to People. Try Stuff. Tell Your Story. By using this approach, starting with humble listening that transitions into iterative prototyping, you can wayfind to designing an effective answer to the challenging and expensive question: "When do we really need to gather in person?"

But Does It Actually WORK?

Is there evidence that a well-executed hybrid organizational design works?

Bill's teaching colleague Eli works for a company that has never had traditional offices and everyone, from their first day on the job, is a remote worker. InVision, one of the leading companies making software tools to design better digital products (software that designs software), has a thriving corporate culture without an office or the traditional trappings of status that comes with it. They have employees scattered all over the world—in the United States, Europe, Asia; twenty-eight countries in all—anywhere they can find great talent. How do they do it? They have a radically "flat" organization, very little hierarchy, a project-oriented team structure, and extreme accountability expected of all of their employees. They use lots of micro-techniques to build culture, starting with small, focused teams, no "supervision" as that term is traditionally used, a ten-minute stand-up meeting at the start of every day for team check-ins, lots of unstructured one-on-one time, and great communication and archiving tools so that teams always know where they stand in regard to their project deliverables. They hold what they call an IRL Conference for the whole company once a year. "IRL" stands for

**"in real life"—a humorous reframe of the traditional on-site/
off-site thinking. InVision, founded as a virtual office company in 2011, has engaged employees and financial success
in their business niche—evidence that you can go all-virtual
and still organize and support corporate culture and people
development.**

Engagement Matters

We began this book talking about the majority of workers feeling
disengaged at work—a problem demanding a solution. We spend
so many of our life hours at work, and perhaps more than ever, we
realize how much our time matters.

How truly short and fragile life can be.

It was true before the pandemic.

It was true during the pandemic.

And it's true after the pandemic.

Workers want to be more engaged at work. Managers want their
staff to be more engaged at work. Customers want the people who
serve them or make products for them to be more engaged.

And now more than ever, designing our work life is all about
creating work and work environments that facilitate more
engagement. More engaged workers do better work, make better
products, deliver better services, get more done in less time, are
happier at home as well as at work, and grow more personally and
professionally.

And now that home and work are blended, both leaders and

individual contributors must use the tools and resources available to increase their engagement in the new hybrid work model that has become the next normal.

Grab the ideas here that can work for you and your organization, and develop your own ideas modeled on the designs we offer as you deal with your own disruptions—whether personal, regional, or global.

Permission to be happy has never been more critical.

And our work life is really just our life.

Design a life where you and others can thrive—no matter what disruption comes your way.

We need each other.

We always have and we always will.

And in the end, that's what matters most.

And we are here cheering you on, knowing that there is always a way to design your way toward whatever comes next.

Try Stuff

Workview and Lifeview

Workview Reflection

Write a short reflection about your Workview. We're not looking for a term paper here (and we're still not grading you), but we do want you really to write this down. Don't do it in your head. This should take about thirty minutes. Try to shoot for 250 words—less than a page of typed writing.

A Workview should address the critical issues related to what work is and what it means to you. It is not just a list of what you want from or out of work, but a general statement of your view of work. It's your definition for what good work deserves to be. A Workview may address such questions as:

- **Why work?**
- **What is work for?**
- **What does work mean?**
- **How does it relate to the individual, others, society?**
- **What defines good or worthwhile work?**
- **What does money have to do with it?**
- **What do experience, growth, and fulfillment have to do with it?**

Lifeview Reflection

Just as you did with the Workview, please write a reflection on your Lifeview. This should also take no more than thirty minutes and be 250 words or so. Below are some questions often addressed in a Lifeview, just to get you started. The key thing is to write down whatever critical defining values and perspectives provide the basis for your understanding of life. Your Lifeview is what provides your definition of what have been called "matters of ultimate concern." It's what matters most to you.

- **Why are we here?**
- **What is the meaning or purpose of life?**
- **What is the relationship between the individual and others?**
- **Where do family, country, and the rest of the world fit in?**
- **What is good, and what is evil?**

- Is there a higher power, God, or something transcendent, and if so, what impact does this have on your life?
- What are the roles of joy, sorrow, justice, injustice, love, peace, and strife in life?

Read over your Lifeview and Workview, and answer each of these questions:

a. Where do your views on work and life complement one another?
b. Where do they clash?
c. Does one drive the other? How?

Conclusion

Permission to Be Happy

Now we've written another book—and now a revised edition to that second book.

Many of the tools and ideas are new, but our core message is the same. You are the creative designer of your life. How you spend your days is how you spend your life. You are never stuck. Perhaps paused on occasion, but never totally stuck. Whether it's a small change in you or the job, or a huge global disruption, you always have at least *some move* that you can make to design your way forward and build toward more thriving and aliveness. Remember that it's not the size of the move, but the movement itself that counts.

When we first got together for a few beers at Zotts, a local beer garden that has been part of the Stanford community forever, and started plotting what has become the worldwide Designing Your Life movement, Bill stated the obvious: "You know, if we teach people this stuff about designing a well-lived, meaningful, coherent, and joyful life, we have only two options: We do everything we ask our students to do ourselves, or we risk turning into the biggest hypocrites on campus."

Since that day, we have been working hard on researching and developing the ideas and tools we teach and write about—and working even harder at living what we teach.

The truth is, Life Design is always a work in progress.

We completed this revised edition at what appeared to be the beginning of the end of the global coronavirus pandemic. As we pondered our next phase of life, we realized that there is nothing better than not knowing what comes next—that's what makes life interesting and exciting and endlessly fascinating. Sometimes we fail, take a step backward, or get thoroughly disrupted and have to start over at the beginning. But with design thinking, we are immune to failure because we always have a way forward.

And other times we succeed—sometimes in ways that are so beyond what we imagined could happen, we forget for a moment to be grateful and let our lives be joyful.

Sometimes we all just need a little permission to be happy.

As for us, Bill keeps redesigning his job at Stanford and as an artist, and redesigning his lifestyle with Cynthia and their family. Dave keeps working to maintain the right mind-set and adjusting his mix of public impact in the world and private impact with his growing brood of grandkids.

We both actively try to focus on what's good enough . . . for now.

But because our lives are constantly changing, the story of our life is constantly changing as well. We have to practice generative acceptance just like everyone else. After his wife died, Dave slowly started learning how to redirect his love for Claudia to their grandkids and his friends and neighbors. Bill and Cyndie, following the passing of both their moms, grabbed the moment and realized a lifelong dream by buying some rural land where they hope to build a family haven that can last for generations.

And of course the people we tell you about in our books—real people—have life design stories that are constantly evolving and changing.

Bonnie, whom we mentioned in the Introduction and who had

been bouncing around the job world, finally got clear about what she was looking for. The problem was that her Maker Mix was way out of whack—she was valuing impact-making more than she realized, and more than she wanted to. She came to understand that being an idealistic Millennial and working to change the world was okay and all, but it was driving her a little crazy. No single job had the global impact she thought she wanted. But when she really sat down with herself and reframed her search around a Minimum Actionable Problem, zoomed in, and stripped out all the drama, it turned out that having some stability (money-making) and some creativity (expression-making) was just as important as impact. She found a midsize company (start-ups are too risky for her current mix) and a good creative job managing their social media marketing. It is definitely more of a job than a calling. In her spare time—and she finally got some—she started training to be a yoga instructor and simultaneously building up her meaning-making and social connections. It's a good balance and it feels good enough for her, for now.

And remember Louis, our midcareer sales manager and Talking Heads fan? He was able to redesign his job in place, and by maximizing the application of his StrengthsFinder strengths, he now enjoys more autonomy and has fun mastering the skills required to do his new job.

And Marie, our bored doctor, made the decision to leave medicine. It was a tough call— her identity as a doctor had been part of the "story" she defined herself with ever since she was a little girl. But living the "doctor story" no longer worked for her, and she is prototyping what comes next and feels excited and thrilled with the process. She completed the Maker Mix exercise and discovered that she values expression-making more than she realized. She decided her next job needed to lean into her creative side more than doctoring did. She realized she was actually redesigning her life as well as her work, so she also returned to key exercises and practices in *Designing Your Life,* especially developing her Odyssey Plans.

And Anna, the disruption-displaced hotel worker, surprised herself by redesigning her home life as well as her career. A few months after being laid off by the hotel and housebound by the pandemic shelter-in-place orders, she got tired of feeling stuck at home and started prototyping how to make home more fun. She did a small remodel to make more play space for the kids and started prototyping activities she could do with them at home. She discovered she loves being a supermom, and as she heads into a new career in the construction industry, she does so with a wonderfully renewed energy and enthusiasm for her family.

All of the people you've read about in our books, along with our students, colleagues, clients, and readers, keep designing and building their way forward. It's our immense privilege to be invited into this important conversation about life and work with so many people, including you. It's a very life-giving experience to get to help someone else design their way forward in building a well-lived and joyful life. We'd like to invite you to join us in having that experience—in being part of the movement that has grown up around *Designing Your Life* and *Designing Your New Work Life.* These books exist because people are tired of being stuck in dysfunctional beliefs and want better, doable, and more actionable ideas about how to get unstuck and get moving toward better work and a better life. We're genuinely thrilled if this book has helped you. We'd be ecstatic if our readers—the growing community of life designers that you are now a part of—were successful in actually reducing the incidence of dysfunctional beliefs simply by designing their lives and telling their stories to facilitate real change for their friends, their families, their workplaces, and our culture as a whole. If these ideas have been powerful for you, please consider sharing them with others.

We often think that work frustration, overwhelm, disengagement, disruption, and burnout are personal problems. It's our job and our fault if it's not working, or our boss's fault, or someone's fault. The truth is, it's not a personal problem alone. It's a societal problem and a global problem. Disengagement at work is epidemic, and the reason is that our organizations are filled with dysfunctional beliefs. This is not just a huge loss of productivity and performance; it's a huge loss for our world. So much of work is wasted or lacking in purpose. We have real problems to solve, real challenges to face, and we need to transform our work culture so that it works for individuals, for organizations, and for societies. By transforming your beliefs about work and sharing these reframes with others, you are contributing to far greater meaning and impact.

We realize that no matter how many people we help, we'll never be done. Not individually or collectively. But we know that there are so many people who could have more joy and purpose in their lives—more impact, more meaning, and yes, more money. We are hoping that this book has helped you to be a life designer, and that you will help many others to be as well.

Life design is never done. It's never perfect.

But it's good.

Sometimes it's very good.

The one thing we know with absolute certainty is this: Life's too short to be disengaged at work.

And life's too precious to be disengaged at life.

Acknowledgments

Designing Your Work Life grew out of the worldwide response to *Designing Your Life,* and would not have been possible without the collective contributions of many amazing people.

Our writer, chief confessor, literary conscience, and ever-patient listener, Lara Love. Lara helped us find our voice and continues to reliably ensure we speak with it. This book would a-b-s-o-l-u-t-e-l-y not have happened without her effort.

Our editor, Vicky Wilson, who informed us that "It's not a book; it's a movement. You simply *have* to keep it going and write the next book." So we did. She decided which of eight books it should be. She advocated for all the frustrated workers. She pressed to ensure we spoke to everyone. In short, she played the role of editor brilliantly. Again. You had us at "darlings . . ." four years ago and you've still got us.

Doug Abrams, our agent, provocateur, and publishing-world docent. Doug got this magic carpet ride started and he continues to be our genie in a bottle. We happily depend on his extraordinary powers to bring big ideas to the world in meaningful ways.

Doug also brought us our great international team (Camilla Ferrier and Jemma McDonagh) at the Marsh Agency and our U.K. team (Caspian Dennis and Sandy Violette) at Abner Stein.

Poppy Hampson and the entire U.K. force at Vintage. Thank you for your brilliant and devoted attention. You had us at the cactus.

Savannah Peterson, our media maven extraordinaire. Every movement is driven by community and community doesn't happen by itself. Someone makes it happen. Our someone is our dear Savvy, a true believer in this work and a global catalyst if there ever was one.

Kim Ingenito and her team at the Penguin Random House Speakers

Bureau. We had no idea how many miles you'd have us flying to literally hundreds of venues worldwide to engage with tens of thousands of people. Thanks for making the book business the people business, and for doing so with such grace.

Kristin Jensen, who makes our workshops happen seamlessly and lets us do what we love—teach.

Trainer Super Pro Susan Burnett is a triple asset—advancing women's empowerment through life design, delivering the goods to corporate clients, and conceiving and delivering our trainer training. You simply do well at all the things we can't or won't. You make us both bigger and better.

Our international collaborators all over the world and especially in Japan, where Manami Tamaoki is leading the charge to bring Designing Your Life workshops to Japanese workers who have one of the most challenging office cultures on the planet, and to Permsit Lamprasitipon, our courageous Thai coach and design thinking workshop leader, who is working hard to make sure that everyone in Thailand has the opportunity to build a well-lived, joyful life.

Stanford Life Design Lab Managing Director Kathy Davies. In the early days, people didn't think this work could survive beyond Bill & Dave. You are the proof that life design is a Big Idea and it can be taught by lots and lots of people, at Stanford and elsewhere. You caught the leadership baton from us with a flourish. We are so grateful for how you've grown the work and freed us to serve our readers beyond the campus.

To our amazing Stanford d.Life Fellows. First, a special shout-out to Gabrielle Santa-Donato for her amazing work in creating the Life Design Studio to empower more than a hundred universities serving more than a million students. Talk about getting the word out! And to our superlative team of teachers and designers—John Armstrong, Emily Tsiang, and Chris Simamora—you continue to wow students and everyone who gets the privilege of collaborating with you. Well done.

The terrific team at Creative Live, whose careful crafting of a personalized online experience has finally made the answer to the question "Can I take the course?" be "YES!" for anyone anywhere anytime.

Special friend Dan Pink, an amazing author, thought leader, and mentor. You have been instrumental in assisting us newbies by generously sharing your experience and insight. We are most grateful for the help.

To all the dozens of great bosses and collaborators who we have worked with and for over our combined seventy-five-plus-year careers. You have taught us so much, and your wisdom (and forgiveness) is the solid ground underneath this book.

And to these terrific communities of life designers, supporters, and mentors:

The more than three hundred educators who've participated in the Stanford Life Design Studio and are dedicated to advancing the mission of higher education.

The more than one hundred dedicated life and executive coaches who have been certified to coach effectively and help groups and individuals make real changes and realize the well-lived and joyful life.

The nearly two hundred event hosts who have invited us to come and speak to you and your communities all over the world. You made the connections that have made all this real and personal for so many people, including us.

The more than three hundred community leaders and more than thirty thousand members of our online community. Your dedication, persistence, and support are the rocket fuel of this movement.

Thank you.

Notes

Introduction Making It Work at Work

3 We showed: See *Designing Your Life,* chapter 6 (New York: Knopf, 2016) or visit designingyour.life.

3 We also heard from people: See *Designing Your Life,* chapter 5 or visit www.designingyour.life.

7 And yet, in poll after poll: *State of the Global Workplace* (Gallup Press, 2017), p. 183.

7 Globally, the number of workers unhappy: *State of the Global Workplace* (Gallup Press, 2017), p. 22.

8 More than 93 percent of Japanese workers: *State of the Global Workplace* (Gallup Press, 2017), p. 133.

14 We'll show you how: For additional resources on storytelling, check here:

www.storycorps.net

www.themoth.org

www.wnycstudios.org/shows/radiolab

14 Dr. Paul J. Zak, director of the Center: *Brain World,* Summer 2018, pp. 16–18.

Chapter 1 Are We There Yet?

19 If asked the same question: See *Designing Your Life,* chapter 1, or visit designingyour.life.

21 Studies of lottery winners show: E. Lindqvist, R. Östling, and D. Cesarini, "Long-run Effects of Lottery Wealth on Psychological Well-being," NBER Working Paper No. 24667, May 2018.

21 Another secret to a happy life: www.adultdevelopmentstudy.org.

21 "Happiness is love. Full stop": George E. Vaillant, *Triumphs of Experience: The Men of the Harvard Grant Study* (Cambridge, MA: Belknap Press, 2012).

23 Garth listened as she explained: We will help Garth and you figure out how "politics" actually work in organizations in chapter 6.

29 It is estimated that 90 percent of: J. C. Norcross, M. S. Mrykalo, and M. D. Blagys, "Auld Lang Syne: Success Predictors, Change Processes, and Self-Reported Outcomes of New Year's Resolvers and Nonresolvers," *Journal of Clinical Psychology* 58 (2002): 397–405.

30 The Set the Bar Low method: See the research of Stanford professor B. J. Fogg. You can also view this TEDx video: www.youtube.com /watch?v=AdKUJxjn-R8.

31 Studies show that: www.dominican.edu/academics/lae/under -graduate-programs/psych/faculty/assets-gail-matthews/research summary2.pdf.

Chapter 2 Money or Meaning

50 The coherent life is: See chapter 12 in *Designing Your Life.*

60 Finding and maintaining the right: If you want an amazing take on "What Teachers Make," go to YouTube and look up the poem by the spoken-word poet Taylor Mali: www.youtube.com /watch?v=RxsOVK4syxU.

74 Adjust the location of: The Maker Mix settings include a number of things. Obviously they include time, but it isn't just a percentage allocation of hours/week spent on each component. Some things just take more time than other things (like commuting or laundry), but that doesn't make them necessarily more valuable or more important. Some things that take a small amount of time feel big and some things that take tons of time feel small. Let your mix represent how you value what you're making and how "loud" it feels to you relative to other things you do. In the example of Bill's current Maker Mix, he set "Expression" at about 20 percent, but it's not fully 20 percent of his time (not yet, anyway . . .). However, his experience of making art is pretty intense for him and

very important. It may be getting only a few hours a week of his attention (compared to fifty-plus hours in his regular job), so it's not literally getting one-fifth of his waking time, but *it feels* like at least 20 percent. (You be the judge.) There's not a right or wrong way to think about your relative weighting of your different types of making. The whole idea here is just to give you a tool to help you articulate how things are going for you as a maker and how you might design your mix a little differently if you want to.

80 After you've plotted your roles: Note that there may be more than one place on the map where you could put a role. The way you think about and describe what that role means, the way that role feels to you—that's what determines where it belongs. If Bill thinks about his role as a teacher primarily in terms of the students he's teaching in a particular course, he'd plot "teacher" in one place. If he thinks about it primarily in terms of the 1,000 students he's worked with over a decade, then the "teacher" role goes in a different place, and if he thinks about it primarily in terms of how his program paves the way for changing design education in other universities, then it's in a different place. They're all "right"; it just depends on how Bill thinks about who he's working with and what impact comes from that role.

Chapter 3 What's the Problem?

96 He has videotaped more than: www.gottman.com.
105 Okay, a moment of sadness for: One kind of poet makes a lot of money. Songwriters like Bob Dylan and rappers like Jay-Z have found a way to turn their poetry into a pretty good business. But it's a long shot—a one-in-a-million chance that you will become a famous rapper. You should probably have a back-up reframe.

Chapter 4 My Overwhelm Is Overwhelmed

111 If you're not sure if you've crossed: See the Mayo Clinic's "Job Burnout: How to Spot It and Take Action" (www.mayoclinic.org /healthy-lifestyle/adult-health/in-depth/burnout/art-20046642).

Chapter 5 Mind-set, Grit, and the ARC of Your Career

134 Research from our Stanford colleague: Carol Dweck. *Mindset: The New Psychology of Success* (New York: Ballantine Books, 2016).

135 Dweck writes: Dweck, *Mindset*, pp. 6–7.

135 "People with a fixed mind-set": Dweck, *Mindset*, p. 18.

139 There are four factors that Duckworth: Angela Duckworth, *Grit: The Power of Passion and Perseverance* (New York: Scribner, 2016), chapters 6–9.

142 ". . . human motivation seemed to": Daniel Pink, *Drive: The Surprising Truth About What Motivates Us* (New York: Riverhead, 2009), introduction.

143 "At a phenomenological level": E. L. Deci and R. M. Ryan, "The 'What' and 'Why' of Goal Pursuits," *Psychological Inquiry* 11, no. 4 (2000): 227–68.

146 "Hello World": The motherboard of any computer is where the main computer chip, the CPU, resides, along with a bunch of other control and memory chips. And there is what's called a "boot ROM" on this board that contains just enough code to start the CPU and memory and establish enough capability to load the operating system. Windows and Macs all have a boot ROM, and so did our little computer. There is a long tradition in Silicon Valley that, when the boot ROM has established functionality and lit up the display, the very first thing it does is display the words "Hello world."

150 All of this adds to the time: Suzanne Lucas, "How Much Employee Turnover Really Costs You," *Inc.,* August 30, 2013, www.inc.com /suzanne-lucas/why-employee-turnover-is-so-costly.html.

Chapter 6 Power and Politics

157 Now for a little 2x2 model: Jim Holden and Ryan Kubacki, *The New Power Base Selling: Master the Politics, Create Unexpected Value and Higher Margins, and Outsmart the Competition* (Hoboken, NJ: Wiley, 2012).

Among the many books on power that we know of, this is the one that is the primary source and reference for the political ideas in this chapter. It's a sales training book. "Sales training? What's that got to do with life design?" you might well ask.

Let us explain . . . A salesperson's job is to help buyers make good decisions in favor of their company's product or service. Good sellers want repeat customers, and the only repeat customers are ones who are happy with their prior purchases. So good sellers want buyers to make good buying decisions. The challenge is that a salesperson is powerless. A salesperson has zero authority over their prospective customers to make them buy something, so the only thing they can do is attempt to orchestrate the wielding of influence on the buying decision. And further, the influence they're orchestrating is not their own—it's the influence of other people within the buying organization. The whole process is done indirectly through others. And sellers have to do that as outsiders. It's a very tough job to do well, so top salespeople are, by necessity, really good at the artful facilitation of healthy influence. Successful salespeople are pros at managing healthy politics.

The truth is we all spend a lot of energy trying to influence others' decisions—trying to advocate in favor of something we care about (like going out for pizza versus Chinese)—which is why one of our favorite writers, Dan Pink, wrote *To Sell Is Human.* If you're curious how we're all sellers in one way or another, check out both Jim Holden's and Pink's books.

Chapter 7 Don't Resign, Redesign!

194 She had heard about a test: www.gallupstrengthscenter.com. (The assessment test costs money, and we do not receive any money for writing about it or sharing this link.)

195 six times: https://www.gallup.com/cliftonstrengths/en/253790/science-of-cliftonstrengths.aspx.

Chapter 8 Quitting Well

227 Employers respond: https://qz.com/955079/research-proves-its-easier-to-get-a-job-when-you-already-have-a-job/ and the base-

data for this conclusion comes from an article by Liberty Street Economics https://libertystreeteconomics.newyorkfed.org/2017/04 /how-do-people-find-jobs.html.

228 When backpacking in the woods: Attributed, perhaps apocryphally, to British military officer Robert Baden-Powell, the founder of the worldwide scouting movement for both boys and girls, circa 1910.

Chapter 10 Being Your Own Boss

268 That's going to: See *Designing Your Life*, p. 70.

271 If you want to dive deeper: uxmastery.com/how-to-create-a -customer-journey-map.

275 "Capabilities such as creativity and sensing": www.linkedin.com /pulse/mckinsey-study-concludes-automation-physical-knowledge -saf-stern/?articleId=6085882246508658688.

Chapter 12 Now Where Are We?

295 Elisabeth Kübler-Ross's: Elisabeth Kübler-Ross, *On Death and Dying: What the Dying Have to Teach Doctors, Nurses, the Clergy, and Their Own Families* (New York: Scribner, 2011, reissue edition).

296 Finding Meaning: David Kessler, *Finding Meaning: The Sixth Stage of Grief* (New York: Scribner, 2019).

Chapter 13 Disruption Design

307 a billion dollars industry-wide: https://www.nytimes.com/2008/03 /18/technology/18check.html. The article estimated $500 million in savings in 2011 by switching from magstripe boarding passes to bar code–scanned boarding passes, with the move to e-mobile phone boarding passes eliminating printed boarding passes far exceeding those savings; https://adventure.howstuffworks.com/destinations /travel-guide/tips/how-airline-e-tickets-work.htm. The article esti- mated the complete conversion to e-ticketing to save $3 billion annually, of which e-boarding passes are a portion.

307 world headquarters in San Francisco: Katie Dowd, "Pinterest Pays $89.5 Million to Terminate San Francisco Office Lease," SFGATE,

August 30, 2020; https://www.sfgate.com/business/article/Pinterest
-terminate-SF-office-lease-88-Bluxome-15525421.php.

309 prove you have a remote job: Monica Buchanan Pitrelli, "The List
of Countries Where Travelers Can Go Live and Work Remotely Is
Growing," CNBC, September 18, 2020; https://www.cnbc.com
/2020/09/18/countries-that-gives-visas-to-remote-workers-during
-covid-19-pandemic.html.

311 increase in depression: https://www.aetnainternational.com/en
/about-us/press-releases/2020/lockdown-mental-health-pressures
-hinder-work-productivity.html. The Aetna report concludes,
"According to the new research over 4,000 office workers across UK,
USA, Singapore and UAE, commissioned by Aetna International,
a leading provider of health and wellness benefits and population
health solutions worldwide, three quarters stated that performance
and productivity has suffered considerably due to mental health
pressures related to the COVID-19 pandemic with younger workers
in particular, 88% of those aged 18–24, most affected. For businesses, the findings highlight potential major issues to come with
the many factors negatively impacting worker performance so far
since the COVID-19 outbreak began. These include poor mental
health (74%), long working hours (70%), blurred lines between
work and home life (67%), as well as remote working set-up (66%)."

314 tool for tracking your energy: Chapter 3: Wayfinding, page 50.

315 improvement in productivity: https://www.fastcompany.com/90
601567/how-covid-19-has-us-doing-more-in-less-time. Original
data from Prodoscore (https://www.businesswire.com/news/home
/20201217005250/en/Prodoscore-Research-Productivity-of
-Remote-Workforce-Remains-Strong-During-Pandemic): "The
data revealed a 5% increase in productivity comparing May–August
2019 to May–August 2020, challenging the assumption by business
leaders that employees working from home are less productive than
when working on-site in an office."

319 writing will improve immensely: You can also check out these other
grammar books, some of which are a little less dry and others that

are the go-to for professional writers who still struggle (who knows what Strunk and White would think of our excessive usage of the em dash in this book):

Mignon Fogarty, *Grammar Girl's Quick and Dirty Tips for Better Writing*. New York: St. Martin's Griffin, 2008.

Verlyn Klinkenborg, *Several Short Sentences About Writing*. New York: Knopf, 2012.

Geoffrey Leech, Benita Cruickshank, and Roz Ivanic, *The A–Z of English Grammar & Usage*, 2nd ed. New York: Addison-Wesley Longman, 2001.

Patricia O'Conner, *Woe Is I: The Grammarphobe's Guide to Better English in Plain English*, 4th ed. New York: Riverhead Books, 2019.

Steven Pinker, *The Sense of Style: The Thinking Person's Guide to Writing in the 21st Century*. New York: Viking, 2014.

Michael Swan, *Practical English Usage*, 4th ed. New York: Oxford University Press, 2017.

Lynne Truss, *Eats, Shoots & Leaves: The Zero Tolerance Approach to Punctuation*. New York: Avery, 2004.

Jan Venolia, *Write Right! A Desktop Digest of Punctuation, Grammar, and Style*, 4th rev. ed. New York: Ten Speed Press, 2001.

319 a hundred times over: Bill remembers a time before digital projectors when a slide presentation was made with real 35mm Kodak Ultramax film slides. He was in a start-up in the eighties that made a desktop color slide maker to make these slides (it failed). He also has all the old "foils" that he used for his lectures in the nineties. These were made on a Xerox machine or by hand and were placed on an overhead projector—mostly black and white, no pictures, and all in one font, Helvetica. Ah, the good old days.

320 "not necessarily in that order": https://www.brainyquote.com/quotes/jeanluc_godard_108249.

320 backbone of all human stories: Christopher Booker, *The Seven Basic Plots: Why We Tell Stories* (New York: Bloomsbury Continuum, 2019).

327 Zoom cats: https://www.youtube.com/watch?v=762tbD1lLxI.

336 take risks on a team: https://rework.withgoogle.com/blog/five-keys
-to-a-successful-google-team/.

Chapter 14 The Humans in the Room

353 staffer who cared about you and your work: Gallup-Purdue Study
Report—Big Six College Experiences Linked to Life Preparedness,
https://news.gallup.com/poll/182306/big-six-college-experiences
-linked-life-preparedness.aspx.

355 "Sometimes you're the bug": "The Bug" by Mark Knopfler, Dire
Straits, 1991.

Conclusion Permission to Be Happy

366 the people we tell you about: For those of you who read our first
book—the lives of the people whose stories are told there continue
as well. Here's what's up with some of them . . .

Ellen, the girl who likes rocks in *Designing Your Life,* is still rock-
ing it at the same company, although she has been promoted three
times and now manages a fairly large group. "I never would have
predicted I'd still be here five years later, but I keep finding ways
to make it interesting and learn new stuff." And there's our friend
Tim, the very coherent life guy who designed just enough moneymaking for security and a good family life, but ample room and
resources for his primary interests: music and cocktail-making.
After twenty-plus years as the go-to guru at his firm, Tim got laid
off. Getting pink-slipped left him understandably disoriented. But
after a bit he revved up his networks and started talking to people,
which finally resulted in a call from a former colleague about an
unlisted opening in her company. Tim got the job and is well on
his way to reestablishing the stable lifestyle and workstyle he's used
to. "I never saw it coming until right at the end, but I ended up
with a promotion and a raise. I was able to design my way out."